Basic Strategy

The Dealer Is Showing:	2	3	4	5	6	7	8	9	10	Ace
Your Total Is: 4–11	H	H	H	H	H	H	H	H	H	H
12	H	H	S	S	S	H	H	H	H	H
13	S	S	S	S	S	H	H	H	H	H
14	S	S	S	S	S	H	H	H	H	H
15	S	S	S	S	S	H	H	H	H	H
16	S	S	S	S	S	H	H	H	H	H

S = Stand   H = Hit

Soft Hand Strategy

The Dealer Is Showing:	2	3	4	5	6	7	8	9	10	Ace
You Have: Ace, 9	S	S	S	S	S	S	S	S	S	S, H
Ace, 8	S	S	S	S	S	S	S	S	S	S
Ace, 7	S	D	D	D	D	S	S	H	H	S
Ace, 6	H	D	D	D	D	S	H	H	H	H
Ace, 5	H	H	D	D	D	H	H	H	H	H
Ace, 4	H	H	D	D	D	H	H	H	H	H
Ace, 3	H	H	H	D	D	H	H	H	H	H
Ace, 2	H	H	H	D	D	H	H	H	H	H

S = Stand   H = Hit   D = Double Down

Splitting Strategy

The Dealer Is Showing:	2	3	4	5	6	7	8	9	10	Ace
You Have: 2, 2	H	H	SP	SP	SP	SP	H	H	H	H
3, 3	H	H	SP	SP	SP	SP	H	H	H	H
4, 4	H	H	H	H	H	H	H	H	H	H
5, 5	D	D	D	D	D	D	D	D	H	H
6, 6	H	SP	SP	SP	SP	H	H	H	H	H
7, 7	SP	SP	SP	SP	SP	SP	H	H	H	H
8, 8	SP	SP	SP	SP	SP	SP	SP	SP	SP	SP
9, 9	SP	SP	SP	SP	SP	S	SP	SP	S	S
10, 10	S	S	S	S	S	S	S	S	S	S
Ace, Ace	SP	SP	SP	SP	SP	SP	SP	SP	SP	SP

S = Stand   H = Hit   SP = Split   D = Double Down

Doubling Down

The Dealer Is Showing:	2	3	4	5	6	7	8	9	10	Ace
Your Total Is: 11	D	D	D	D	D	D	D	D	D	H
10	D	D	D	D	D	D	D	D	H	H
9	H	D	D	D	D	H	H	H	H	H

H = Hit   D = Double Down

Las Vegas For Dummies, 1st Edition

Cheat Sheet

The Hierarchy of Poker Hands

Royal Flush

A-K-Q-J-10 all of the same suit.

Straight Flush

Five cards in any *sequence*, all of the same suit. (e.g., Q-J-10-9-8 of clubs.)

Four of a Kind

Four cards of the same rank, one in each suit, plus an additional card that doesn't matter.

Full House

Three cards of one rank plus another two cards of another rank.

Flush

Any five cards of the same suit, in any order.

Straight

Any five cards in sequence.

Three of a Kind

Three cards of the same rank, plus two additional cards.

Two Pairs

Two cards of one rank and two cards of another rank, plus an additional card.

One Pair

Two cards of the same rank plus three additional cards.

No Pair

All five cards of different ranks and not all of one suit.

Here's How the 36 Craps Combinations Stack Up

Number Rolled	How Many Ways to Roll the Numbers?	True Odds	Winning Combinations
Two	1	35 to 1	
Three	2	17 to 1	
Four	3	11 to 1	
Five	4	8 to 1	
Six	5	6.2 to 1	
Seven	6	5 to 1	
Eight	5	6.2 to 1	
Nine	4	8 to 1	
Ten	3	11 to 1	
Eleven	2	17 to 1	
Twelve	1	35 to 1	

IDG BOOKS WORLDWIDE

For Dummies™: *Bestselling Book Series for Beginners*

Dear Tom & Mom~

Happy Honeymooning!

Enjoy !

All our love,

Karen & Phil

xo

Las Vegas

FOR

DUMMIES®

1ST EDITION

by Mary Herczog

IDG
BOOKS
WORLDWIDE

IDG Books Worldwide, Inc.
An International Data Group Company

Foster City, CA ✦ Chicago, IL ✦ Indianapolis, IN ✦ New York, NY

Las Vegas For Dummies, 1st Edition

Published by
IDG Books Worldwide, Inc.
An International Data Group Company
919 E. Hillsdale Blvd.
Suite 300
Foster City, CA 94404
www.idgbooks.com (IDG Books Worldwide Web Site)
www.dummies.com (Dummies Press Web Site)

Library of Congress Control Number: 00-109403

ISBN: 0-7645-6162-6

ISSN: 1528-2147

Printed in the United States of America

10 9 8 7 6 5 4 3 2 1

1B/QW/RR/QQ/IN

Distributed in the United States by IDG Books Worldwide, Inc.

Distributed by CDG Books Canada Inc. for Canada; by Transworld Publishers Limited in the United Kingdom; by IDG Norge Books for Norway; by IDG Sweden Books for Sweden; by IDG Books Australia Publishing Corporation Pty. Ltd. for Australia and New Zealand; by TransQuest Publishers Pte Ltd. for Singapore, Malaysia, Thailand, Indonesia, and Hong Kong; by Gotop Information Inc. for Taiwan; by ICG Muse, Inc. for Japan; by Intersoft for South Africa; by Eyrolles for France; by International Thomson Publishing for Germany, Austria and Switzerland; by Distribuidora Cuspide for Argentina; by LR International for Brazil; by Galileo Libros for Chile; by Ediciones ZETA S.C.R. Ltda. for Peru; by WS Computer Publishing Corporation, Inc., for the Philippines; by Contemporanea de Ediciones for Venezuela; by Express Computer Distributors for the Caribbean and West Indies; by Micronesia Media Distributor, Inc. for Micronesia; by Chips Computadoras S.A. de C.V. for Mexico; by Editorial Norma de Panama S.A. for Panama; by American Bookshops for Finland.

For general information on IDG Books Worldwide's books in the U.S., please call our Consumer Customer Service department at 800-762-2974. For reseller information, including discounts and premium sales, please call our Reseller Customer Service department at 800-434-3422.

For information on where to purchase IDG Books Worldwide's books outside the U.S., please contact our International Sales department at 317-572-3993 or fax 317-572-4002.

For consumer information on foreign language translations, please contact our Customer Service department at 1-800-434-3422, fax 317-572-4002, or e-mail rights@idgbooks.com.

For information on licensing foreign or domestic rights, please phone +1-650-653-7098.

For sales inquiries and special prices for bulk quantities, please contact our Order Services department at 800-434-4322 or write to the address above.

For information on using IDG Books Worldwide's books in the classroom or for ordering examination copies, please contact our Educational Sales department at 800-434-2086 or fax 317-572-4005.

For press review copies, author interviews, or other publicity information, please contact our Public Relations department at 650-653-7000 or fax 650-653-7500.

For authorization to photocopy items for corporate, personal, or educational use, please contact Copyright Clearance Center, 222 Rosewood Drive, Danvers, MA 01923, or fax 978-750-4470.

About the Author

Mary Herczog lives in Los Angeles and works for the film industry when she's not writing *Las Vegas For Dummies.* She is also the author of *Frommer's New Orleans* and *Frommer's Las Vegas,* and contributes to *Frommer's Los Angeles* and *Frommer's Southeast Asia* — you can never have too much of a good thing, something she learned in Vegas (although she still doesn't know how to play craps).

ABOUT IDG BOOKS WORLDWIDE

Welcome to the world of IDG Books Worldwide.

IDG Books Worldwide, Inc., is a subsidiary of International Data Group, the world's largest publisher of computer-related information and the leading global provider of information services on information technology. IDG was founded more than 30 years ago by Patrick J. McGovern and now employs more than 9,000 people worldwide. IDG publishes more than 290 computer publications in over 75 countries. More than 90 million people read one or more IDG publications each month.

Launched in 1990, IDG Books Worldwide is today the #1 publisher of best-selling computer books in the United States. We are proud to have received eight awards from the Computer Press Association in recognition of editorial excellence and three from Computer Currents' First Annual Readers' Choice Awards. Our best-selling ...For Dummies® series has more than 50 million copies in print with translations in 31 languages. IDG Books Worldwide, through a joint venture with IDG's Hi-Tech Beijing, became the first U.S. publisher to publish a computer book in the People's Republic of China. In record time, IDG Books Worldwide has become the first choice for millions of readers around the world who want to learn how to better manage their businesses.

Our mission is simple: Every one of our books is designed to bring extra value and skill-building instructions to the reader. Our books are written by experts who understand and care about our readers. The knowledge base of our editorial staff comes from years of experience in publishing, education, and journalism — experience we use to produce books to carry us into the new millennium. In short, we care about books, so we attract the best people. We devote special attention to details such as audience, interior design, use of icons, and illustrations. And because we use an efficient process of authoring, editing, and desktop publishing our books electronically, we can spend more time ensuring superior content and less time on the technicalities of making books.

You can count on our commitment to deliver high-quality books at competitive prices on topics you want to read about. At IDG Books Worldwide, we continue in the IDG tradition of delivering quality for more than 30 years. You'll find no better book on a subject than one from IDG Books Worldwide.

IDG BOOKS WORLDWIDE

John Kilcullen
Chairman and CEO
IDG Books Worldwide, Inc.

VIII
WINNER

Eighth Annual Computer Press Awards ≥1992

IX
WINNER

Ninth Annual Computer Press Awards ≥1993

X
WINNER

Tenth Annual Computer Press Awards ≥1994

XI
WINNER

Eleventh Annual Computer Press Awards ≥1995

IDG is the world's leading IT media, research and exposition company. Founded in 1964, IDG had 1997 revenues of $2.05 billion and has more than 9,000 employees worldwide. IDG offers the widest range of media options that reach IT buyers in 75 countries representing 95% of worldwide IT spending. IDG's diverse product and services portfolio spans six key areas including print publishing, online publishing, expositions and conferences, market research, education and training, and global marketing services. More than 90 million people read one or more of IDG's 290 magazines and newspapers, including IDG's leading global brands — Computerworld, PC World, Network World, Macworld and the Channel World family of publications. IDG Books Worldwide is one of the fastest-growing computer book publishers in the world, with more than 700 titles in 36 languages. The "...For Dummies®" series alone has more than 50 million copies in print. IDG offers online users the largest network of technology-specific Web sites around the world through IDG.net (http://www.idg.net), which comprises more than 225 targeted Web sites in 55 countries worldwide. International Data Corporation (IDC) is the world's largest provider of information technology data, analysis and consulting, with research centers in over 41 countries and more than 400 research analysts worldwide. IDG World Expo is a leading producer of more than 168 globally branded conferences and expositions in 35 countries including E3 (Electronic Entertainment Expo), Macworld Expo, ComNet, Windows World Expo, ICE (Internet Commerce Expo), Agenda, DEMO, and Spotlight. IDG's training subsidiary, ExecuTrain, is the world's largest computer training company, with more than 230 locations worldwide and 785 training courses. IDG Marketing Services helps industry-leading IT companies build international brand recognition by developing global integrated marketing programs via IDG's print, online and exposition products worldwide. Further information about the company can be found at www.idg.com.   1/26/00

Author's Acknowledgments

A very special thank-you to Rick Garman.

Thanks also to Steve Hochman (for being my gambling guinea pig), Naomi Kraus, Jen Michaels, Culver City Herczogs, and An and Arlene for last-minute travel companionship and dining opinions.

Publisher's Acknowledgments

We're proud of this book; please register your comments through our IDG Books Worldwide Online Registration Form located at http://my2cents.dummies.com.

Some of the people who helped bring this book to market include the following:

Editorial

Editors: Jennifer Ehrlich, Naomi Kraus

Cartographer: Elizabeth Puhl

Editorial Assistant: Jennifer Young

Senior Photo Editor: Richard Fox

Assistant Photo Editor: Michael Ross

Production

Project Coordinator: Nancee Reeves

Layout and Graphics: Beth Brooks, LeAndra Johnson, Kristin Pickett, Jill Piscitelli, Brent Savage, Julie Trippetti, Jeremey Unger

Proofreaders: John Bitter, Susan Moritz, Christine Pingleton, Charles Spencer

Indexer: Sherry Massey

General and Administrative

IDG Books Worldwide, Inc.: John Kilcullen, CEO; Bill Barry, President and COO

IDG Books Consumer Reference Group

> **Business:** Kathleen A. Welton, Vice President and Publisher; Kevin Thornton, Acquisitions Manager

> **Cooking/Gardening:** Jennifer Feldman, Associate Vice President and Publisher

> **Education/Reference:** Diane Graves Steele, Vice President and Publisher; Greg Tubach, Publishing Director

> **Lifestyles:** Kathleen Nebenhaus, Vice President and Publisher; Tracy Boggier, Managing Editor

> **Pets:** Dominique De Vito, Associate Vice President and Publisher; Tracy Boggier, Managing Editor

> **Travel:** Michael Spring, Vice President and Publisher; Suzanne Jannetta, Editorial Director; Brice Gosnell, Managing Editor

IDG Books Consumer Editorial Services: Kathleen Nebenhaus, Vice President and Publisher; Kristin A. Cocks, Editorial Director; Cindy Kitchel, Editorial Director

IDG Books Consumer Production: Debbie Stailey, Production Director

IDG Books Packaging: Marc J. Mikulich, Vice President, Brand Strategy and Research

♦

The publisher would like to give special thanks to Patrick J. McGovern, without whom this book would not have been possible.

♦

Contents at a Glance

Cartoons at a Glance

By Rich Tennant

"Welcome to 'Jungle Jungle', Las Vegas' newest theme hotel. You're in treehouse 709. The vines are around the corner to your left. I'll have a monkey bring up your luggage."

page 35

"The level of service at this hotel is really wonderful, but I'd have been just as happy to walk to the Men's Room and back."

page 7

"We heard that your final vacation was spent 'killing 'em at the craps tables' in Vegas."

page 99

"The buffet at this place is incredible, isn't it?!"

page 125

FOR THE BUDGET MINDED: LAS VEGAS SHOW GOERS CAN TAKE IN "WHIP RENALDO AND HIS WILD BALLOON ANIMAL ACT."

page 239

"...and do you promise to love, honor, and always place maximum bets on the dollar slots?"

page 263

"Would you mind not sitting at that machine? It throws off the feng shui in this row."

page 161

Fax: 978-546-7747
E-mail: richtennant@the5thwave.com
World Wide Web: www.the5thwave.com

Maps at a Glance

- -

Table of Contents

· ·

Introduction

●●●

*W*elcome to Las Vegas, a truly original city, where the greatest
landmarks are all reproductions and the name of the game is
gambling. This neon jungle is, at turns, classy, tacky, cheesy, and
sleazy, but it's always entertaining. If there's one sure bet in this town,
it's that you'll never be bored — even if you don't pull a single slot
handle.

But navigating your way through the sensory overload that is Sin City
without exhausting yourself should be a priority; you are, after all, on
vacation. All you need to ensure an enjoyable trip to Las Vegas is some
patience, some advance planning, and a little luck (hitting it big can do
wonders for one's mood).

About This Book

Pay full price? Read the fine print? Do it their way?

Excuse me. There's no need for any of that.

You picked this book because you know the . . . *For Dummies* brand
and you want to go to Las Vegas. You also probably know how much
you want to spend, the pace you want to keep, and the amount of planning you can stomach. You may not want to tend to every little detail,
yet you don't trust just anyone to make your plans for you.

In this book I give you the lowdown on Las Vegas, which is fast challenging Orlando as the number-one tourist destination in the U.S.
Rising from its modest beginnings as a small, old-time gambling town,
the city has more hotel rooms (more than 120,000) than any other, and
is currently home to eight of the ten biggest hotels in the world. And
for sheer spectacle, it's hard to beat this town. Here you can watch a
volcano explode, see a pirate ship sink, stroll by the Arc de Triumph,
and cross the Brooklyn Bridge — all on the same street. And did I mention that you can gamble?

To say that taking it all in can be overwhelming, and exhausting, would
be a massive understatement. No need to worry. As a Vegas veteran
with years of experience, I've scoured the city from the Strip to downtown to find the best deals around. In this book I guide you through Las
Vegas in a clear, easy-to-understand way, allowing you to find the best
hotels, restaurants, and attractions without having to read this book
like a novel — cover to cover. Although you can read this book from
cover to cover if you so choose, you can also flip to only those sections
that interest you. I also promise not to overwhelm you with too many
choices. All that you'll find here are the best, most essential ingredients
for a winning vacation.

Please be advised that travel information is subject to change at any time — and this is especially true of prices. I therefore suggest that you write or call ahead for confirmation when making your travel plans.

Conventions Used in This Book

Because Las Vegas does its best to make you max them out, I use the following abbreviations for commonly accepted credit cards:

- ✔ AE: American Express
- ✔ CB: Carte Blanche
- ✔ DC: Diners Club
- ✔ DISC: Discover
- ✔ JCB: Japan Credit Bank
- ✔ MC: MasterCard
- ✔ V: Visa

I also include some general pricing information to help you decide where to unpack your bags or dine on the local cuisine. I've used a system of dollar signs to show a range of costs for one night in a hotel or a meal at a restaurant. Unless I say otherwise, the lodging rates are for a standard double room during high season. Included in the cost of each meal is soup or salad, an entrée, dessert, and a nonalcoholic drink. Check out the following table to decipher the dollar signs.

Symbol	Hotel	Restaurant
$	Less than $40 per night	A mind-blowing deal
$$	$40 – $59	$5 – $9
$$$	$60 – $79	$10 – $14
$$$$	$80 – $99	$15 – $19
$$$$$	$100 and up per night	$20 and up, up, and away

Another helpful feature of this book is the use of **bold type.** Where appropriate, all hotels, restaurants, attractions, and important resources have been put into bold type so you can find essential information in this guide with a minimum of fuss.

Foolish Assumptions

As I wrote this book, I made some assumptions about you and what your needs might be as a traveler. Here's what I assume about you:

- ✔ You may be an inexperienced traveler looking for guidance when determining whether to take a trip to Las Vegas and how to plan for it.

- ✔ You may be an experienced traveler, but you don't have a lot of time to devote to trip planning or you don't have a lot of time to spend in Las Vegas once you get there. You want expert advice on how to maximize your time and enjoy a hassle-free trip.

- ✔ You're not looking for a book that provides all the information available about Las Vegas or that lists every hotel, restaurant, or attraction available to you. Instead, you're looking for a book that focuses on the places that will give you the best or most unique experience in Las Vegas.

How This Book Is Organized

Las Vegas For Dummies is divided into seven parts. The chapters in each part lay out the specifics within each part's topic. Likewise, each chapter is written so you don't have to read what came before or after, though I sometimes refer you to other areas for more information.

Here's a brief look at the parts:

Part I: Getting Started

Think of this part as the hors d'oeuvres. In this part, I tempt you with the best experiences, hotels, restaurants, and attractions in Las Vegas. I also throw in a weather forecast and a look at special events, and then help you plan a budget. I also provide special tips for families, seniors, travelers with disabilities, and gay and lesbian travelers.

Part II: Ironing Out the Details

Should you use a travel agent? How about buying a package tour? Where can you find the best airfare? I answer those questions, and then talk about booking tips and online sources in this part. I also give you a menu of area hotels and motels, and talk about travel insurance, renting a car, and packing tips.

Part III: Settling In to Las Vegas

I introduce you to the neighborhoods and explore some of the *modus transporto* (local buses, trolleys, taxis, shuttles, and other vehicles to get from hither to yonder). I also discuss money matters, such as ATMs and taxes.

Part IV: Dining in Las Vegas

From buffets to brunches, this is where I discuss reservations (you'll need them), the dress code (surprisingly casual), and show you how to eat at the best for less. I also rate the restaurants and recommend the best buffets and cheap meal deals in town.

Part V: Exploring Las Vegas

Jackpot! In this part, I take you on a stroll through Sin City, enabling you to do your best at adding to the coffers of the casinos. After introducing you to Las Vegas, I take a thorough look at the attractions, entertainment (and yes, some people consider getting married at a drive-through window entertaining!), shopping, and recreational opportunities in the city. Oh, and if you've managed to miss this until now, there's a lot of gambling. Since you'll probably want to press your luck at least once, I've included everything you need to know to play the most popular games and find the best casinos. I even provide a few helpful itineraries to help you cruise Vegas' hot spots in the most efficient manner.

Part VI: Living It Up After the Sun Goes Down: Las Vegas Nightlife

An adult playground, Las Vegas really heats up after the sun sets, offering numerous opportunities to party all night long. In this part, I explore the city's life after dark, from big, splashy production shows, such as **Cirque du Soleil,** to some of the hottest dance clubs in town.

Part VII: The Part of Tens

Every . . .*For Dummies* book offers the delightful Part of Tens. Finding this part is as certain as the casino coming out ahead at the gambling tables. In this part, I serve up a bunch of cool facts about Las Vegas, and salute some of the city's past greats.

You'll also find two other elements near the back of this book. I've included an appendix — your Quick Concierge — containing lots of handy information you may need when traveling in Las Vegas, such as phone numbers and addresses of emergency personnel or area hospitals and pharmacies, contact information for babysitters, lists of local newspapers and magazines, protocol for sending mail or finding taxis, and more. Check out this appendix when searching for answers to lots of little questions that may come up as you travel.

I've also included a bunch of worksheets to make your travel planning easier. Among other things, you can determine your travel budget, create specific itineraries, and keep a log of your favorite restaurants so you can hit them again next time you're in town. You can find these worksheets easily because they're printed on yellow paper. Feel free to tear them out and take them along with you as you make the trek through Las Vegas.

Icons Used in This Book

You'll find several icons (those little pictures in the margins) scattered throughout this guide. Consider them your road map for finding the information you need.

The Tip icon tells you how to save time (including ways to beat the lines) and it highlights other handy facts.

Watch for the Heads Up icon to identify annoying or potentially dangerous situations such as tourist traps, unsafe neighborhoods, budgetary rip-offs, and other things to be aware of.

This icon flags bits of information that are important to keep in mind. They may help save your sanity!

I use this icon to identify particularly kid-friendly hotels, restaurants, and attractions. Keep in mind that Las Vegas is not that receptive to small fries, so it's not the ideal spot for a family vacation.

Keep an eye out for the Bargain Alert icon as you seek out money-saving tips and/or great deals. Hey, you may as well go home with a little jingle left in your pockets (which isn't an easy task in Vegas!).

Because you're likely to press your luck at some point during your stay in Las Vegas, look to the Gambling Tip icon for a little guidance on maximizing your chances and minimizing your losses.

Where to Go from Here

I've briefed you on what to expect from this book and told you how to plan a successful vacation to Las Vegas. So roll the dice and start reading. You have lots to do before you arrive, from arranging a place to snatch a few hours' sleep between poker sessions to finding the best places to spend your winnings. Like the Boy Scouts' creed, the successful Vegas traveler needs to "be prepared"; follow the advice in this book and the odds that you'll have a great vacation will be hard to beat. And, last but not least, have fun — the city is designed to entertain you, so open your mind and enjoy it!

Part I
Getting Started

The 5th Wave   By Rich Tennant

"The level of service at this hotel is really wonderful, but I'd have been just as happy to walk to the Men's Room and back."

In this part . . .

To get the most enjoyment out of a vacation — with the least amount of hassles — it helps to know what's awaiting you in your chosen paradise before the landing gear lowers. If you want your Las Vegas vacation to pay off in spades, you'll need to plan it as far in advance as possible. In this part, I highlight the joys of a trip to Sin City and help you sort out the logistics of planning your trip, from choosing the best times to go, to planning your vacation budget. But before I get into the nitty-gritty details, I take a look at some of the best things Las Vegas has to offer.

Chapter 1

Discovering the Glam and Glitz of Las Vegas

. . . .

In This Chapter

▶ Introducing Las Vegas

▶ Hunting down a hotel

▶ Betting the house

▶ Filling your belly

▶ Taking in a show

▶ Contemplating a side trip

. . . .

"**I**t's *Vegas,* baby!" is the catchphrase from the independent movie hit *Swingers* — and that's all you need to know.

Okay, maybe you need to know a little more. But if a city exists that has its heart — and all sorts of other body parts — right on its sleeve, a city that keeps all its goods in the shop window (which is, by the way, subtly outlined in blazing bright neon), it's Las Vegas. This is not a coy metropolis, nor an unassuming city. Vegas is a gaudy monstrosity of delight: a city designed solely to take your money and break your heart while making you love it and beg for more. And people do keep coming — Las Vegas is the number-one tourist spot in America and the fifth most-popular destination in the world. Don't come here looking for culture and self-improvement, but do come here looking for a whale of a good time. You're sure to have it.

Brother, Can You Spare a Room?

Las Vegas may well be the only city in the world where the skyline is made up entirely of other cities. New York, Egypt, Paris, Venice — all are represented in the facades of extraordinary hotel-resort complexes, behemoths of more than 3,000 rooms. And their themes span the globe and the ages. Visit the Sphinx at **Luxor,** watch pirates battle at **Treasure Island,** ride a gondola through **The Venetian,** take in a joust at **Excalibur,** ride a Coney Island roller coaster at **New York-New York,** or climb the Eiffel Tower in **Paris Las Vegas.** In other cities, the hotels are built near the tourist attractions. In Vegas, they *are* the tourist attractions. Makes

Las Vegas at a Glance

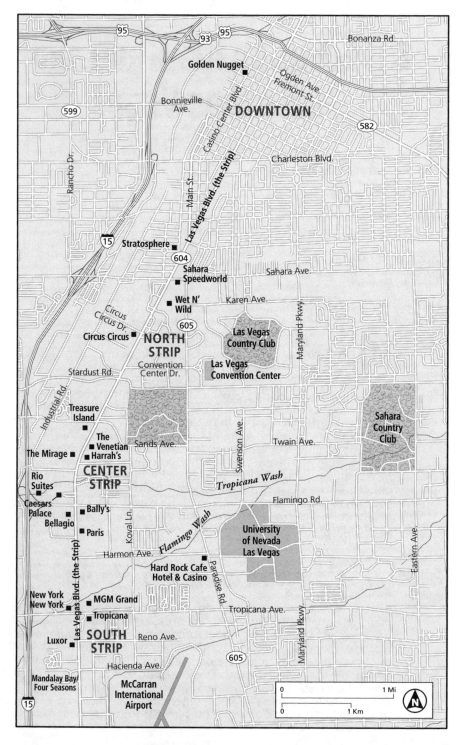

things simple, doesn't it? And as awesome as the scene is in the daytime, it's even more spectacular at night when the eye-popping lights assault your senses and seem to turn night into day.

The upside to this hotel explosion is that there are more than 120,000 hotel rooms out there waiting for you to occupy them. The bad news is that the city's popularity means that many of them are going to be filled by other pleasure seekers when you roll into town. And that doesn't even take into account conventions and other business travel, which means that you, John Q. Public, just have that much more competition for space. Las Vegas is a city that doesn't sleep, but if you want some shut-eye, you need to reserve your room as soon as you can. (I discuss hotels in more detail in Chapters 6, 7, and 8. Check them out before it's too late!)

Oh, Craps!

You may have heard a vague rumor along the lines that there is gambling in Vegas. Boy, oh boy, is there ever! Get off the plane, and you see slot machines right there in the airport, just waiting for you to lay your eager hands on them. But don't; the gambling odds at the airports are notoriously bad. Try to control yourself; if I make one, absolute promise to you in this book, it's that you will have ample time and opportunity to lose your money. Casinos beckon with numerous games of chance, from blackjack to poker to roulette.

Don't kid yourself; Vegas has presented itself as many things over the years (it started out as an "adult playground" and has recently moved into and back out of the arena of "family destination"), and will come up with still more personas in years to come. But this desert oasis was built for one purpose and one purpose only: to part you from your money. Luckily, however, spending a little money can be a very enjoyable thing, if you, er, play your cards right. (And with some luck and a peek at Chapter 15, I hope that you do.)

Salute the Chef

Vegas used to have a terrible reputation, richly deserved, for really crappy food. No one minded that much, however, because the prices were so cheap. The good news is the quality has skyrocketed; the bad news is, so have many of the prices. Vegas now has a restaurant from many (if not most) of the celebrity chefs and name-brand eateries in America and can stand proudly alongside more traditionally lauded culinary cities. You wonder what that Emeril guy on the Food Network is all about? Bam! He's got two restaurants in Vegas. You figure it's too hard to get into **Spago** in Los Angeles? Vegas has one of its own. Feast on French cuisine at **Lutece,** dine under the works of the master at **Picasso,** or down vodka and caviar at **Red Square.** But if all you care about is stuffing yourself — and hey, I'm right there with you — the famous Vegas buffets are still in action, presenting each and every diner with enough food to feed a small country, or at least, several very hungry football teams. And if you crave some Mickey D's in the middle of the night, you'll find it and about a billion (okay, maybe I'm exaggerating a little — but not by much) other fast food joints spread all over town. Check out Chapters 13 and 14 for more information on finding good eats, whatever your budget.

Giggles and Jiggles

Frank Sinatra and his Rat Pack buddies made Vegas the hot destination, and by the time Elvis established himself as a regular performer, Vegas shows were legendary. While those glamour days are somewhat behind the town, top performers still consider it a must-stop. At any given time you can see a number of big production shows — ranging from the exquisite artistry of the **Cirque du Soleil** to the high-kicking showgirls of the *Follies Bergère* and a host of other options, from renowned magicians to comedians to free lounge singers and bands. And yes, the topless revues, while no longer the main attraction, still have their place. If you want to dig right in and find out what shows are waiting for you, jump over to Chapter 20.

And if sweating it out on the dance floor is more to your taste, Las Vegas' club scene will more than satisfy your appetite. Sashay your way into the city's appropriately snooty rendition of the legendary **Studio 54,** down almost any kind of alcoholic brew you can imagine as you dance the night away at **Drink,** tackle the two-step at **Sam's Town Western Dance Hall,** or party on at **The Beach.** If I can offer one sure bet when it comes to Sin City's after-dark action, it's that you'll find at least one club that caters to your demographic. If you want to delve further into the club and bar scene, check out Chapter 21.

Ditching the Glitz

Las Vegas is designed to make visitors forget about the outside world and such mundane matters as their bank balances. And it does its designers proud. Nevertheless, you may find yourself yearning for something a little less artificial after a few days of sensory overload. And ditching town for a bit probably won't hurt that bank balance either.

None of Las Vegas' monumental hotels would exist without the modern marvel that is **Hoover Dam.** Just 30 miles outside the city, this feat of engineering provides the juice that keeps Las Vegas' cash cows running. For those who want to keep their bodies up and running, numerous recreational opportunities — from swimming to hiking — await visitors to **Lake Mead.** And for sheer natural beauty, it's hard to beat the almost otherworldly terrain of **Red Rock Canyon** and **Valley of Fire State Park.** A day trip out of town doesn't mean you'll run out of spectacles to see, it's just that natural wonders tend to be more restful than blinking lights and feathered showgirls (for most people anyway). If you want to schedule your hiatus from the hype right away, head over to Chapter 19.

Chapter 2

Deciding When to Go

• •

In This Chapter

▶ Considering the pros and cons of each season

▶ Checking out a calendar of special events

• •

*A*lthough, by most standards, Las Vegas remains a busy town throughout the year, certain seasons hold advantages over others. Deciding when to take your trip may affect how much you pay, what you're able to see, and how crowded it will be at the gambling tables. In this chapter, I analyze the advantages and disadvantages of visiting during various times of the year so you can decide on the time of year that works best for you. You can also turn to Chapter 9 to find some handy resources to help you decide what's going on and when.

The Secret of the Seasons

Las Vegas is a year-round city. While the weather can be tricky and strange, you aren't going to get blizzards or tons of rain and other fun-dampening problems. Sure, it can get hot — oh, man, can it! — but that's why they invented swimming pools and air conditioning, both of which are found in Vegas in abundance (see Table 2-1 for average temperatures in Las Vegas). But, because it is a year-round city, you may find that when it's off-season for other popular tourist destinations, Vegas' hotel rooms can be full thanks to conventions, a highly publicized boxing match, or some other crowd-drawing event.

Do remember that weekdays here are considerably less crowded than weekends, which means you're likely to find the best hotel rates on weekdays.

Flip to the section "Vegas Calendar of Events" at the end of this chapter to find out how you can plan for — or around — all the festivities throughout the year.

Springtime in Vegas

Spring is a popular vacation time for most travelers, and Vegas is no different. Some of the best reasons to go to Vegas in the springtime follow:

✔ It's not hot yet!

✔ Kids are still in school, so adults have the run of this most adult of destinations.

✔ It's a good time to go hiking in **Red Rock Canyon,** where the wild-flowers will be blooming. (If you want to find out more about out-of-town excursions, go to Chapter 17.)

But keep in mind the following springtime pitfalls:

✔ **Softbank Comdex,** one of the three biggest regular Vegas conventions, happens in the spring.

✔ Just because it's not hot doesn't mean the weather is necessarily nice. Strong winds can blow, making lying by the pool a nasty adventure, and producing cold nights. And it can rain. (One year, a heavy downpour loosed so much water on the Strip, people were using rowboats!)

✔ Some production shows take time off during the spring to rest up. See Chapter 20 for more information on finding schedules for these events.

Summer heats up the scene

Another popular travel time is summer. Ahhh, summer. The lazy days and quiet nights. . . . Well, not in Vegas! Vegas is a bustling metropolis at all times of the year and summer is no different. Here are some points to consider:

✔ It may be hot but at least it's not humid. Yes, dry heat really does feel less stifling!

✔ June and July are traditionally among the slowest times of the year, meaning smaller crowds and often much better hotel rates.

✔ All those wonderful hotel pools are fully open and operational, as is the city's water park.

But, again, keep in mind the following:

✔ It gets really stinkin' hot in the summer. Like 118 degrees hot (see Table 2-1 for average temperatures in Las Vegas).

✔ Between conventions, family vacations, and savvy travelers, it's rapidly becoming as popular a time to go as any other.

✔ Did I mention that it gets really hot in the summer?

✔ Because of the heat, everyone is at the pool (even though it's probably too hot to stay outside for long), making the pool areas less peaceful and more party-hearty.

✔ School is out and the Strip is swarming with kids, who don't have that much to keep them occupied.

Fall in the desert

In my opinion, fall is a beautiful time of year — no matter where you are. Here are some autumn bonuses for the Las Vegas scene:

✔ You get the best weather in the fall; still warm enough to swim, but not so hot you want to shrivel up and die.

✔ The kids are back in school and adults have the city to themselves again.

Some things to look out for, however:

✔ The **Softbank Comdex** convention, the absolute biggest convention of the year, happens then. Vegas is overrun with a quarter of a million computer geeks — and you.

✔ Beware of unpredictable September or October Indian summer heat waves (don't forget the summer duds and sunscreen — just in case!).

Winter in the West

Winter brings visions of softly falling snowflakes (and slick roads and salt trucks) to most travelers. But that's not often the case in Las Vegas. You should consider the following when planning a winter vacation in Vegas:

✔ Next to June and July, the week before Christmas and the week after New Year's are the two slowest times of the year. In fact, December generally isn't a bad month for crowds.

✔ Hotel prices sink during the slowest weeks of the winter, making it much easier to get a good room at a great rate.

Winter does have its downside, however. Consider the following:

✔ Tourists are quickly catching on to the fact that winter travel is slower in Vegas, so eventually those cold months may become as crowded as any other.

✔ Desert winters can get surprisingly cold — some years, you may even see snowfall!

✔ Because the weather is nippy, hotels (assuming fewer people want to swim) can close part or all of their pool areas for maintenance purposes.

✔ It's the other time of year (along with springtime) when shows can close for a week; remember, performers need vacations, too.

✔ New Year's Eve crowds in Vegas are starting to rival those in New York's Times Square, and Valentine's Day brings waves of people to town looking for a romantic quickie wedding.

✔ The final big convention, the **Consumer Electronics Show,** happens during this season.

✔ And don't forget the **Super Bowl** and the **NCAA's March Madness,** both of which bring out the sports-book gamblers (see the section "Vegas Calendar of Events" for more details).

Table 2-1 gives you the lowdown on the average temperatures in Las Vegas. Remember, though, that these are only averages. You may want to pack an outfit or two for cooler or warmer weather, depending on when you plan to travel.

Gift shops and malls carry lots of clothes — from cheesy logo fare to designer-label duds. They also have raincoats, umbrellas, swimwear, and other weather-related items that you may forget to pack. But be aware that you're likely to pay a premium!

Table 2-1	Las Vegas Average Temperatures											
	Jan	*Feb*	*Mar*	*Apr*	*May*	*June*	*July*	*Aug*	*Sept*	*Oct*	*Nov*	*Dec*
Average	44°F (7°C)	50°F (10°C)	57°F (14°C)	66°F (19°C)	74°F (23°C)	84°F (29°C)	91°F (33°C)	88°F (31°C)	81°F (27°C)	67°F (19°C)	54°F (12°C)	47°F (8°C)
Avg. High	55°F (13°C)	62°F (17°C)	69°F (21°C)	79°F (26°C)	88°F (31°C)	99°F (37°C)	105°F (41°C)	103°F (39°C)	96°F (36°C)	82°F (28°C)	67°F (19°C)	58°F (14°C)
Avg. Low	33°F (1°C)	39°F (4°C)	44°F (7°C)	53°F (12°C)	60°F (16°C)	68°F (20°C)	76°F (24°C)	74°F (23°C)	65°F (18°C)	53°F (12°C)	41°F (5°C)	36°F (2°C)

Vegas Calendar of Events

Following is a sampling of the events that I think showcase the best Vegas has to offer. To get a more detailed listing of convention and event dates call the **Las Vegas Convention and Visitor's Authority** (☎ **800-332-5333;** Internet: www.lasvegas24hours.com) and ask them to send you their brochures on these topics.

You need to order tickets for most events through the hotel or organization sponsoring the affair. Keep in mind that hotel prices and crowds soar when special events and conventions take place, so either avoid coming to town during those times of year, or be prepared to pay the price — in spades.

Wild weather

Las Vegas rests in the middle of a desert, so how wacky could the weather possibly get? A lot crazier than you think. It's common knowledge that Las Vegas' location results in broiling-hot temperatures in the summer, but many people tend to forget that deserts get cold, and they get rained on.

Winter temperatures in Las Vegas have been known to dip below 30°F, and when you toss in 40-mile-an-hour winds, that adds up to a very chilly stroll on the Strip. And snow is not an unheard-of occurrence. Most years see a flurry or two falling on Las Vegas, and since 1949, a total of 11 "storms" have resulted in accumulations of 2 inches or greater, the largest storm pouring 9 inches onto the Strip in January 1949. In the winter of 1998 – 1999, two inches of the white stuff fell on the city, resulting in the truly bizarre spectacle of the Luxor's Sphinx covered in snow. Locals usually find the snow a charming addition to the city (and the stuff usually melts completely within a day or two, so they don't have to shovel it — lucky them).

But while snow is a novel quirk that many Vegas residents and visitors welcome, rain isn't always as well received. The soil in Las Vegas is parched most of the year, making it difficult for the land to absorb large amounts of water in a short time. Between June and August, when most of the area's rainfall takes place, there is a good possibility of flash flooding.

At times, the skies open up and don't shut down, resulting in flooding that wreaks havoc on Sin City. On July 9, 1999, Mother Nature unleashed more than 3 inches of rain in *just a few hours* on a city that averages about 4 inches of rain *a year.* The deluge killed two people, swamped hundreds of cars, and destroyed millions of dollars in property. As the Strip turned into a raging river, tourists took refuge in the hotels, but at least one resort — Caesars Palace — had to close its casino and shopping arcade because of flooding.

Las Vegas also suffered devastating floods in 1984 and 1975. The city is working on putting in a billion-dollar flood-control system to prevent further large-scale disasters, but it will be several years before it's fully operational. In the meantime, visitors can console themselves with the knowledge that, historically, a really bad flood only comes along every 10–15 years, so until 2009, the odds of avoiding a devastating flood are significantly in your favor.

January

Consumer Electronics Show: A major convention with attendance of over 100,000. Usually held the second week in January.

The PBA Players Classic: This major bowling tournament is held at **The Showboat Hotel,** 2800 Fremont St. (☎ **702-385-9123**).

The Super Bowl: Sports fans galore flock to Vegas to wager on this football showdown. Last Sunday in January.

March

March Madness: The Strip turns into a hotbed of hoops betting action during the NCAA's basketball championship. Late March/ Early April.

April

The World Series of Poker: This famed 21-day event takes place at **Binion's Horseshoe Casino,** 128 Fremont St. (☎ **702-382-1600**), in late April and early May, with high-stakes gamblers and show-biz personalities competing for six-figure purses. There are daily events with entry stakes ranging from $125–$5,000. To enter the World Championship Event (purse $1 million), players must put up $10,000. It costs nothing to go watch the action.

Gay & Lesbian Pride Celebration: Festival held every year, usually the last weekend in April. Call ☎ **702-225-3389.**

June

Helldorado: A Western heritage celebration with rodeos, trail rides, and barbecues at the **Thomas and Mack Center** at the University of Nevada Las Vegas (UNLV). Sponsored by the Elk's Lodge. Call ☎ **702-870-1221** for details.

September

Oktoberfest: This boisterous autumn holiday is celebrated from mid-September through the end of October at the **Mount Charleston Resort** (☎ **800-955-1314** or 702-872-5408) with music, folk dancers, sing-alongs around a roaring fire, special decorations, and Bavarian cookouts.

October

PGA Tour Las Vegas Invitational: The PGA tour makes a stop in Sin City for a five-day championship golf event. For more details, call ☎ **702-242-3000.**

November

Softbank Comdex: This computer convention is the biggest of the year, with almost 200,000 people expected. Second or third week of November.

Thanksgiving: Loads of people take advantage of the four-day weekend to come to town — and yes, the hotel buffets serve turkey. Fourth Thursday of the month.

December

National Finals Rodeo: The biggest rodeo event in the country, with 170,000 attendees each year. The top 15 male rodeo stars compete in six different events: calf roping, steer wrestling, bull riding, team roping, saddle bronco riding, and bareback riding. And the top 15 women compete in barrel racing. Order tickets as far in advance as possible (☎ **702-895-3900**). This show occurs during the first two weeks of the month.

New Year's Eve: More than 200,000 visitors jam the city to count down the year, and the Las Vegas Strip is closed off to accommodate nearly twice that number of revelers, rivaling the attendance in Times Square! The closing of the **Desert Inn** in 2000 may mean that the 2001 festivities will include that most Vegas of New Year's activities — a hotel implosion. You've got to book your room well in advance to enjoy this party.

Chapter 3

Planning Your Budget

● ●

In this Chapter:

▶ Managing your dollars and cents

▶ Avoiding surprise expenses

▶ Debating traveler's checks, credit cards, ATMs, and cash

▶ Gathering cost-cutting tidbits

● ●

*O*nce upon a time — last week, it seems to me — Las Vegas had a reputation for being a cheap vacation. The theory held that if rooms and food were cheap (if not free) and shows were bargains, then patrons would feel more comfortable spending lots of money gambling. Even if they lost their shirts, the reasoning went, they would think "well, but my room was free, and I ate myself into a coma at the buffet for $2, so really, the trip was a bargain!" Buoyed by such feelings of good will, a repeat visit was thus ensured.

If that is the picture you have of Vegas, wipe it from your mind. This town has massive casino hotel resorts to pay for. See those chandeliers up there? Enjoy them — you're gonna pay for them. Here I show you both the best cheapest and best high-end options in all the important travel categories, so you can decide where you want to spend your money — and it's just fine with me if that place is the craps table.

Adding Up the Elements

Budgeting your trip shouldn't be difficult. Use the yellow worksheets at the end of the book to get an approximate idea of how much your trip will cost. Remember to include transportation to Vegas and food, drinks (if you buy them), hotel, entertainment, and tips. The best travel-related financial advice I ever got was this: Figure out how much money you need, and then take twice that amount. I don't necessarily recommend that you do that, but do bring perhaps 20 percent more than your highest estimate, if you can. Remember Las Vegas was designed to lighten your wallets and it does an excellent job of it.

Lodging

This is a tricky thing in Vegas. The same hotel room can go for $29 (because, say, it's a summer weekday) on one night and the very next day, go for $250 (because a huge convention just started, or it's Super Bowl weekend). Consequently, it's difficult to give you an "average" rate, although you can figure on spending around $70 per night based on double occupancy, but can spend significantly more or less, depending on what you're looking for. The higher profile a hotel is, the more it's going to cost. So for the fancy theme resorts, figure at least $100 for a double. If you can get in **The Mirage,** for example, for less (and surprisingly often, you can), that's a good deal. See Chapter 8 for a listing of great hotels.

Transportation

I suggest you rent a car in Vegas (see Chapter 9 for more information), because even though the traffic is terrible, which can make driving a chore, it's still better than paying ridiculous taxi rates or relying on the limited public transportation. You can walk — everywhere is flat and just about everything is in a straight line — but it's not the most pleasant activity, particularly on a hot summer day. Parking is free and ample, and every hotel has free valet parking (tip the nice folks $1; they will often have your air conditioning already going when you get in). Plan on spending about $40 a day for a rental car.

Dining

The good news is that Vegas has had a boom in world-class restaurants.

The bad news is this has happened only in the high-end restaurants. Most of the places I feel most comfortable recommending, in terms of quality, are costly — upwards of $100 per person and that's before alcohol. You can certainly eat more cheaply; there are still inexpensive (under $10) all-you-can-eat buffets and "meal deals" ($5.99 complete steak dinners) but those don't make for any memorable dining experiences. I suggest trying a little of both; have one great expensive meal and then seek out the cheaper options. Plan on spending anywhere from $40 to $70 a day per person for food, although the truly frugal, and those with humble tastes, can do just fine on about $25 per day.

Attractions

Wonderfully, this town has a number of free attractions. The hotels themselves, of course, are the main sights of interest and several of them (**The Mirage, Treasure Island, MGM Grand, Rio, Bellagio**) have free shows and attractions. And it costs nothing to watch the curiously entertaining spectacle of other people risking their cash inside the casinos.

Unfortunately, most of the other attractions in town, while not expensive in terms of actual cost, are overpriced for what they are. (For example, the recently closed **Bellagio Art Gallery** consisted of just one or two rooms, but cost more than the entrance fee to the bigger-than-big

Louvre and Vatican museums!) While I will tell you what options are out there, there are only a couple of oughta do's in town (see Chapter 16); after you visit them, you can plan on picking only a couple of other "I need some relief from gambling/I need to distract the kids" selections.

Shopping

This is one area where you can save mucho dinero on your vacation bill. Although Vegas has lots of great shopping, it's mostly of the variety you would find anywhere, so you shouldn't feel an urgent need to buy anything. Some of the major stores here are attractions in their own right — **The Forum Shops** and **Grand Canal Shoppes,** to name a couple — so they're perfect places to stroll if you'd rather browse than buy. If you're the type who can't come back from a vacation without having made a major purchase, you will find some cool places to spend your money, as well as some outlet centers that offer bargain-basement merchandise. See Chapter 18 for shopping suggestions.

Entertainment

Here is another place where you can stretch your budget. You need never spend any money on nightlife — and yet, you can still have nightlife. Most casinos offer free drinks to gamblers, even if they aren't spending much of anything, and every hotel has at least one lounge with free live music nightly.

I think you ought to see **Cirque du Soleil,** because it is so memorable, but tickets cost from $65 – $100. You can, however, find cheaper shows ranging from about $15 – $75.

If you want to see comedy headliners such as **George Carlin** or **Rita Rudner,** tickets will average $35 – $45. If you don't care where you get your laughs, a ticket to one of Las Vegas' many comedy clubs will set you back approximately $20, and that may even include a few drinks.

Cover charges for the city's dance clubs range from free (**Cleopatra's Barge Nightclub** at Caesars) to the ridiculously overpriced (**Club Rio** at the Rio). The gentler sex will be happy to know, however, that sexism (of a sort) still reigns in Sin City in that women — even at the high-priced clubs — invariably pay a cheaper cover (and sometimes, no cover at all) than men. Don't forget to tack on the price of the alcohol that you may consume while boogying the night away; the possible damage too many drinks can do to your wallet should be enough to spur you to limit your alcohol intake.

Lastly, if you plan to sample the city's famous (or infamous) strip clubs, you'll have to cough up a cover charge of about $10. And if you want to get up-close-and-personal service, keep in mind that lap dances start at $20 and escalate from there. A few too many of those and you'll strip-mine your wallet in no time.

Gambling

And then there is gambling. How much should you budget for gambling? Figure out how much you can afford to lose. That's right; assume that you are going to lose every penny; if you don't, count yourself lucky. If you come back with the same amount you brought, you are very lucky. And if you come back with more, well, break out the champagne and enjoy it, because it won't happen again. At least, you have to assume it won't.

Be strict with yourself. Decide in advance exactly how much you can afford to lose, and gamble that much and that much only. Make your goal not so much to win, but to make your money last as long as possible. If you blow it all in the first hour, that's no fun at all. If you plop your last quarter in a slot at the airport on your way home, well, you can pat yourself on the back. Remember that gambling is entertainment, not a way to raise funds.

Table 3-1 gives you a bird's-eye view of what you're likely to pay to live it up in Las Vegas.

Table 3-1	What Things Cost in Las Vegas	
Transportation *(As of this writing, $1.46=1£)*	*U.S.$*	*U.K.£*
Taxi from airport to the Strip	$8 – $12	5.52£ – 8.28£
Taxi from airport to downtown	$15 – $18	10.35£ – 12.42£
Accommodations *(As of this writing, $1.46=1£)*	*U.S.$*	*U.K.£*
Double room at The Venetian	$179	123.51£
Double room at MGM	$129	89.01£
Double room at Circus Circus	$79	54.51£
Food and Beverages *(As of this writing, $1.46=1£)*	*U.S.$*	*U.K.£*
5-course tasting with wine at Napa	$90	62.10£
3-course dinner at Olives	$35 – $40	24.15£ – 27.60£
Dinner buffet at The Mirage	$14.95	10.32£
Dinner buffet at the Luxor	$11.49	7.93£
Attractions *(As of this writing, $1.46=1£)*	*U.S.$*	*U.K.£*
Show tickets (including tax & two drinks) for Legends in Concert	$34.50	23.81£
Show tickets for Cirque du Soleil's *Mystère* at Treasure Island (taxes and drinks extra)	$69.85	48.20£

Attractions (As of this writing, $1.46=1£)	U.S.$	U.K.£
Show tickets for headliners at the Hard Rock Hotel	$20 – $100	13.80£ – 69.00£
Show tickets for headliners at Caesars Palace	$50 – $100	34.50£ – 69.00£
Show tickets (including tax, two drinks, gratuity, and souvenir brochure) for Siegfried and Roy	$95	65.55£

Keeping a Lid on Hidden Expenses

As if their crimes against today's budget traveler weren't grave enough already, Vegas has really loaded the deck with all kinds of hidden costs. Want to work out in the hotel's fab health club? Most of the hotels charge from $15 – $25 just for you to use the equipment. Want to rent a cabana by the pool? It'll set you back $40–$75 (and up up up) a day. Want a spa service? It's $50 for a basic facial and don't even get me started on seaweed wraps. Want to use the printer in your room? Usually $2 a page.

Hotels generally charge 9 percent sales tax per night on rooms, and restaurants do the same on meals. Don't forget tipping, because you'll be doing a lot of it. In a restaurant, the average tip is 15 percent of the total (before tax) — more if the service was superb. In hotels, plan to tip a bellboy $1 – $2 per bag, and the valet parker who returns your car $1. Leave $3 a day for the maid who cleans your room (at least, if you want good karma). Rental car agencies charge a whopping 23¼ percent fee on top of the daily charge.

Using Paper, Plastic, or Pocket Change

You can choose from a number of options to pay for your vacation (including meals, souvenirs, and so on). In this section, I explore the available options to help you determine the one that's right for you. For information on safety and money, see Chapter 12.

Relying on ATMs

One thing you can count on in Las Vegas is the ability to get ready cash. They want you to have access to your money so you can give it to them. After all, if you run out of cash and can't use your ATM card at 3 a.m., you can't drop any more quarters in that Double Diamond slot machine that you're just *sure* is going to pay off big at any moment. There are cash machines every five feet in Las Vegas, which is mighty convenient. However, they clip you $2 or more for each transaction.

Many banks also impose a fee ranging from 50¢ – $3 every time you use an ATM in a different city. Your own bank most likely charges you a fee for using ATMs from other banks, too. Try to anticipate your cash needs to cut down on the number of trips you'll make to the ATM; it will leave you with more cash to hand over to those other one-armed bandits.

Cirrus (☎ 800-424-7787) and **Plus** (☎ 800-843-7587) are the two most popular ATM networks; check the back of your ATM card to find out what network your bank affiliates with. (The toll-free numbers also provide ATM locations where you can withdraw money.)

Some of you may be in the habit of carrying cash when you're on vacation. I really can't recommend carting more than 1 – 2 days' worth of money around with you in Las Vegas. While security in the casinos is tight, pickpocketing on the Strip is the crime of choice, and when you consider how easy it is to access an ATM, there's no reason to tote a wad of cash. If you do choose to carry cash, make certain that you never flash it around; you may attract the wrong kind of attention.

Using traveler's checks

Traveler's checks are a throwback to the days before ATM machines gave you easy access to your money. Because you can replace them if they're lost or stolen, traveler's checks are a sound alternative to stuffing your wallet with cash. However, you may have trouble cashing them in some places. Foreign travelers should note that you get a better exchange rate using ATMs or credit cards.

Still, if you feel you need the security of traveler's checks and don't mind the hassle of showing identification every time you want to cash a check, you can get them at almost any bank. **American Express** offers checks in denominations of $10, $20, $50, $100, $500, and $1,000. You'll pay a service charge ranging from 1 – 4 percent, although AAA members can obtain checks without a fee at most AAA offices. You can also get American Express traveler's checks over the phone by calling ☎ 800-221-7282; Amex gold and platinum cardholders who call this number are exempt from the 1 percent fee.

Visa also offers traveler's checks, available at Citibank locations across the country and at several other banks. The service charge ranges between 1.5 – 2 percent; checks come in denominations of $20, $50, $100, $500, and $1,000. **MasterCard** also offers traveler's checks. Call ☎ 800-223-9920 for a location near you.

Charging up a storm

Travelling with credit cards is a safe alternative to carrying cash. Credit cards also provide you with a record of your vacation expenses after you return home. Plus, foreign travelers get a better exchange rate. You can also get cash advances with your credit cards at any bank (although you start paying interest on the advance the moment you receive the cash, and you don't receive frequent-flyer miles on an airline credit card). At most banks, you don't even need to go to a teller; you can get a cash advance at the ATM if you know your PIN number. If you've forgotten your PIN number or didn't even know you had one, call the phone number on the back of your credit card and ask the bank to send it to you. It usually takes five to seven business days, although some banks will do it over the phone if you tell them your mother's maiden name or give them some other security clearance.

 Most casinos make it easy to get a cash advance with your credit card. Isn't that nice of them? The problem is that they charge outrageous processing fees — usually 7 – 10 percent of the amount you are advancing ($200 costs you an additional $16). Don't do it!

Tips for Cutting Costs

 You can conserve your cash in more than just a couple of ways when you vacation in Las Vegas. Use these tips to keep your vacation costs manageable:

- ✔ **Go during the off-season.** If you can travel at non-peak times (notably, summer), you'll find hotel prices that are significantly reduced from those in peak months.

- ✔ **Travel on off-days of the week.** Airfares vary depending on the day of the week. If you can travel on a Tuesday, Wednesday, or Thursday, you may find cheaper flights to your destination. When you inquire about airfares, ask if you can get a cheaper rate by flying on a different day. Also, keep in mind that hotel rates in Las Vegas tend to be cheaper on weekdays then on weekends.

- ✔ **Try a package tour.** You can book airfare, hotel, ground transportation, and even some sightseeing just by making one call to a travel agent or packager, and it may cost a lot less than if you tried to put the trip together yourself. (See Chapter 5 for specific companies to call.)

- ✔ **Always ask for discount rates.** Membership in AAA, frequent-flyer plans, trade unions, AARP, or other groups may qualify you for discounted rates on car rentals, plane tickets, hotel rooms, and even meals. Ask about everything; you may be pleasantly surprised.

- ✔ **Ask if your kids can stay in your room with you.** A room with two double beds usually costs the same as a room with a queen-size bed. And many hotels don't charge you the additional-person rate if the additional person is pint-sized and related to you. Even if you have to pay $10 or $15 for a rollaway bed, you save hundreds by not taking two rooms (and you can keep a closer eye on your little scamps).

- ✔ **Try expensive restaurants at lunch instead of dinner.** If you want to try a top restaurant (see Chapter 14 for some of the best), consider having lunch instead of dinner. Lunch tabs are usually much cheaper and the menu often boasts many of the same specialties.

✔ **Skip the souvenirs.** Your photographs and your memories should be the best mementos of your trip. If you're worried about money, you can do without the T-shirts, key chains, Elvis salt-and-pepper shakers, fuzzy dice for your dashboard, and other trinkets.

✔ **Grab every free tourist magazine that you can get your hands on.** You can find these little gems in all Las Vegas hotel rooms and in hotel lobbies. They often contain valuable coupons for restaurant and attraction savings. (Feel free to skip the X-rated ones that solicitors try to push off on you in the streets!)

✔ **Eat out.** Try to eat outside your hotel whenever possible; the giant hotel complexes figure, correctly, that you are a captive audience and so even when they do provide more moderately priced food, there are usually long lines between you and it. The usual chain suspects (fast food joints and so on) are all over town, and while the food's not terribly interesting, they are certainly more budget-minded. Many of the lower-profile hotels also offer late night meal deals (steak dinners for $6, full breakfasts for $3, prime rib meals for $4.99 and so forth), which may mean eating at strange hours, but are worth taking advantage of.

✔ **Don't gamble your life's savings away.** Really, the biggest pitfall for the Vegas visitor is the gambling. If you get that gleam in your eye when you're near a blackjack table and have a hard time exercising self-restraint, you really need to take some extraordinary measures, such as leaving your ATM card at home or in your hotel room and carrying only as much cash as you're willing to lose. And frankly, the person with $10 playing nickel slots is having just as much fun as the high rollers (well, maybe not if the high rollers are winning!).

Chapter 4

Tips for Travelers with Special Needs

*W*orried that your kids are too young for Sin City or that you're too old to enjoy a Las Vegas show? Afraid you may experience barriers blocking your access or lifestyle? In this chapter, I dispense a little advice for travelers with specific needs.

Making Family Travel Fun

The Vegas masterminds decided, a few years ago, to try to go after the family market. Family-oriented attractions such as amusement parks, roller coasters, and arcades sprang up to try to get parents to bring their kids along with them to the Las Vegas wonderland (instead of, say, Walt Disney World). The resorts included such family perks as hotel childcare centers. In fact, many of the hotels were initially designed with the kids in mind. **MGM Grand,** for example, had a mammoth Wizard of Oz theme as soon as you entered the hotel, and the **Stratosphere** and **Excalibur** hotels had similar kiddie themes.

Let's just say that the plan didn't work too well.

The kid-friendly hotels, along with many others, have scaled back their offerings and, in some cases, ditched them altogether. Now there just isn't a lot for the wee ones to do.

Regardless of the extravagant facades, the main lure of Vegas is, of course, gambling. You have to be at least 21 to even enter a casino (although most hotels allow your kids to walk through the casino en route to somewhere else — after all, you usually can't get *anywhere* in a hotel without walking through the casino!). In other words, your little good-luck charms can't stand next to you at the craps table to blow on your dice. The upshot is this: If you intend to spend much time gambling (or indulging in any of the other "adult" pastimes), you'll have to find a safe and fun spot to leave the kids while you hit the tables. And, quite frankly, you'll probably wind up spending more to do this than you'll win.

Don't get me wrong, with a little bit of creativity and a few extra bucks, you can bring your entire family and everybody will have a good time.

The first thing to do to ensure that your family vacation doesn't end up like a National Lampoon nightmare is to go through this book and look for hotels, restaurants, and attractions with the kid-friendly icon.

When planning a family trip to Las Vegas, think about what you need to get through a typical day in your own household. Then consider what you need to meet those requirements outside the comforts of home. For example, if you have a very small child who requires a car seat, don't forget to ask the car-rental company if they provide them. And if you want to go out for a night at **EFX,** check into getting a childcare service (many hotels offer baby-sitting services — just be sure to inquire about costs, references, and arrangements before you arrive at the front desk).

If your children are old enough to understand, let them help you plan your adventure: Read some of the descriptions in the following chapters to them and let them decide which ones they think sound like fun. If they feel like they've helped plan the trip, they'll be more likely to have a good time. (Start out by browsing through Chapters 16 and 17.)

Being Part of the Senior Set

People over the age of 60 are traveling more than ever before, and they're coming to Vegas in droves. Unless your idea of a good time is rubbing elbows with the "youngsters" at Studio 54 (and maybe it is!), you will find that the tourists in Vegas come from all walks of life. The only requirement to fully enjoy everything the town has to offer is being *at least* 21.

Becoming a member

Many organizations cater to seniors. And many of them can save you some money. The following are some safe bets (maybe the only safe bets you'll find when traveling to Las Vegas!):

> ✔ **AARP (American Association of Retired Persons)** (601 E St. NW, Washington, DC 20049. ☎ **202-434-AARP.**) If you're not currently a member, you should consider joining. You're sure to get discounts on car rentals and hotels.

✔ **Mature Outlook** (P.O. Box 9390, Des Moines, IA 50306-9519. ☎ **800-336-6330.** Fax: 847-286-5024.) This is a similar organization you may want to look into. Here again you can get discounts on car rentals and hotel stays at many **Holiday Inn, Howard Johnson,** and **Best Western** hotels. For a mere $20 annual membership fee, you also get $100 in Sears coupons and a bimonthly magazine. All **Sears** customers (18 and over) are eligible for membership, but the organization's primary focus is on the 50-and-over market.

Another perk for having so much life experience is that most of the major domestic airlines — including **American, United, Continental,** and **U.S. Airways** — offer discount programs for senior travelers. Just be sure to ask about them when you book a flight.

In Las Vegas, people over the age of 62 can get discount fares on the local bus system by obtaining a *Reduced Fare Identification Card* from the **Downtown Transportation Center** (300 North Casino Center, Las Vegas, NV 89101; ☎ **702-229-6025.**) You need to apply for the card in person and must provide proof of age.

Some theaters, museums, and other attractions offer discounts to seniors — the **Stratosphere Tower** and the **Liberace Museum,** to name a couple — so ask about discounts when you pay your admission fee. As always, you'll need to show identification with proof of age.

Saving money with publications

Seniors can also get some great deals through publications that make their money by saving you money. Following is a sampling:

✔ *The Mature Traveler,* GEM Publishing Group (Box 50400, Reno, NV 89513-0400. ☎ **800-460-6676.**) This monthly, 12-page newsletter on senior-citizen travel is available by subscription ($30 a year).

✔ *The Book of Deals,* also published by GEM (see the preceding bullet). Here you find a collection of more than 1,000 senior discounts on airlines, lodging, tours, and attractions around the country that sells for $9.95.

✔ *101 Tips for the Mature Traveler,* Grand Circle Travel (347 Congress St., Suite 3A, Boston, MA 02210. ☎ **800-221-2610** or 617-350-7500. Fax: 617-350-6206.) Grand Circle Travel is also one of the literally hundreds of travel agencies specializing in vacations for seniors.

Many of these vacations are of the tour-bus variety, with free trips thrown in for those who organize groups of 20 or more. If you're looking for more independent travel, you should probably consult a regular travel agent. **SAGA International Holidays** (222 Berkeley St., Boston, MA 02116; ☎ **800-343-0273**), offers inclusive tours for those 50 and older.

Traveling without Barriers

Las Vegas is truly for everyone and a disability shouldn't stop you from visiting and having a great time. Vegas has really gone to great lengths to accommodate individuals with special needs. All of the major hotels come equipped with the basics, such as ramps and elevators, and most have rooms outfitted with the latest technology designed for accessibility.

In order to get the most out of your visit, be sure to inform your reservations agent of your requirements.

Having said that, keep in mind the vastness of the massive hotel resorts. It can be a long haul from the front entrance to your room, to the pool, or to anywhere at all. Some casinos don't have a lot of aisle space, making them hard to maneuver. And you can count on encountering a whole lot of people and a whole lot of stuff between you and your ultimate destination.

Resources for those with disabilities are wide and varied. I give you a sampling of some of the best in the following list:

- ✔ **Avis** (☎ **800-331-1212**) and **Hertz** (☎ **800-654-3131**) offer hand-controlled cars for drivers with disabilities. Avis can provide such a vehicle at any of its locations in the U.S. with 48-hour advance notice; Hertz requires between 24 and 72 hours notice at most of its locations.

- ✔ **Wheelchair Getaways** (☎ **888-790-6749**; Fax: 606-873-8039; Internet: www.blvd.com/wg.htm). This company rents specialized vans with wheelchair lifts and other features for the disabled in Las Vegas.

- ✔ **A World of Options,** Mobility International USA (P.O. Box 10767, Eugene, OR, 97440; ☎ **541-343-1284,** voice and TTY; Internet: www.miusa.org). This is a 658-page book of resources for physically-challenged travelers, covering everything from biking trips to scuba outfitters. The book costs $35. Another place to try is **Access-Able Travel Source** (Internet: www.access-able.com), a comprehensive database of travel agents who specialize in disabled travel that is also a clearinghouse for information about accessible destinations around the world.

- ✔ **Flying Wheels Travel** (P.O. Box 382, Owatonna, MN 55060; ☎ **800-535-6790**; Fax: 507-451-1685). This is one of the best operators to help you join a tour that caters specifically to the physically challenged. They offer various escorted tours and cruises, as well as private tours in minivans with lifts.

- ✔ **FEDCAP Rehabilitation Services** (211 W. 14th St., New York, NY 10011; ☎ **212-727-4200**; Fax: 212-727-4373). This is another great resource to help you book an escorted tour.

- ✔ **American Foundation for the Blind** (11 Penn Plaza, Suite 300, New York, NY 10001; ☎ **800-232-5463**). If you're vision-impaired, these are the folks to contact for information on traveling with a seeing-eye dog.

Traveling Tips for Gays and Lesbians

The hotels and casinos in Las Vegas want your money — regardless of your lifestyle. Many of the megaresorts actively advertise in gay and lesbian papers with the hopes of luring some of those disposable-income dollars away from you.

I list a few of the best gay bars in Chapter 21. For your traveling pleasure, you can also check out the following list of some of the better resources:

✔ *The Las Vegas Bugle* (☎ 702-369-6260). This is Vegas' local monthly gay and lesbian newspaper that lists all the bars, restaurants, and events in town. When you arrive in Vegas, grab one for the latest information on what's happening. You can often find them in hotel lobbies, at the bars themselves, or in the media boxes on the streets.

✔ *The Damron Guide* (☎ 415-255-0404). This is a great nationwide travel guide for the gay community. It's available at most gay and lesbian bookstores. An abbreviated version is available online at www.damron.com.

✔ **Gay Las Vegas** (Internet: www.gaylasvegas.com). Here is a terrific Web site, including information on gay bars, gay-friendly restaurants, and even weather forecasts.

Part II

Ironing Out
the Details

The 5th Wave By Rich Tennant

"Welcome to 'Jungle Jungle', Las Vegas' newest theme hotel. You're in treehouse 709. The vines are around the corner to your left. I'll have a monkey bring up your luggage."

In this part . . .

Okay, it's nitty-gritty time. I open this part of the book by chatting a little about travel agents, package tours, and getting the best airfare. Then, it's time to find a place to rest your bones. I help you shuffle through Las Vegas' neighborhoods, zero in on a room that's right for you, get it booked, and send you packing.

So, if you're ready, let's start the ball rolling!

Chapter 5

Making the Trek to Las Vegas

* *

In This Chapter

▶ Deciding whether to use a travel agent

▶ Checking out package tours

▶ Getting the best airfares

▶ Arriving in Las Vegas by car

* *

An oasis plopped down in the middle of a barren desert and surrounded by nothing but miles and miles of sand, Las Vegas is the most isolated metropolis in the U.S.

Since there is no train service to Las Vegas, you'll either have to fly or drive to reach the city. (The city has had long-standing plans to institute rail service, and they may have come to fruition by the time you read this. Check with Amtrak at ☎ **800-USA-RAIL;** Internet: www.amtrak. com). Without further ado, read this chapter to find out your traveling options — somewhere out there is a roulette table with your name on it!

Using a Travel Agent — or Not

The best way to find a good travel agent is the same way you find a good plumber or mechanic or doctor — through word of mouth. If your circle of friends and coworkers are more homebodies than frequent fliers, try the American Society of Travel Agents' (ASTA) Web site at www.astanet.com. The site offers a directory of its certified agents, and allows you to search for agents that specialize in several different categories of travel, including adventure, family, and gambling.

Any travel agent worth their salt can help you find a great deal on airfare, hotel rates, or rental car prices. A good travel agent can also stop you from ruining your vacation by trying to save a few dollars. The best travel agents can tell you how much time you should budget for a destination, where to find a cheap flight that doesn't require you to change planes 17 times, how to upgrade your hotel room for about the same price, how to arrange for a competitively priced rental car, and can even give you restaurant recommendations. (Be sure to ask for this type of information if you're interested.)

To get the most out of your travel agent, do your homework (my apologies if I sound a bit like your third-grade teacher). The best place to begin is to flip through my sections on accommodations (see Chapter 8) and choose a few that appeal to you. If necessary, get an additional travel guide such as *Frommer's Las Vegas*. If you have access to the Internet, check prices on the Web (see the section "Getting the best airfare," later in this chapter).

After you've done your homework, document your choices on the yellow worksheets at the back of this book, take them to the travel agent of your choice, and ask him to make the arrangements for you. Because he has access to more resources than even the most complete travel Web site, your travel agent can often get you a better price than you can get by yourself. And he can even issue your tickets and vouchers on the spot. If he can't get you into your first-choice hotel, ask him to recommend an alternative (and be sure to look for an objective review in this book).

Don't forget that most commercial travel agents work on commission. The good news is that *you* don't incur that added cost; the airlines, accommodations, and tour companies do. The bad news is that unscrupulous travel agents often try to persuade you to book the vacations that allow them the most money in commissions. But over the past few years, some airlines and resorts have begun to limit or eliminate travel agent commissions altogether. The immediate result has been that travel agents don't bother booking certain services unless the customer specifically requests them. Some travel agents have started charging customers for their services. When that practice becomes more commonplace, the best agents should prove even harder to find. So feel free to use a travel agent — you can get a great deal through one. But do it wisely. And don't jump into any "deals" that you feel uncomfortable with. With a little research and your own good, common sense, you're sure to come away with a great vacation plan.

Buying It All at Once: The Ins and Outs of Package Tours

Package tours, put simply, are a way of buying your airfare and accommodations in one fell swoop. It's probably a good bet for a popular destination like Las Vegas. In many cases, you pay less for a package that includes airfare, hotel, and transportation to and from the airport than you pay for the hotel alone if you book it yourself. The reasoning is simple: Packages are sold in bulk to tour operators, who resell them to the public.

It's kind of like buying your vacation at Sam's Club — except the tour operator is the one who buys the 1,000-count box of garbage bags and resells them at a cost that undercuts what you'd pay at your average neighborhood supermarket.

Package tours can vary by leaps and bounds, however. Some offer a better class of hotels than others. Some offer the same hotels for lower prices. Some offer flights on scheduled airlines; others book charters. Some even limit your choice of accommodations and travel days. The upshot here is to make sure you get what you want at a price you are comfortable with. A great starting point when looking for a package is the travel section of your local Sunday newspaper. Also check the ads in the back of national travel magazines such as *Travel & Leisure, National Geographic Traveler,* and *Condé Nast Traveler.* **Liberty Travel** (☎ 888-271-1584; Internet: www.libertytravel.com) is one of the biggest packagers in the Northeast, and usually boasts a full-page ad in Sunday papers. **American Express Vacations** (☎ 800-346-3607; Internet: http://travel.americanexpress.com/travel/) is another option.

Don't forget another good resource: the airlines themselves! They often package their flights together with accommodations. When choosing the airline, pick the one that has frequent service to your home town and lets you accumulate frequent-flyer miles. **Southwest Vacations** (☎ 800-423-5683; Internet: www.swavacations.com/) recently offered a Las Vegas package out of Los Angeles that included airfare, accommodations at **Luxor,** hotel taxes, and a discount coupon book for $269 per person. A package offered by **Delta Vacations** (☎ 800-872-7786; Internet: www.deltavacations.com) out of New York City included airfare, accommodations at the **Mandalay Bay,** hotel taxes, numerous discount offers, and some souvenirs for $599 per person. Other airline packagers include the following:

- ✔ **American Airlines Vacations** (☎ 800-321-2121; Internet: www.aavacations.com)

- ✔ **Continental Airlines Vacations** (☎ 888-898-9255; Internet: www.coolvacations.com)

- ✔ **National Airlines Vacations** (☎ 888-757-5387; Internet: www.nationalairlines.com)

- ✔ **US Airways Vacations** (☎ 800-455-0123; Internet: www.usairwaysvacations.com)

Some of the biggest hotels also offer packages. If you have your heart set on staying at a particular hotel, call them and ask if they can offer land/air packages. I include a list of the major resorts and their contact information in Chapter 8.

Becoming an Independent Traveler

If you're more the independent type and have your heart set on planning your own perfect vacation, go for it! Doing so can be a very gratifying experience. Just browse the following sections to ensure that your toils don't end up spoiled.

Who flies there?

The following airlines have regularly scheduled flights into Las Vegas (some of these are regional carriers, so they may not all fly from your point of origin): **Air Canada** (☎ 888-247-2262; Internet: www.aircanada.ca; does not offer direct service but will book on partner airlines, usually with a change in San Francisco), **Alaska Airlines** (☎ 800-426-0333; Internet: www.alaskaair.com), **Allegiant Air** (☎ 877-202-6444; Internet: www.allegiantair.com; service only from Long Beach and Fresno, CA), **America West** (☎ 800-235-9292; Internet: www.americawest.com), **American/American Eagle** (☎ 800-433-7300; Internet: www.americanair.com or www.aa.com), **American Trans Air** (☎ 800-543-3708; Internet: www.ata.com; currently only has service to Vegas through Chicago or Indianapolis), **Continental** (☎ 800-525-0280; Internet: www.flycontinental.com), **Delta/Skywest** (☎ 800-221-1212; Internet: www.delta-air.com), **Frontier Airlines** (☎ 800-432-1359; Internet: www.frontierairlines.com), **Hawaiian Airlines** (☎ 800-367-5320; Internet: www.hawaiianair.com), **Legend Airlines** (☎ 800-452-2022; Internet: www.legendairlines.com; a small start-up airline that currently only offers service from Dallas, Los Angeles, and Washington, D.C.), **Northwest** (☎ 800-225-2525; Internet: www.nwa.com), **Reno Air** (☎ 800-736-6247), **Southwest** (☎ 800-435-9792; Internet: www.iflyswa.com), **Sun Country** (☎ 800-752-1218; Internet: www.suncountry.com), **TWA** (☎ 800-221-2000; Internet: www.twa.com), **United** (☎ 800-241-6522; Internet: www.ual.com), and **US Airways** (☎ 800-428-4322; Internet: www.usair.com).

The newest low-cost airline on the Las Vegas scene, **National Airlines** (☎ 888-757-5387; Internet: www.nationalairlines), debuted in 1999 and has its hub at McCarran Airport. It offers nonstop service to several major U.S. cities and offers free unlimited stopovers in Vegas on its transcontinental flights.

Getting the best airfare

Competition among the major U.S. airlines is unlike that of any other industry. A coach seat is virtually the same from one carrier to another (you know: small, cramped, and basically uncomfortable), yet the difference in price may run as high as $1,000. If you're a business traveler and need the flexibility to purchase your tickets at the last minute, change your itinerary at a moment's notice, or want to get home before the weekend, you'll wind up paying the premium rate (known as the *full fare*). If you don't require this level of flexibility, you can probably get a better deal. Consider the following:

- ✔ **Plan ahead:** On most flights, even the shortest hops, the full fare is close to $1,000 or more, but a 7-day or 14-day advance-purchase ticket is closer to $200 – $300.

- ✔ **Be flexible about the dates you travel:** You can often get a bargain-basement deal (usually a fraction of the full fare) if you can book your ticket long in advance, don't mind staying over Saturday night, or are willing to travel on a Tuesday, Wednesday, or Thursday.

✔ **Check out consolidators:** Also known as *bucket shops, consolidators* are a good place to check for the lowest fares. Their prices are much better than the fares you could get yourself, and are often even lower than what your travel agent can get you. You see their ads in the small boxes at the bottom of the page in your Sunday travel section. Some of the most reliable consolidators include **Cheap Tickets** (☎ 800-377-1000; Internet: www.cheaptickets. com), **1-800-FLY-CHEAP** (Internet: www.flycheap.com) and **Travac Tours & Charters** (☎ 877-872-8221; Internet: www. thetravelsite.com). Another good choice, **Council Travel** (☎ 800-226-8624; Internet: www.counciltravel.com), caters especially to young travelers, but their bargain-basement prices are available to people of all ages.

✔ **Look for sales:** Don't forget that the airlines periodically lower the prices on their most popular routes. These fares have advance-purchase requirements and date-of-travel restrictions, but you can't beat the price: usually no more than $400 for a cross-country flight. To take advantage of these airline sales, watch for ads in your local newspaper and on TV and radio, and call the airlines or check out their Web sites.

These fare sales tend to take place during seasons of low travel volume. You'll rarely see a sale around the peak summer vacation months of July and August, or around Thanksgiving or Christmas, when people are more willing to pay a premium.

Booking your ticket online

If you're on the prowl for a super deal, grab that mouse and scour the Internet. Computers are great at sifting through millions of pieces of data and returning information in rank order.

Because there are too many travel-booking sites to mention, I'll just give you a few of the better-respected (and more comprehensive) ones: **Travelocity** (Internet: www.travelocity.com), **Microsoft Expedia** (Internet: www.expedia.com), and **Yahoo Travel** (Internet: http:// travel.yahoo.com). Each has its own little quirks, but all provide variations of the same service. Simply enter the dates you want to fly and the cities you want to visit, and then sit back and let your computer look for the lowest fares. Several other features have become standard to these sites: the ability to check flights at different times or dates in hopes of finding a cheaper fare; e-mail alerts that tell you when fares drop on a route you have specified; and a database of last-minute deals that advertises super-cheap vacation packages or airfares for those who can get away at a moment's notice.

Another great way to find a last-minute deal is to check directly with the airlines themselves through a free e-mail service called **E-savers.** With this service, you get a weekly list of discounted flights, most of which leave the upcoming Friday or Saturday and return the following Monday or Tuesday. The easiest way to go about this is to sign up for all the major airlines at once. Just log on to **Smarter Living** (Internet: www.smarterliving.com), or go to each individual airline's Web site (see the appendix at the back of the book for a list of airline Web sites). These sites offer schedules, flight booking, and information on late-breaking bargains.

Hitting the Road

Check your oil, top off your fluids, get out that map, and hit the road, Jack!

Sometimes getting there is half the fun. If you're one of those folks who wants to put the pedal to the metal, the rubber to the road (even if it means having a longer journey), you may enjoy driving to Vegas.

 Keep in mind that if you plan on hitting the highway, **AAA** (☎ 800-222-4357; Internet: www.aaa.com) and some other automobile clubs offer free maps and optimum driving directions to their members. If you have access to the Internet, **MapQuest** (www.mapquest.com) provides driving directions, and it even gives step-by-step maps to help those of us with no sense of direction.

 Be sure to check out the weather forecast before setting out on your journey: A snowstorm approaching through the Rockies or a heat wave across the Southwest may cause you to reconsider your travel route. If your local TV station or newspaper doesn't give you enough information, check out **The Weather Channel** on cable, or on the Web at www.weather.com. The channel also offers a 24-hour weather hotline (☎ 1-900-WEATHER), which costs 95 cents per minute.

Las Vegas is located on the southern tip of Nevada right along Interstate 15, the major north-south route from Los Angeles to the Canadian border. I-15 actually runs through the city, past downtown and less than a mile from the famed Vegas Strip.

You should check with a reliable source before actually planning your route (unless you're in no hurry and just want to ramble along), but the following are some good choices from some of the major U.S. regions:

  ✔ **California:** If you're coming from Northern or Central California, consider taking Highway 99 from Sacramento to Highway 58 in Bakersfield, which will take you to I-15 in Barstow. Portions of that route are still a two-lane, undivided highway, but most of the trip is freeway-style driving. From Southern California, take I-15 all the way.

  ✔ **Upper Midwest:** If you're coming from the upper Midwest, your best bet is probably I-80, which stretches from Pennsylvania all the way to San Francisco. It may not be an extremely scenic drive, but it's the safest and fastest route to the point where it intersects with I-15 in Utah. Another option is I-70, which runs from Missouri to I-15 in Utah.

Highway Access to Las Vegas

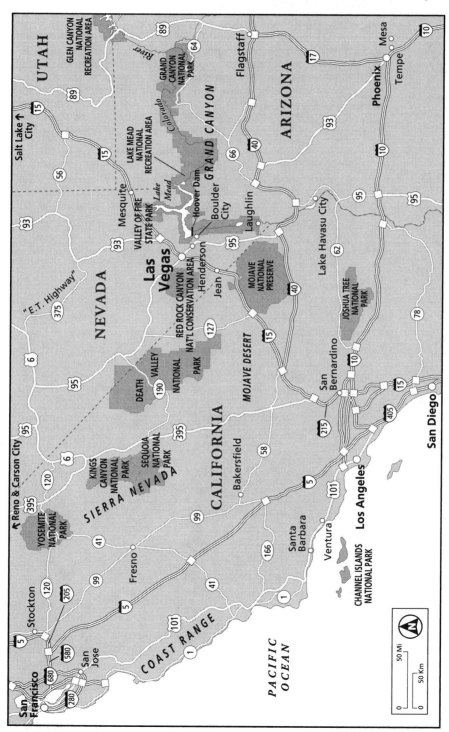

✔ **The Great Northwest:** The best way to travel from the Northwest is probably I-84 running from Oregon to I-15 in Utah.

 ✔ **East of Sin City:** If you're coming from anywhere east of Las Vegas, you may get your kicks by taking historic Route 66. Parts of this route have been replaced by interstates, but for the most part, it still meanders from Chicago to Los Angeles, offering more than 2,000 miles of beautiful Americana. You can take it all the way to Kingman, Arizona, where you hook up with Highway 93. This takes you past the famous Hoover Dam (see Chapter 19 for more information on the Dam and other side trips) and then right into Las Vegas. You can't beat it if you have the time or a sense of wanderlust!

Chapter 6

Deciding Where to Stay

● ●

In This Chapter

▶ Finding a hotel room that meets your needs

▶ Choosing the neighborhood in which you want to stay

▶ Selecting a hotel that falls in your price range

● ●

*H*ave you ever dreamed of seeing the pyramids of Egypt? Imagined you're on a pirate ship preparing to do battle? Is hanging out in Times Square your kind of activity? What about attending a circus, complete with acrobats and trapeze artists? You can be everywhere at once, and yet nowhere but Las Vegas.

Remember that, in most other cities, hotels are built near the attractions, but in Vegas, the hotels *are* the attractions.

If you tend to think of a hotel stay in terms of amenities and ambiance, you'll need to readjust your thinking before arriving in Vegas. The hotels here go way beyond room service and a swimming pool. I'm talking roller coasters, wildlife, beautiful décor, and slot machines out the wazoo. It's not exactly your everyday choice between a Marriott and a Motel 6.

But you don't need to feel overwhelmed by the Vegas scene, because in this chapter I tell you what you need to know to make the choices that are right for you. Trust me, you'll walk into this glittering city with a firm grasp on where you want to go and what you want to do.

Having It Your Way

So you've chosen a general location, and you know from the size of your bank balance what kind of price range you can afford (and if you don't, turn to Chapter 3). Unfortunately (or *fortunately*, really), there are still a few things you need to consider.

Stay where you play — or not

This is a big decision. Don't kid yourself: Gambling is a major Vegas activity, so you won't lack for casino action. If you're itching to spin the roulette wheel, it may be nice to have immediate access to one 24 hours a day. Those of you who don't consider it a high priority might feel differently. Regardless of your preference, here's basically what you need to know:

- **Casino hotels:** If you opt for a casino hotel, you're in for 'round-the-clock entertainment, dining, and action. Casino hotels are often loud, crowded, enormous places that actively discourage relaxing (it hinders your gambling, don't you know!).

- **Non-casino hotels:** Most non-casino hotels provide you with a room, a pool (maybe), and a parking space. But they can also offer a quiet getaway from the hustle and bustle of this happening town.

In the end, only you can decide whether you'd rather stay in the middle of the fray or quietly slip away for a little peace and quiet at the end of the day.

One popular misconception is that non-casino hotels offer cheaper rooms. That's not necessarily true. You may find a good deal occasionally, but most non-casino hotels have to make up for a lack of gaming revenue by charging higher room rates.

The big and the small of it

There really is no such thing as a small hotel in Las Vegas. So your options are not really big versus small — they're gargantuan versus big. (For the sake of this argument, however, I call it big versus small.)

- **Small fry:** On one hand, you have the small hotels, which often give more-personalized service. These are the places where you don't need to leave a trail of breadcrumbs to find your room, and you don't get stuck for an eternity in a line at the front desk. However, the smaller hotels usually offer less in the way of amenities like pools, health clubs, and restaurants.

- **Big cheeses:** On the other hand, you have the big hotels. These cities unto themselves have spared no expense in keeping you entertained and pampered (and they're full of gambling action and boutiques). However, these hotels give you a map when you check in. (Nope, I'm not joking.) Consider a 15-minute walk from your room to the spa — in your workout clothes — right through the middle of a crowded casino. Scary thought.

In Chapter 8, I give you the rundown on the relative size of each hotel. This has to do with more than just the number of rooms and how many people can fit into the main dining room — it's about the *sprawl,* or how far you have to walk from the elevator to the front door, and how easily you can negotiate the place. When you make your final decision, you need to weigh the tradeoff between convenience and personal service and having every conceivable amenity and amusement available without ever having to smell the desert air. It's a tough choice, I know, but you'll do just fine.

To theme or not to theme

Here's the basic question: Do you want to stay in a place that smacks of Venice at every turn? Or one whose décor screams "rock 'n' roll" throughout? While some visitors love the fact that they can enter a different world for a while, others prefer a more low-key approach. It's really your call.

Many of the theme hotels fall into the "gargantuan" category. If you want a smaller venue, you may want to check out a non-theme hotel. Chapter 8 gives you a peek at which hotels, in particular, give you which type of experience.

Into everybody's life a little chain must fall

Actually, most non-theme hotels in Vegas, at least, the ones I recommend, belong to high-profile chains: **Marriott, Holiday Inn, Best Western,** and so on. Now, normally I like to tout Mom and Pop over Big Business, but there isn't much of the former, hotel-wise, in Vegas. But while hard-core travelers may snort at your lack of adventure, there really isn't anything wrong with choosing the reliability and the certain quality assurance — easier, in theory, to maintain in the smaller properties — of a chain. Although staying at a theme hotel is absolutely a first priority for Vegas, their rooms, in many cases, aren't much different from the dull standard hotel comforts found in a generic chain. After all, you can — and should — leave your room and go explore the theme hotels at length and leisure. So don't fret if the theme hotels are booked, or if you really just like the coffee served at a Marriott. Just don't let me hear of you making that kind of choice when you eventually go to Istanbul.

Even the big hotels have the whiff of chain about them. **Harrah's** is a famous casino-hotel line, while **Bellagio, The Mirage, Treasure Island, Golden Nugget, MGM Grand, New York-New York** and half of **Monte Carlo** are owned by the same company. Another company owns **Circus Circus, Luxor, Excalibur** and **Mandalay Bay,** while still another has **Bally's** and **Paris.** (Remember that any or all of this ownership information will likely change: Hotel ownership is shuffled faster than a poker deck.)

Family fun or adult action

When I say *adult hotels,* I don't mean trashy décor and mirrors everywhere. I simply mean that some places aim for the grown-up market by deliberately leaving out the things that appeal to children, like video arcades and water rides. In some cases, they even actively discourage guests from bringing children. The **Bellagio** actually bars kids who aren't staying at the hotel from entering after 6 p.m. — and yes, the staff does check room keys.

If you have kids who will be joining you on your vacation, look for the kid-friendly icon when you read the hotel reviews in Chapter 8. These icons highlight the places that cater to families.

Location, Location, Location

Las Vegas' major hotels and attractions are concentrated in three main areas: *the Strip*, *downtown*, and *Paradise Road*.

Your mission, should you choose to accept it, is to read the pros and cons of each area and decide which part of town to choose as your base of operations (but, being a nice person, I haven't rigged this book to self-destruct when you're done).

Staying on the Strip

Officially known as Las Vegas Boulevard South, this four-mile stretch of road is home to the biggest, splashiest, and (in some cases) gaudiest hotels on earth. All the major players you've heard about are here: **Bellagio, The Venetian, New York-New York, MGM Grand, Caesars Palace,** and **The Mirage,** just to name a few.

No matter how it may seem, the Strip is very spread out. If it's a nice day and you're feeling frisky (and wearing sensible shoes), you can try walking from one end to the other — just be sure to bring cab fare with you in case your legs give out. To make things a bit more manageable, I've divided the Strip into three sections:

- ✔ **The South Strip** runs roughly from Harmon Avenue south and includes the **MGM Grand, New York-New York,** and the **Luxor.**

- ✔ **The North Strip** is everything north of Fashion Show Lane up to the **Stratosphere Tower;** it's here that you'll find **Circus Circus,** the **Sahara,** and the **Stardust,** to name a few.

- ✔ **The Center Strip** is basically everything in between and includes **Bellagio,** the **Flamingo, Caesars Palace, The Mirage,** and **Treasure Island.**

Las Vegas Accommodations Overview

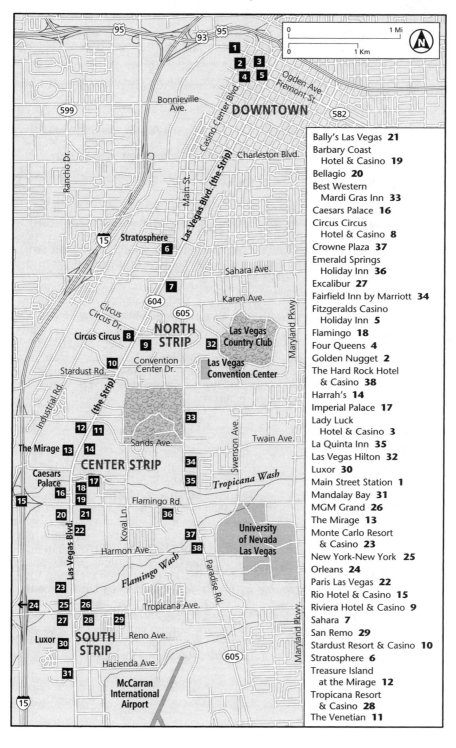

Bally's Las Vegas **21**
Barbary Coast
  Hotel & Casino **19**
Bellagio **20**
Best Western
  Mardi Gras Inn **33**
Caesars Palace **16**
Circus Circus
  Hotel & Casino **8**
Crowne Plaza **37**
Emerald Springs
  Holiday Inn **36**
Excalibur **27**
Fairfield Inn by Marriott **34**
Fitzgeralds Casino
  Holiday Inn **5**
Flamingo **18**
Four Queens **4**
Golden Nugget **2**
The Hard Rock Hotel
  & Casino **38**
Harrah's **14**
Imperial Palace **17**
Lady Luck
  Hotel & Casino **3**
La Quinta Inn **35**
Las Vegas Hilton **32**
Luxor **30**
Main Street Station **1**
Mandalay Bay **31**
MGM Grand **26**
The Mirage **13**
Monte Carlo Resort
  & Casino **23**
New York-New York **25**
Orleans **24**
Paris Las Vegas **22**
Rio Hotel & Casino **15**
Riviera Hotel & Casino **9**
Sahara **7**
San Remo **29**
Stardust Resort & Casino **10**
Stratosphere **6**
Treasure Island
  at the Mirage **12**
Tropicana Resort
  & Casino **28**
The Venetian **11**

If you're a first-time visitor to Vegas and want to be close to all the glitzy sites, the Strip is your best bet. Consider the pros and cons, however:

✔ **Pros:** All the megaresorts are here — many within walking distance of one another (and trust me, you'll want to spend time gawking at these hotels).

The Strip offers a wide variety of choices, from super-luxurious casino resorts to standard motels. And don't forget: This is really why you're coming to Vegas!

✔ **Cons:** This is why *everyone* comes to Vegas, so this is where the crowds are. Don't overlook the fact that most places are on the expensive side, and the few cheap hotels are cheap in every sense of the word. Finally, with so much to do on the Strip, it's easy to miss out on the rest of the city.

Note also that the extreme end of the North Strip (near the **Stratosphere** particularly, but even closer down toward the **Sahara**) is not nearly as bustling as it once was; in fact, it's kinda desolate and creepy in spots. The closer you get to the center, the better, although the South Strip, with the **MGM Grand, Excalibur, New York-New York,** and **Tropicana** on four corners, is pretty happening.

The Las Vegas Strip is one of the most popular destinations in the country and, as such, tourist traps are everywhere. Be aware that anything you buy on the Strip — a meal, film, a souvenir, or a can of shaving cream — costs more than anywhere else in town. Be careful to pack enough film and an adequate supply of all your toiletries so that you don't run out and get price-gouged. And by all means, try to resist buying souvenirs until you're in another part of town. (For more information on shopping in Vegas, see Chapter 18.)

Doing the downtown thing

Downtown is really where the Las Vegas phenomenon began. Hotels and casinos sprang up here long before the Strip was anything more than a gleam in Bugsy Siegel's eye. The area is informally known as *Glitter Gulch* (narrower streets make the neon seem brighter here).

The bulk of the action is concentrated on and around Fremont Street between Main and 9th (about a five-minute drive from the north end of the Strip), putting any number of casinos within a block or two of each other. Downtown had, in the not-so-distant-past, fallen victim to the high-profile aura surrounding the Strip. Revitalized by the *Fremont Street Experience* (see Chapter 17), downtown has been transformed from a seedy, unsafe row of low-rent hotels and strip joints to a more pleasant, friendly row of medium-rent hotels (with only the *occasional* strip joint). And it's all tied together by a pedestrian mall topped with a canopy that features a regular light show set to music.

Again with the pros and cons:

✔ **Pros:** Downtown is less crowded and overwhelming than the Strip. You'll often get better bargains on hotels and entertainment. And if you don't want to rent a car, you'll save on transportation because everything in the downtown area is within walking distance.

✔ **Cons:** You'll find fewer choices of hotels and places to play than on the Strip. It's also somewhat isolated from all the really famous, big-ticket venues in town. And, if you're bringing your family, keep in mind that downtown is still seedy in spots and doesn't cater much to families.

The good news is that staying downtown usually saves you a few bucks on your hotel bill and cab fares. And, as a general rule, meals, shows, and attractions are cheaper.

Playing on Paradise Road

This section of town, near the **Las Vegas Convention Center,** is the main choice for convention-goers. The road runs parallel to Las Vegas Boulevard, about a mile away, and most hotels and casinos are located between Harmon and Sahara Avenues. (Keep in mind when you read the hotel reviews in Chapter 8 that a "Paradise Road" designation does not necessarily mean the hotel is right *on* Paradise Road, but rather in the vicinity.)

Hotels here are mostly of the generic, if not outright chain variety, which could take a big chunk of fun out of your Vegas experience. Many boast that they are an easy walk to the Strip, but that depends on your definition of "easy."

✔ **Pros:** This area offers more non-casino hotels as a quiet alternative to the busy Strip and downtown. And it's within close proximity to all the action without being right in the middle of it. If you're a budget-conscious traveler, you're likely to find the best deals here.

✔ **Cons:** Paradise Road has fewer hotel, entertainment, and recreation choices than either the Strip or downtown. And it doesn't have the fun stuff within true walking distance. Finally, if there's a convention in town, forget it!

Choosing a Hotel That's Right on the Money

Pricing a hotel is a tricky thing in Vegas; the same room that you can have for a mere $29 on one night can, the following night, be as much as $250. No lie. In theory, the more you pay, the plusher the furnishings and linens, the faster the service, the posher the place. But again, come to Vegas on a busy weekend, and you may well pay $200 or more for a very basic hotel room.

Unfortunately, the days of the super-cheap room at a famous, big-name hotel are over. At the risk of giving away my, um, years of experience, I remember staying at the **Dunes Hotel** (before it was blown up in 1993, of course) for $19! — and that was a deluxe tower room facing the Strip. Now you just can't find a clean, safe room for less than $30.

The other problem is that Vegas is presently remaking itself as a "luxury resort" vacation destination, and this is not conducive to budget travel. Most of the newer hotels — **Bellagio, Mandalay Bay, The Venetian, Four Seasons** — intend to have their prices start high and go higher. It remains to be seen whether they can consistently sell enough rooms that way in order to justify their high prices, or whether lack of demand will force them to rethink this annoying trend. Feel free to let them know you would just simply *love* to stay in their gorgeous digs, but you've gotten a better bargain elsewhere — and that elsewhere's casino is also going to be getting your money.

Chapter 7

Booking Your Room

• •

In This Chapter

▶ Getting a good deal on your hotel room

▶ Shopping for a hotel on the Internet

▶ Arriving in town without a reservation

• •

$\mathcal{S}$ ome people call a hotel, ask for a rate, and pay it — no questions asked. These are also the same people who go to a car lot and pay sticker price. There are, however, better ways to burn your cash in Las Vegas — slot machines and blackjack tables, for example. In this chapter, I show you how to find the best hotel rates so you can spend your money on more, um, interesting things.

The Truth about Rack Rates (And Why You Don't Have to Pay Them)

The *rack rate* is the maximum rate that a hotel charges for a room. It's the rate you'd get if you walked in off the street and asked for a room for the night. You sometimes see the rate printed on the fire/emergency exit diagrams posted on the back of your hotel-room door.

Hotels are happy to charge you the rack rate, but you don't have to pay it. Hardly anybody does. Perhaps the best way to avoid paying the rack rate is surprisingly simple: Just ask for a cheaper or discounted rate. You may be pleasantly surprised.

A rack rate is kind of like a full-fare ticket on an airplane. The only people who end up paying full price are the ones who didn't plan in advance, don't care what they're paying, or who have inflexible travel dates.

Although Las Vegas hotels average an annual occupancy rate of 92 percent, that still leaves a lot of rooms to fill. And hotels make no money on empty rooms, so they compete with each other to fill up vacancies. During off-season lulls, when occupancy rates drop even more, the big resorts aggressively court travelers with discounted room rates.

Tips for Getting the Best Room at the Best Rate

Finding the best room and getting the best rate seems like a tall order — and it is if you aren't armed with some great tips and general guidelines. Allow me to make the task a little less stressful for you.

Finding a room that's right for you

If you're looking for general guidelines for getting a great room, here are some of my strategies:

- ✔ **Always ask for a corner room.** They're usually larger, quieter, closer to the elevator, and have more windows and light than standard rooms, and they don't always cost more.

- ✔ **Steer clear of construction zones.** Be sure to ask if the hotel is renovating; if it is, request a room *away from the renovation work.* The noise and activity may be a bit more than you want to deal with on your vacation.

- ✔ **Request your smoking preference.** Be sure to ask for either a smoking or no-smoking room, if you have a preference. Otherwise, you're likely to get stuck with a room that doesn't meet your needs.

If you are booking your room through a travel agent, ask the agent to note your room preferences on your reservation. When you check in at your hotel, your preferences pop up when the reception desk pulls your reservation. Special requests cannot be guaranteed, but it can't hurt to make them in advance.

A word about smoking

All Las Vegas hotels have at least some no-smoking rooms; most have entire floors set aside for those who eschew the habit. As far as the rest of the hotel is concerned, however, it's pretty much open season — smoking is allowed just about everywhere. If you're a non-smoker, it's important that you request a smoke-free room when you reserve it, or you may regret it.

Some casinos offer small no-smoking sections of slot machines or no-smoking gaming tables, but it really doesn't mean much because these areas aren't really separate from the rest of the casino. If you're especially sensitive to cigarette/pipe/cigar smoke, don't plan on spending a lot of time in the casino area.

All hotel restaurants have no-smoking areas, but most bars and nightclubs don't.

If you do smoke, Vegas is one of the few places in the U.S. where you can light up just about anywhere. Enjoy!

✔ **Inquire about the location of the restaurants, bars, and discos.** These areas of the hotel could all be a source of irritating noise. On the other hand, if you want to be close to the action, or if you have a disability that prohibits you from venturing too far very often, you may choose to be close to these amenities. (See Chapter 4 for more information about getting around town if you have a disability.)

✔ **Ask for a room with a view.** Ask for a room that overlooks the Strip (if you're staying in a hotel situated in that part of town), otherwise, the only view you may get is of the parking garage. Rooms with Strip views usually don't cost more, although some hotels do charge for the privilege of soaking in the Las Vegas skyline from the privacy of your room. For example, **Paris** charges more for a room with a view of the **Bellagio's** fountain show across the street.

Remember, if you aren't happy with your room when you arrive, talk to the front desk. If they have another room, they should be happy to accommodate you, within reason.

Sniffing out a great room rate

Assuming you don't have an unlimited vacation budget — face it, very few of us do — here are some tips for navigating the labyrinth of Vegas hotel rates:

✔ **Travel with a group:** If you're traveling with your family or a group of friends who are willing to share a room, you can save big bucks. Be sure to ask the reservations agent at each hotel about its policy on occupancy. Most room rates are based on *double occupancy* (two people), and charges for extra guests vary wildly. Some hotels let small children stay for free in their parents' room, but charge anybody else up to $30 a night extra; other hotels allow up to four people to a room at no extra charge.

✔ **Use the toll-free number.** Reserving a room through the hotel's toll-free number may also result in a lower rate than if you call the hotel directly. On the other hand, the central reservations number may not know about discount rates at specific locations. (Local franchises may offer a special group rate for a wedding or a family reunion, for example, but they may neglect to tell the central booking line.)

Your best bet is to call both the local number and the toll-free number to see which one gives you a better deal.

✔ **Call around — twice.** Every hotel listed in this book has a toll-free phone number. It doesn't cost you anything, so call around and see who is offering the best prices. When you're finished, wait a day and call again. You'll often get different prices — maybe higher — but possibly an even better deal.

✔ **Time your reservation.** Unless your boss is dictating your vacation schedule, try to think in year-round terms. Room rates change with the season and as occupancy rates rise and fall. As you would probably expect, you can get the best bargains during off-peak times (Sunday through Thursday, during slower summer months, and the weeks in December leading up to Christmas are good times). If a hotel is close to full, it is less likely to extend discount rates; if it's close to empty, it may be willing to negotiate. Resorts are most crowded on weekends and usually offer discounted rates for midweek stays.

The reverse is true for business and convention hotels. See Chapter 2 for a list of dates for the biggest Vegas conventions; these are expensive times to go, so try to avoid them if you can.

Room prices are subject to change without notice, so even the rates quoted in this book may be different from the actual rate you get when you call. Rates can and do swing *wildly* in Las Vegas, so comparison shopping and being flexible with your dates is the best advice I can give.

Here's living proof: A friend of mine recently booked a trip for his parents, who were willing to travel either the first or second weekend in November. One hotel quoted a rate of $189 a night for the first set of dates but only $69 for the second — a savings of $120 per night! Another place offered the same rooms for $85 one week and $28 the next — that second rate is better than what you'd pay at the local Motel 6, and this was at a major Las Vegas hotel.

And while it's always wise to book far ahead for a particularly busy time, if your trip came up suddenly, don't despair. Occasionally, if bookings are unexpectedly slow, you can snag a real bargain at the last minute. After all, a hotel makes no money on an empty room, so they want to sell it.

✔ **Put your membership to use.** Be sure to mention your membership in AAA, AARP, frequent-flyer programs, and any other corporate rewards program when you make your reservation. You never know when it might be worth a few dollars off your room rate. It never hurts to ask!

✔ **Go low-key.** The boom in "luxury resort hotels" has meant a corresponding boom in hotel prices, much to the budget traveler's dismay. But here's a prediction from me to you (it's only an educated guess, mind you): The older hotels will probably find it hard to compete with their newer, flashier brethren on the "gee whiz" level, so instead they may make up for it by lowering their prices. They may do this in an attemp to lure the savvy — that's you, of course! — over to their side. Sure, you may have to give up a spiffier room and service, but if you save as much as $100 a night, it's worth it!

The hotels in Las Vegas *are* the tourist attractions, so you don't have to actually stay in the biggest and brightest to experience most of what it has to offer. Unless you've got your heart set on a spa or you plan to do a lot of relaxing at a fabulous pool at your own hotel, it doesn't matter where you sleep, right? Consider checking in to a cheaper, more out-of-the-way hotel, drop your luggage off, and then explore!

✔ **Try a package tour.** Package tours combine airfare and accommodations in one purchase. Because package-tour companies buy in bulk, they can pass major savings along to you. Just be sure that you understand their restrictions and can live with the terms. For more information on package tours to Las Vegas, see Chapter 5.

I've talked a lot in this chapter about landing great deals, but be careful when shopping for a bargain that you aren't getting stuck in an older section of the hotel that isn't as nice as the rest. Ask for details on amenities and conditions from hotel reservation agents and tell them that you are writing it down. If your room doesn't match the description when you get there, cause a stink!

Surfing the Web for Hotel Deals

While the major travel booking sites (**Travelocity, Expedia, Yahoo! Travel,** and **Cheap Tickets;** see Chapter 5 for details) offer hotel booking, it's probably best to use a site devoted primarily to lodging, because you may find properties that aren't listed on more general online travel agencies. Some lodging sites specialize in a particular type of accommodations, such as bed and breakfasts, which you won't find on the more mainstream booking services. Others, such as **TravelWeb** (see below), offer weekend deals on major chain properties, which cater to business travelers and have more empty rooms on weekends.

✔ **All Hotels on the Web** (Internet: www.all-hotels.com): Although the name is something of a misnomer, the site *does* have tens of thousands of listings throughout the world. Bear in mind, however, that each hotel has paid a small fee to be listed, so it's less an objective list and more like a book of online brochures.

✔ **hoteldiscount!com** (Internet: www.180096hotel.com): This site lists bargain room rates at hotels in many cities, including Las Vegas. The cool thing is that this site pre-books blocks of rooms in advance, so sometimes it has rooms — at discount rates — at hotels that are "sold out." Select your city, input your dates, and you get a list of best prices for a selection of hotels. This site is notable for delivering deep discounts in cities where hotel rooms are expensive. The toll-free number is printed all over the site (☎ 800-96-HOTEL); call it if you want more options than are listed online.

✔ **TravelWeb** (Internet: www.travelweb.com): This site lists more than 26,000 hotels in 170 countries, focusing on chains such as **Hyatt** and **Hilton,** and you can book almost 90 percent of these online. TravelWeb's **Click-It Weekends,** updated each Monday, offers weekend deals at many leading hotel chains.

✔ **Other sites:** A number of other good Vegas-specific reservations sites reside on the Web. These include the following: www.lasvegashotel.com; www.lasvegasreservations.com; www.lvholidays.com; and www.lasvegasrooms.com. All these sites offer discounted rooms at the major hotels and at some cheaper properties.

What to Do If You Arrive without a Reservation

Okay, so you're standing in the bookstore in the Las Vegas airport having just arrived in town on a last-minute whim. Now you realize that you don't have hotel reservations, and the prospect of sleeping at the bus station looms large. What do you do? Well, first find a pay phone.

Most of the hotels in this book have local numbers listed in addition to their toll-free numbers (which usually don't work in Las Vegas). You can find this information in Chapter 8. This may sound obvious at first, but stick with me: Start by calling a few and seeing if they have any vacancies. If they do, you can relax and take your time in selecting a hotel that fits your needs and budget. If you get nothing but "Sorry, sold out," read on.

You could go through the phone book and call numbers at random, but you risk getting stuck in a bad neighborhood or an overpriced dump. Instead, try a hotel reservations service that can find a place for you to sleep and book the room for you — without charging a service fee: **The Las Vegas Convention and Visitors Authority** (☎ 702-892-0711) is open weekdays from 8 a.m. – 6 p.m. and weekends from 8 a.m. – 5 p.m.; **Las Vegas Reservations Systems** (☎ 702-369-1919) is open 24 hours a day; **Reservations Plus** (☎ 702-795-3999) is also available around the clock.

I've listed a few reservations agencies in this section in case you arrive without reservations and aren't having any luck finding a vacancy. But I don't recommend these agencies for anybody else, because these services are usually tied, in some way or another, to specific businesses. This means that they often try to steer you toward a place where they collect a commission instead of helping you find another option that may suit you better.

If you still have no luck finding a room, you're going to have to do some real work: Go get a rental car (you can't do what I have in mind on foot or by taxi) and start driving. (For information on renting a car, see Chapter 9.) There are lots of little hotels near the airport, so you can begin there. If you strike out there, head to the **Strip** — that's where most of the rooms in Las Vegas are located. Even if you got a "sold out" on the phone, try the front desk anyway, in case there's been a last-minute cancellation.

Your next hunting ground should be **Paradise Road** and the streets crossing it, like **Flamingo, Convention Center,** and **Harmon.** This area has lots of nice, smaller hotels that might not be a top pick in this book or be included in the reservations systems, but are fine in a pinch.

Also, don't forget that many of the hotels are owned by the same companies (like **Luxor, Excalibur,** and **Circus Circus** are). Throw yourself on the mercy of the front-desk clerk and ask if any "sister" hotels have vacancies.

 Finally, go **downtown,** but be careful — some areas are not very safe.

Chapter 8

Checking In to Las Vegas' Best Hotels

· ·

In This Chapter

▶ Browsing hotels by location and price

▶ Getting reviews of the best hotels in the city

▶ Finding an alternative hotel

· ·

*F*inding a great place to hang your hat in Vegas may or may not be tops on your list, but you'll need to sleep somewhere. In this chapter, I make the decision easier by breaking down some of my favorite hotels by neighborhood and price. I then give you a quick review of each one so you can choose the one that best suits your needs. Looking for a great location but don't want to spend a bundle? Check out the "Hotel Index by Price" section (which also gives you a brief idea of the location). Looking for a super (read *expensive*) room with all the amenities? Again, look at the "Hotel Index by Price" section and then cross-reference the "Las Vegas Hotels A to Z" section. I've worked hard on this research so you don't have to. Hey, vacations should be about fun, right?

Note that I purposefully didn't include every single hotel in town. That would defeat the purpose of giving you some helpful advice, now wouldn't it? The goal here is to save you the time and energy of having to slog through endless descriptions of hotels that, ultimately, I wouldn't recommend. I'm sending you straight to my favorites, but I've tried to give you a broad range of choices in size, cost, location, family friendliness, amenities, and the like. I've also scattered some helpful maps throughout the chapter. Chapter 6 has an overview map that lists all the hotels in one convenient spot.

Because price is such a big factor for most travelers, I note rack rates in the listings and also precede each with dollar signs to make them easy to reference. The more dollar signs under the name, the more you pay. Remember, however, that the prices listed here are the "official" rack rates; they're rarely what you're going to wind up paying (you can usually get a better deal). If one of these hotels sounds good to you but appears to be out of your price range, don't give up too quickly. It may be having a special promotion or a slow week that could get you in for a lower rate than normal. You may as well give them a call to find out.

All the hotels listed have free parking for guests (usually self and valet), so I don't waste your time by rehashing that point in every listing.

Pricing the Competition

I provide a dollar rating for each hotel listing in this chapter. Here's how the symbols break down:

$$$$$	Very expensive	$100 and up per night
$$$$	Expensive	$80 – $99 per night
$$$	Moderate	$60 – $79 per night
$$	Inexpensive	$40 – $59 per night
$	Unbelievably cheap	$40 or less per night

Because I've done my research, I base the ratings on what you can expect to pay *on average* for a standard room with single or double occupancy. The ratings don't necessarily correspond with the rack rates that are printed with the listing, simply because you can normally get a much better deal. Trust me on this one.

To give you a slightly better idea of what you get for your money in Vegas, here's a more detailed description of my price categories.

- ✔ **$ ($40 and under):** In this category, you can stay in a smallish room in an older, no-frills motel or hotel (with a private bath). You won't be located in the thick of things and you probably won't have a casino on the premises. Your room will be clean, and probably have a TV and phone. Don't expect room service or chocolates on the pillow.

- ✔ **$$ ($40 – $59):** The rooms in this category can be pretty plain, but you can count on a TV (most likely with cable hook-up), and other amenities (coffee maker, soaps, and shampoos). You're apt to find more uniformed men and women offering their services (don't forget to tip). Some of the downtown casinos and lesser Strip casinos fall into this category.

- ✔ **$$$ ($60 – $79):** Amenities such as hair dryers, on-site restaurants, health clubs (on- or off-site), cable TV; larger rooms, bathrooms, and closets are standard in this category. You may get a modem jack for your PC. Room service may or may not be standard. The second-tier mega resorts on the Strip and some of the lesser non-casino hotels fall into this category.

- ✔ **$$$$ ($80 – $99):** Besides a large, well-decorated room, you can count on a larger-than-a-closet bathroom with ample towels. The casino hotels in this category will definitely be sporting a theme, and you can count on finding several restaurants, a health club, and several thousand rooms. Non-casino hotels usually sport a business center and data ports in the rooms.

✔ **$$$$$ ($100 and up):** You're paying for the prestigious name, location, and/or service. Expect round-the-clock concierge service, sumptuous lobbies, an elegant theme, and beautiful room furnishings. You'll find a full range of amenities, multiple phones (some people like this; I travel to get away from phones), a data port, minibars, bathrobes, and in-room safes. Rooms may actually be junior suites. There will be one or more restaurants for fine dining, a bar and/or lobby cocktail lounge, and an on-site spa/health club. Non-casino hotels (and even some of the casino ones) have full business centers.

Hotel Index by Price

$$$$$
Bally's Las Vegas — Center Strip
Bellagio — Center Strip
Caesars Palace — Center Strip
Crowne Plaza — Paradise Road
Las Vegas Hilton — Paradise Road
Mandalay Bay — South Strip
The Mirage — Center Strip
The Venetian — Center Strip

$$$$
Flamingo — Center Strip
Hard Rock Hotel & Casino — Paradise Road
Harrah's Las Vegas — Center Strip
MGM Grand Hotel/Casino — South Strip
Monte Carlo Resort & Casino — South Strip
New York-New York — South Strip
Paris Las Vegas — Center Strip
Rio Hotel & Casino — Center Strip
Treasure Island — Center Strip
Tropicana Resort & Casino — South Strip

$$$
Emerald Springs Holiday Inn — Paradise Road
Fairfield Inn by Marriott — Paradise Road
Four Queens — Downtown
Golden Nugget — Downtown
La Quinta Inn — Paradise Road
Riviera Hotel & Casino — North Strip
Sahara Hotel & Casino — North Strip
Stratosphere Las Vegas — North Strip

$$
Barbary Coast Hotel & Casino — Center Strip
Best Western Mardi Gras Inn — Paradise Road
Excalibur — South Strip
Fitzgeralds Casino Holiday Inn — Downtown
Lady Luck Casino Hotel — Downtown
Luxor — South Strip
Main Street Station — Downtown
Stardust Resort & Casino — North Strip

$
Circus Circus — North Strip
Hotel San Remo — South Strip
Imperial Palace — Center Strip
Orleans — South Strip

Hotel Index by Location

South Strip
Excalibur — $$
Hotel San Remo — $
Luxor — $$
Mandalay Bay — $$$$$
MGM Grand Hotel/Casino — $$$$
Monte Carlo Resort & Casino — $$$$
New York-New York — $$$$
Orleans — $
Tropicana Resort & Casino — $$$$

Center Strip

Bally's Las Vegas — $$$$$
Barbary Coast Hotel & Casino — $$
Bellagio — $$$$$
Caesars Palace — $$$$$
Flamingo — $$$$
Harrah's Las Vegas — $$$$
Imperial Palace — $
The Mirage — $$$$$
Paris Las Vegas — $$$$
Rio Hotel & Casino — $$$$
Treasure Island — $$$$
The Venetian — $$$$$

North Strip

Circus Circus — $
Riviera Hotel & Casino — $$$
Sahara Hotel & Casino — $$$

Stardust Resort & Casino — $$
Stratosphere Las Vegas — $$$

Downtown

Fitzgeralds Casino Holiday Inn — $$
Four Queens — $$$
Golden Nugget — $$$
Lady Luck Casino Hotel — $$
Main Street Station — $$

Paradise Road

Best Western Mardi Gras Inn — $$
Crowne Plaza — $$$$$
Emerald Springs Holiday Inn — $$$
Fairfield Inn by Marriott — $$$
Hard Rock Hotel & Casino — $$$$
La Quinta Inn — $$$
Las Vegas Hilton — $$$$$

Las Vegas Hotels A to Z

Aladdin Resort & Casino
$$$$ South Strip

Though as a sentimentalist, I was sorry to see the old Aladdin go — didja know Elvis married Priscilla there? — but as a practical person who likes my creature comforts, I have to admit that the old girl was a dump and a half. The new one promises to be another of these fabbo theme places, although whether or not it makes good on its other promises — you are never less than seven doors from an elevator at any time, the Arabian Nights themed shopping mall will rival the Roman fantasm over at **Caesars** — remains to be seen, as it was not yet open at press time.

3667 Las Vegas, S. ☎ **877-333-WISH.** *Internet:* www.aladdincasino.com. *2600 units. Rack rates: $119 – $149 double. AE, DC, DISC, MC, V.*

Bally's Las Vegas
$$$$$ Center Strip

Poor Bally's. Here they are, the very epitome of a Las Vegas hotel, all glitzy, glamour and neon (not to mention home to the best topless show in town), but more and more, they just get overlooked. They are too upscale to have a theme, so they lack that cartoon appeal, but they aren't upscale enough to compete with the new lux wonders on the Strip. They are even getting upstaged by their very own **Paris Las Vegas,** right next

South Strip Accommodations

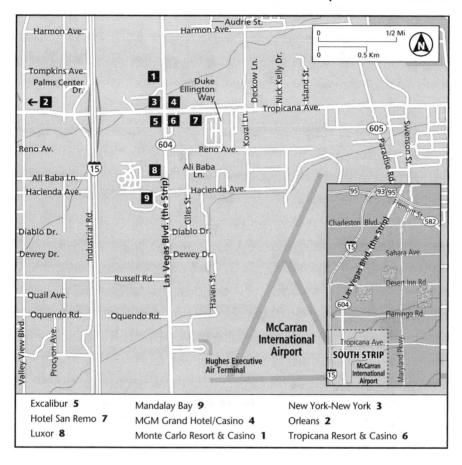

Excalibur **5**	Mandalay Bay **9**	New York-New York **3**
Hotel San Remo **7**	MGM Grand Hotel/Casino **4**	Orleans **2**
Luxor **8**	Monte Carlo Resort & Casino **1**	Tropicana Resort & Casino **6**

door. If only they had built in the shape of a pyramid or put a pirate ship out front. But their loss might translate into your eventual gain; it's not out of the question that in order to keep their profile high, they may bring their prices down. And if that's the case, Bally's would be quite the deal. Centrally located, you enter from the Strip via moving sidewalks that pass through muted neon-light pillars, waterfalls, and lush landscaping. Bright and cheerful marble, wood, and crystal are the rule throughout. The oversized rooms contain a sofa — a rarity in Las Vegas. The hotel is not huge in comparison to other Vegas hotels, but it does have more than 2,800 rooms, a light and airy casino, a noteworthy spa and fitness center, tennis and basketball, a handsome Olympic-sized swimming pool, and a whole range of restaurants.

3645 Las Vegas Blvd. S. (at Flamingo Rd.). ☎ *800-634-3434 or 702-739-4111. Fax: 702-967-3890. Internet:* www.ballyslv.com. *Rack rates: $69 and up double. AE, CB, DC, JCB, MC, V.*

Center Strip Accommodations

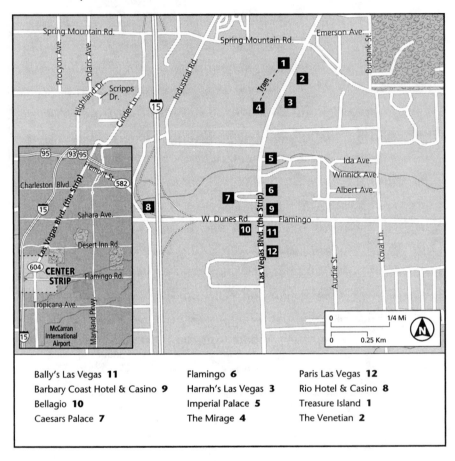

Bally's Las Vegas **11**	Flamingo **6**	Paris Las Vegas **12**
Barbary Coast Hotel & Casino **9**	Harrah's Las Vegas **3**	Rio Hotel & Casino **8**
Bellagio **10**	Imperial Palace **5**	Treasure Island **1**
Caesars Palace **7**	The Mirage **4**	The Venetian **2**

Barbary Coast Hotel & Casino
$$ Center Strip

If you're looking for an inexpensive option right in the heart of all the Strip action, look no further. Since it's (relatively) small, with only 200 rooms, you forego niceties like a pool, health club, and showrooms (although there are two restaurants, two bars, and a casino). But the upside is a perfect location, a friendly, attentive staff, and rooms that border on the tacky (faux-Victorian) but don't fall over the edge.

3595 Las Vegas Blvd. S. (at Flamingo Rd.). ☎ *800-634-6755 or 702-737-7111. Fax: 702-737-6304. Rack rates: $39 – $159 double. AE, CB, DC, DISC, JCB, MC, V.*

Bellagio
$$$$$ Center Strip

A billion dollars will buy you a lot of hotel. **Bellagio** is determined to show you what a grown-up experience Las Vegas can be (so much so they don't want non-guests under 18 to even enter the property) and the result is this enormous, gorgeous, and slightly intimidating property. It has everything the other hotels have, and then some, just more sophisticated. There's an art gallery (in Vegas, no less!), some of the best restaurants in town (including one with Picassos hanging casually on the walls), a conservatory full of fresh flowers and plants that's changed almost monthly to reflect the seasons, a 12-acre lake out front that hosts a water fountain ballet (the coolest, and least-cheesy free show in town), a neo-Classical pool area right out of an Italian villa (a really big villa), plush lush rooms full of nifty amenities, plus big gleaming bathrooms.

Oh, it's grand. Grand, I tell you! (Though honestly just a little too big — 3,000 rooms or so — to provide the kind of intimate service one gets at most in their class and price range. Not that they don't try hard.) What it isn't, is cheap. After all, they want to lure the sort of well-heeled folk who are used to dining with Picassos looking over their shoulder. But just because your own walls may not be graced by Pablo, there is nothing to prevent you from living the Bellagio life for a couple of days, particularly because you can, more often than you might think (but not as often as you'd like), catch the hotel's normally sky-high rates in an affordable mood. Make the call.

3600 Las Vegas Blvd. S. (at Flamingo Rd.). ☎ *888-987-6667 or 702-693-7444. Fax: 702-693-8346. Internet:* www.bellagiolasvegas.com. *Rack rates: $129 – 499 double. AE, CB, DC, DISC, JCB, MC, V.*

Best Western Mardi Gras Inn
$$ Paradise Road

If you've ever stayed at any other Best Western motor inn (a very reliable chain) in the U.S., you'll find more of the same here in terms of quality and cleanliness. Some exceptions, however, are this one's larger-than-normal rooms, manicured lawns, and, of course, a small casino in the lobby. Single king rooms have small sitting areas with convertible sofas, and all units have kitchenettes. And as a bonus, you get a large pool area, two sun decks, and a gazebo-covered picnic area.

3500 Paradise Rd. (between Sands Ave. and Desert Inn Rd.). ☎ *800-634-6501 or 702-731-2020. Fax: 702-733-6994. Internet:* http://www.mardigrasinn.com. *Rack rates: $40 – $125 double. AE, CB, DC, DISC, JCB, MC, V.*

Caesars Palace
$$$$$ **Center Strip**

This is the archetypical sprawling Vegas hotel, where high class meets high kitsch. When in Rome, after all. A major $300-million remodeling made Caesars brighter and more truly elegant, but have no fear: The campy Roman theme lives on, with marble columns, copies of famous statues, and toga-wearing employees. True glamour has replaced most of the tacky stuff (kind of sad for those of us who love all things kitschy), but this still has that great Vegas feel. The newer rooms are generic-beautiful and huge — some with his and hers baths. And even the older rooms have character; some have sunken tubs in the sleeping areas. And for every fabulous new touch — a stunning swimming pool area and health club/spa, each with a classical Roman theme — there remains some of the Vegas cheese we all love so well, like the talking, stiffly moving statues in the shopping area. That shopping area, by the way, is also a Vegas wonder, a reproduction of an Italian street, down to the sky overhead, full of famous-name stores plus a very fine motion simulator ride. Add to this quite a few terrific restaurants (including **Spago,** and the **Palm**) and one of the best casinos in town, and Caesars remains the place to go for all facets of Vegas life.

3570 Las Vegas Blvd. S. (just north of Flamingo Rd.). ☎ *800-634-6661 or 702-731-7110. Fax: 702-731-6636. Internet:* www.caesars.com. *Rack rates: $99 – $500 double. AE, CD, DC, DISC, MC, V.*

Circus Circus
$ **North Strip**

If you have the kids in tow, be sure to consider staying at this massive hotel (with more than 3,700 rooms). Unless you are clownphobic. (Don't laugh. Many people are.) The feel is basically, well, circus, complete with a chaotic carnival and arcade games on the midway. Don't miss the circus acts (trapeze, high wire, jugglers, and so on) that run most of the day and are visible from the midway and much of the casino. The kiddies will be entranced with the myriad amusements: an aerial tramway, an arcade, the **Adventuredome** indoor theme park (much superior to the one offered by the **MGM Grand**), two swimming pools, and even a McDonalds. Despite a recent face-lift, it's still a bit worn-at-the-edges, but it's almost always a great deal for travelers on a budget, and one of the few places in town that actively encourages families to stay. Try to avoid the Manor rooms, which are in glorified motel buildings that have seen better days, though if you do get stuck there (or are lured there by sometimes rock-bottom prices), know that they are going through some much-needed renovations and so ask for a newly redone room.

2880 Las Vegas Blvd. S. (between Sahara Ave. and Convention Center Dr.). ☎ *800-444-CIRC or 702-634-3450. Fax: 702-734-2268. Internet:* www.circuscircus-lasvegas.com. *Rack rates: $39 and up double. AE, CB, DC, DISC, MC, V.*

North Strip Accommodations

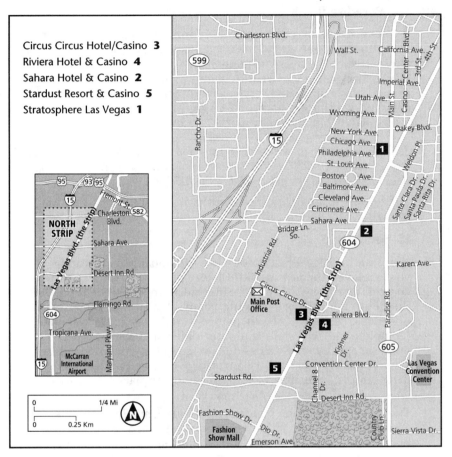

Circus Circus Hotel/Casino **3**
Riviera Hotel & Casino **4**
Sahara Hotel & Casino **2**
Stardust Resort & Casino **5**
Stratosphere Las Vegas **1**

Crowne Plaza
$$$$$ Paradise Road

Crowne Plaza is the upscale division of **Holiday Inn,** and this all-suite hotel caters mostly to business folk. You aren't going to get much Vegas here, nor really anything to indicate you aren't in, say, Des Moines or Miami, but that may be the way you like it and a certain level of quality is assured. A six-story atrium lobby done in marble and muted tones greets guests. Rooms are large, with unique layouts offering separate sleeping quarters, wet bars, and mini-fridges, plus nice touches such as bathrobes. Other nice features include the pool area, where Calypso bands play during the summer, and a small gym.

4255 Paradise Rd. (just north of Harmon Ave.). ☎ ***800-2-CROWNE*** *or 702-369-4400. Fax: 702-369-3770. Rack rates: $125 – $185 double. AE, CB, DC, DISC, MC, V.*

Emerald Springs Holiday Inn
$$$ Paradise Road

If you've stayed in a typical **Holiday Inn,** this one is a bit nicer: It's an exceptionally clean and well-tended place offering a low-key, non-casino alternative to the overwhelming Strip — although it's only three (big) blocks away when you want to go out on the town. The emphasis is on providing friendly, family-style service. Standard rooms are large, with sofas, desks, and wet bars with a fridge. Larger suites with kitchenettes are available, but you'll pay more.

325 E. Flamingo Rd. (between Koval Lane and Paradise Rd.). ☎ *800-732-7889 or 702-732-9100. Fax: 702-731-9784. Internet:* www.holidayinnlasvegas.com. *Rack rates: $69 and up double. AE, CB, DC, DISC, MC, V.*

Excalibur
$$ South Strip

A gigantic, medieval castle, complete with moat and drawbridge — don't you just love a theme run wild? History purists will note all sorts of inaccuracies and cringe at the castle-and-knight themed rooms, but that's not the point. If you're bringing the family, this is a good and reasonably priced choice. Kids will be enchanted with the attractive swimming pools (complete with waterfalls and water slides) and will love the sheer enormity and spectacle of it all. (Adults often quickly tire of the place for the same reasons.) Budget travelers also love its well-priced rooms — good deals happen here more often than any other place.

The vast size of the hotel (more than 4,000 rooms, 7 restaurants, a casino, and medieval-theme video and shopping arcades) means it's mostly hectic and noisy (Camelot was a "shining spot" not a "quiet spot"), but it is perfectly located at the newly bustling south end of the Strip, and is now neatly connected to its southern neighbors, **Luxor** and **Mandalay Bay,** by a handy monorail.

3850 Las Vegas Blvd. S. (at Tropicana Ave.). ☎ *800-937-7777 or 702-597-7777. Fax: 702-597-7009. Internet:* www.excalibur-casino.com. *Rack rates: $49 – $119 for up to four people. AE, CB, DC, DISC, MC, V.*

Fairfield Inn by Marriott
$$$ Paradise Road

Located within walking distance of several major restaurants, but not much else, lies the **Fairfield Inn by Mariott.** Consider staying here if you don't want the full-blownVegas experience. It doesn't even have a casino (in Vegas? Now *that's* different!). Friendly, personal service is the main draw of this small hotel. It offers a continental breakfast, a living room–style lobby, and a "guest of the day" who gets a basket of goodies. Rooms are basic motel-style, but they're clean and comfortable, and they offer sleeper sofas.

3850 Paradise Rd. (between Twain Ave. and Flamingo Rd.). ☎ ***800-228-2800*** *or 702-791-0899. Fax: 702-791-2705. Internet:* www.marriott.com. *Rack rates: $62 – $250 for up to five people. AE, CB, DC, DISC, MC, V.*

Fitzgeralds Casino Holiday Inn
$$ Downtown

Here's a solid, middle-of-the-road choice for affordable downtown accommodations, with a fun and understated luck o' the Irish theme. Rooms are pretty standard but comfortable (slightly larger Jacuzzi units are available for a few bucks more), but the tall tower offers great views of the mountains or the Strip. You won't find a pool or recreational facilities, but you will find a casino and a few restaurants and bars. Be sure to stop by the outdoor balcony off the casino and watch a cool view of the ***Fremont Street Experience.***

301 E. Fremont St. (at 3rd St.). ☎ ***800-274-LUCK*** *or 702-388-2400. Fax: 702-388-2181. Internet:* www.fitzgeraldslasvegas.com. *Rack rates: $40 – $85 double. AE, CB, DC, DISC, MC, V.*

Flamingo
$$$$ Center Strip

Infamous gangster Bugsy Siegel would no longer recognize his baby, which he opened in 1946 on what would eventually become the Strip. More than 50 years and a $130-million renovation later, there is nothing left from Bugsy's day but a rumor of escape tunnels under the grounds. It currently sports a vaguely art deco/tropical theme and is every bit as neon as you would like. The standard rooms and casino are nice but nothing to write home about. The gorgeous, lush pool and spa area, on the other hand, is, with its dense foliage and live birds, worth at least a postcard. There's also a bustling casino, excellent tennis facilities, a wedding chapel, and some indifferent bars and restaurants. It's all too far removed from its past self for nostalgia, but its Central Strip location still makes it a star.

3555 Las Vegas Blvd. S. (just north of Flamingo Rd.). ☎ ***800-732-2111*** *or 702-733-3111. Fax: 702-733-3353. Internet:* www.flamingolv.com. *Rack rates: $69 – $299 double. AE, CB, DC, DISC, JCB, MC, V.*

Downtown Accommodations

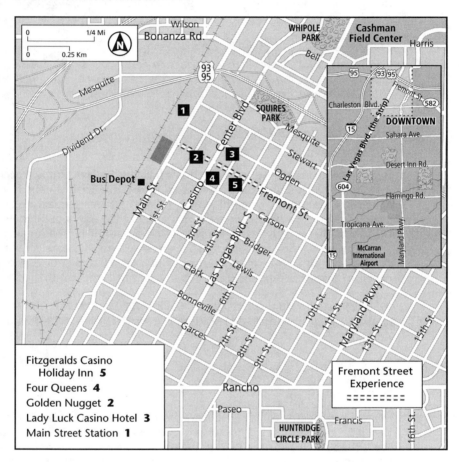

Fitzgeralds Casino
  Holiday Inn **5**
Four Queens **4**
Golden Nugget **2**
Lady Luck Casino Hotel **3**
Main Street Station **1**

Fremont Street
Experience
=========

Four Queens
$$$ Downtown

This is one of the last remnants of the 1960s' Rat Pack glory days of old
Las Vegas. It's rather dated (and a bit worn in spots), especially when
compared to the new mega-resorts on the Strip, but the old-time elegance
still lingers, and the price is right. The clientele is older, and these folks
are definitely here to gamble, not to sightsee. You get clean, comfortable,
quiet rooms and a handful of restaurants on site but alas, no pool.

202 Fremont St. (at Casino Center Blvd.). ☎ ***800-634-6045*** *or 702-385-4011. Fax:
702-387-5122. Internet:* www.fourqueens.com. *Rack rates: $29 – $179 double.
AE, CB, DC, DISC, MC, V.*

Four Seasons
$$$$$ South Strip

If you've got the money to burn, you can't go wrong by joining the other fat cats at Vegas' one true luxury resort. Not only does the **Four Seasons** have a degree in pampering, but with just 400 rooms, they can give far more personal attention than any other high-profile hotel. This is a truly unique experience for Vegas, in that the Four Seasons occupies the top five floors of **Mandalay Bay,** accessible through its own entrance (on the other side of the building), with its own lobby, high-speed elevators, pool, and health club/spa.

You don't, however, have to miss any Vegas fun. On the Four Seasons side, all is calm and serene. But open a door and presto! You're back in the hustle and bustle of Vegas, heading right into Mandalay Bay's casino. It's the best of both worlds, though once you've experienced this kind of serenity, it's hard to return to the typical adrenaline rush. Rooms don't appear all that special, but when you sink into their many comforts (down comforters, fancy amenities, VCRs, bathrobes), you don't mind. The staff is brilliant at fulfilling and even anticipating needs, and loves to pamper your children even more than you. And included delights, such as health club privileges and pool cabanas, that cost extra at other hotels may mean this particularly high ticket isn't all that out of line.

3960 Las Vegas Blvd. ☎ ***877-632-5200*** *or 702-632-5000. Fax: 702-632-5195. Internet:* www.fourseasons.com. *Rack rates: $200 – $500 standard. AE, DISC, MC, V.*

Golden Nugget
$$$ Downtown

Indisputably the nicest downtown hotel, the **Golden Nugget** has miles of white marble and gleaming brass fixtures evoking a French Riviera feel. It's owned by the same folks who run **Bellagio** and **The Mirage,** so the quality you get here is heads above that of other downtown hotels. Larger-than-average rooms — virtually identical but for the use of a different shade of beige to those found at The Mirage — are comfortable and elegant, with marble entryways, armoires, and partially canopied beds. There's also a beautiful health club and spa, a large pool (rare for downtown), and several different restaurants. Like any place in downtown, it can be a little cramped, but at least you won't feel like you are stuck in a time warp. Despite its superior status, the Nugget can be a surprisingly good deal; I once booked a mid-week room there for $39 a night!

129 E. Fremont St. (at Casino Center Blvd.). ☎ ***800-634-3454*** *or 702-385-7111. Fax: 702-386-8362. Internet:* www.goldennugget.com. *Rack rates: $49 – $299 double. AE, CB, DC, DISC, MC, V.*

The Hard Rock Hotel & Casino
$$$$ Paradise Road

Gen X and Baby Boomers should run to the Hard Rock: Your people await! This is one fun hotel. Rock music blares in the wildly and playfully decorated casino, the center of the circular — it's record and CD-shaped, you see — public area, while rock n' roll memorabilia litter the space and cover the walls, and rock references pop up everywhere, even in the elevator. This hotel is not for someone looking for a quiet getaway (it's loud, loud, loud), but is definitely the epicenter of happening Las Vegas. The pool area isn't much for swimming (mostly too shallow) but it is perfect for seeing and being seen, as guests can make like Frankie and Annette and do the Beach Blanket Bingo in the sand (yep) by the stage, or play swim-up blackjack. A new health club/spa is terrific, and they have several fine restaurants. Rooms here are a letdown. They're a bit bleak — ask for a room in the hotel's newly opened expansion — and despite bigger-than-average TVs and French windows that actually open (a rarity for Vegas), who really wants to spend time in them when there is so much fun to be had downstairs?

Music buffs will want to check out the memorabilia in the Hard Rock Hotel & Casino. Some of it's a little lame, but there's some cool stuff, too, such as a smashed guitar from Pete Townsend, James Brown's "King of Soul" cape and crown, menus signed by Elvis and Jimi Hendrix, and Greg Allman's favorite biker jacket.

4455 Paradise Rd. (at Harmon Ave.). ☎ ***800-473-ROCK*** *or 702-693-5000. Fax: 702-693-5010. Internet:* www.hardrock.com. *Rack rates: $75 – $300 double. AE, CB, DC, DISC, MC, V.*

Harrah's Las Vegas
$$$$ Center Strip

Harrah's is one of the friendliest places in town; its location (smack in the center of the Strip), price (another one where good deals can be had), and overall theme make it a solid pick. A great renovation has moved the hotel away from its former cheese and much closer to class (think marble and a grand piano in the lobby), but it's still light and fun (okay, so the piano is painted bright colors). The carnival atmosphere is not overwhelming, and the rooms are large and comfortably furnished. The casino is certainly festive, and you can spend some quality time relaxing in the pool, dining at one of the several restaurants, browsing the shopping and live entertainment plaza, and sweating at an outstanding gym.

3475 Las Vegas Blvd. S. (between Spring Mountain and Flamingo Rds.). ☎ ***800-HARRAHS*** *or 702-369-5000. Fax: 702-369-4147. Internet:* www.harrahs.lv.com. *Rack rates: $65 – $250 double. AE, CB, DC, DISC, MC, V.*

Hotel San Remo
$ South Strip

Here's a fine alternative if you want to be near the Vegas madness but not right in the middle of it. It's a small hotel located just off the Strip (and across the street from the **MGM Grand**) with nice rooms done in a vaguely French provincial decor. Many of the tower rooms include balconies and sleeper sofas. It has a small casino, several moderately priced restaurants (which often feature the cheapest prime rib deal — around $4 — in town), and two lounges featuring daily entertainment.

115 E. Tropicana Ave. (just east of the Strip). ☎ _**800-522-7366** or 702-739-9000. Fax: 702-736-1120. Internet:_ www.sanremolasvegas.com. _Rack rates: $49 – $169 double. AE, CB, D, DISC, JCB, MC, V._

Imperial Palace
$ Center Strip

Now here's a great buy! Even though this place is older and has some rough edges, it's hard to find a better value in cost, facilities, and location. It's in the heart of the Center Strip, within walking distance of many major hotel/casinos. It offers large, inexpensive rooms. Especially hard to pass up are the well-priced "Luv Tub" rooms, which get their name from the big ol' bathtub, sized to comfortably fit two and a couple of bottles of champagne. Outside the rooms, matters are definitely on the tacky and aging side, but location and its sometimes rock-bottom prices ($29! On the Strip! Right in the middle of the Strip!) make it hard to beat. Add in a large casino (with a separate no-smoking area), a tropical pool, an adequate health club, cheap prime rib specials, and entertainment options such as their famous auto collection, and you have to ask: Who needs a brand-new, gleaming hotel?

3535 Las Vegas Blvd. S. (between Spring Mountain and Flamingo Rds.). ☎ _**800-634-6441** or 702-731-3311. Fax: 702-735-8578: Internet:_ www.imperialpalace.com. _Rack rates: $49 – $99 double. AE, CB, DC, DISC, MC, V._

La Quinta Inn
$$$ Paradise Road

This is another good choice if you want to avoid the hectic Vegas atmosphere. Everything here is clean and quiet. The already comfortable decor and facilities were recently upgraded, and again, you've got that chain quality assurance. Rooms range from standard hotel rooms to two-bedroom suites that feel like apartments; some have kitchens and all have whirlpool tubs. You can easily walk to lots of great restaurants from this locale. Also of note are the heated pool and friendly staff, plus the free 24-hour shuttle to and from the **airport** and several casinos on the Strip.

3970 Paradise Rd. (between Twain Ave. and Flamingo Rd.). ☎ *800-531-5900 or 702-796-9000. Fax: 702-796-3537. Internet:* www.laquinta.com. *Rack rates: $79 – $99 double. AE, CB, DC, DISC, MC, V.*

Lady Luck Casino Hotel
$$ Downtown

Unless numbers lie, this hotel has to be doing something right: Eighty percent of the clientele here is repeat business. I attribute it mainly to the friendly atmosphere and bargain rates. There's not as much glitz and glamour as in the newer hotels, but it is brighter and more attractive than many other downtown options. The rooms, although standard, are large and airy, with a Southwestern motif; it even has a pool and sundeck — one of the few downtown. Given how easy it is to get lost in most Vegas behemoths, I am amused by the color-coded neon tubing the hotel uses to help you keep track of where you are. It's like an electric trail of bread crumbs, and especially useful if you are staying in the hotel's second tower, which is actually across the street!

206 N. 3rd St. (at Ogden Ave.). ☎ *800-523-9582 or 702-477-3000. Fax: 702-382-2346. Rack rates: $40 – $155 double. AE, CB, DC, DISC, JCB, MC, V.*

Las Vegas Hilton
$$$$$ Paradise Road

If you are a fan of The King, come worship at the place where Elvis spent the bulk (sorry) of his Fat Years. Aside from E fanatics, this flagship of the Hilton chain caters mostly to business travelers, because it's adjacent to the **Las Vegas Convention Center.** Large and comfortable, if not all that striking, the rooms here are top-of-the-line, with marble desks and bathrooms, plus minibars upon request. Actually, this hotel has a little bit of everything one looks for in Vegas; the casino is small and tucked to the side of the lobby so it's handy but not something you need crawl across every time you leave your room. The atmosphere is more elegant and expensive than not, but with **Star Trek: The Experience** and the **Spacequest Casino** adding a motion simulator ride and a high-tech themed casino annex, respectively, you don't miss out on the Vegas kitsch cache either. (Phew! What a relief.) The Las Vegas Hilton has an extensive selection of restaurants, a superior recreation deck with a swimming pool and tennis courts, and a terrific health club/spa where you'll really feel pampered.

3000 Paradise Rd. (at Riviera Blvd.). ☎ *800-732-7117 or 702-732-5111. Fax: 702-794-3611. Internet:* www.lvhilton.com. *Rack rates: $49 – $349 double. AE, CB, DC, DISC, ER, MC, V.*

Paradise Road Accommodations

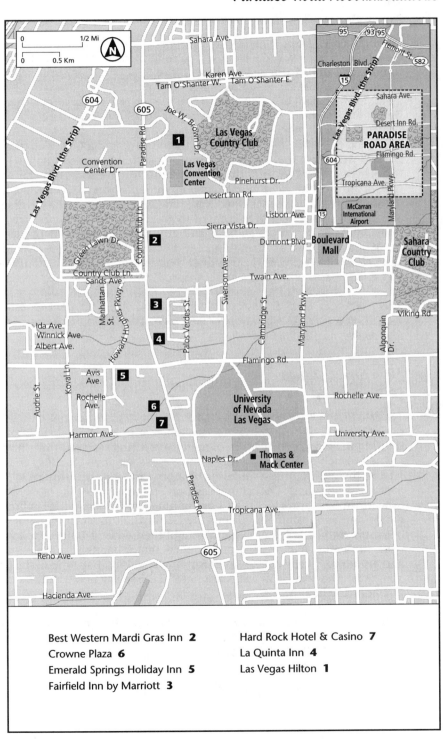

Best Western Mardi Gras Inn **2**

Crowne Plaza **6**

Emerald Springs Holiday Inn **5**

Fairfield Inn by Marriott **3**

Hard Rock Hotel & Casino **7**

La Quinta Inn **4**

Las Vegas Hilton **1**

Luxor
$$ South Strip

Ever fantasize about living life like Cleopatra, except with modern conveniences? Then walk like an Egyptian right over to the **Luxor.** It's hard to miss; it's the 30-story pyramid with the Sphinx in front. And no, the Great Pyramid of Giza is not similarly covered in glass, nor does it have a 315,000-watt light beam shooting from the top. Then again, the Grateful Dead haven't played in front of the Luxor, though if Jerry Garcia hadn't died, it was probably just a matter of time. Where was I? Right, the Luxor. This used to be the epitome of tacky theme park, but a huge renovation worked wonders. The theme still runs amok, thank heavens, so it's just the right sort of silly and a very likable hotel. The rooms in the new towers are most impressive with their Egyptian/art-deco décor, while the pyramid rooms have cool sloped walls, making them larger than average, and have recently been redecorated to great success. It houses five big pools, a shopping arcade, a large and airy casino, numerous places to drink and dine, and an attractions level with games and rides. Friendly staff, affordable rates, and a monorail that connects you with **Mandalay Bay** and **Excalibur** — go down, Moses, to Egypt-land!

3900 Las Vegas Blvd. S. (just south of Tropicana Ave.). ☎ *800-288-1000 or 702-262-4000. Fax: 702-262-4452. Internet:* www.luxor.com. *Rack rates: $49 – $299 double. AE, CB, DC, DISC, MC, V.*

Main Street Station
$$ Downtown

This surprisingly sweet hotel — hard to believe in Vegas, but true — is one of the nicest downtown choices and a really great bargain to boot. It does a good job of evoking turn-of-the-century San Francisco with charming décor, including gas lanterns, stained-glass windows, and lazy ceiling fans in the casino, plus plantation shutters and comfy furniture in the average-sized rooms. Though not right on **Fremont Street** like most other downtown hotels, it's less than a five-minute walk away. And its in-house dining and entertainment options are better than those at many of the other downtown hotels, including one of the two best buffets in downtown (and maybe in all of Vegas), a particularly handsome steakhouse and a microbrewery that is great for snacking, and bar-type nighttime hangouts. The only drawbacks are potential freeway noise and the lack of a pool and health club.

200 N. Main St. (between Fremont and I-95). ☎ *800-465-0711 or 702-387-1896. Fax: 702-386-4466. Internet:* www.mainstreetcasino.com/. *Rack rates: $45 – $175 double. AE, CB, DC, DISC, MC, V.*

Mandalay Bay
$$$$$ South Strip

In case you were wondering, it's named after a Kipling poem. (Who says Vegas can't be educational?) A Kipling-themed hotel? No such luck, no mini-Mowglis or Baloos running around singing about the bear/bare necessities. Perhaps that's just as well. There is much to like about this place, from the immediate access to the guest elevators off the aquarium and bird-studded lobby (avoiding the usual tiring slog through casino mayhem found at so many of its peers), to the superb unimpeded views of the entire Strip, plus the planes landing at the airport. The hotel has particularly handsome and large rooms (king rooms come off better than doubles) with stunning bathrooms (biggest and nicest around; you may never get out of that sunken tub). The pool area is still settling in foliage-wise, but with a wave pool (let's go surfing now! Or, at least as often as the waves get big enough), a lazy "river," and some basic pools, there is something here for every water taste.

Mandalay Bay is also home to the **House of Blues,** where many of the best bands in rock and blues play when they're in town (and it's a better venue overall than its rival the **Hard Rock**). All the restaurants here, many of which are quite good, have extraordinarily striking decor. "But I don't want to be so far south on the Strip," you say. No need to worry. A free monorail takes you to **Excalibur** (also stopping at **Luxor**), and then catty-corner across the street is another one going from **MGM Grand** to **Bally's,** which will leave you smack in the center of the Strip. What more could you want?

3950 Las Vegas Blvd. S., at Hacienda. ☎ *877-632-7000 or 702-632-7000. Fax: 702-632-7228. Internet:* www.mandalaybay.com. *Rack rates: $99 and up standard double. Extra person $35. AE, CB, DC, DISC, JCB, MC, V.*

MGM Grand Hotel/Casino
$$$$ South Strip

This is not the biggest hotel in the world. It's only the second biggest hotel. In the world. Rhode Island could comfortably fit inside its casino, which by the way, *is* the biggest in the world. Big-a-phobes, stay away. But if you, like Godzilla, believe size does matter, read on. Clearly, this is not a cozy, intimate locale, but some recent renovations have tried to tone the thing down, and have sort of succeeded. The original Wizard of Oz theme, with its vile overuse of emerald green, is mostly gone, as are most of the family-friendly aspects of the hotel (though a carnival midway and a recommended children's activity/daycare center remain). Now the theme is classic MGM movies, and the rooms (the most distinctive in this price range on the Strip), in addition to stand-out minimalist 30's glamour-evoking furniture, also feature black and white movie star photos. The staff somehow manages to be attentive despite the overwhelming hugeness.

The newly redone pool area is fabulous, with big bodies of water, a lazy river, and many acres to play and splash around in. The theme park has been downgraded in importance and is probably skipable, unless you are here with kids, as many of the guests seem to be. The new spa is luxurious and grown-up. The **MGM Grand** has a fine lineup of restaurants: **The Wolfgang Puck Café, Emeril Legasse's New Orleans Fish House, Gatsby's,** an outpost of Hollywood's **Brown Derby,** and a newly added **Rain Forest Café,** to name just a few. The whole thing is overseen outside by a four-story-tall gleaming gold lion, and while he's photo-op ready, the new **Lion Experience** allows you to visit and even have your photo taken with real-life Simbas.

3799 Las Vegas Blvd. S. (at Tropicana Ave.). ☎ *800-929-1111 or 702-891-7777. Fax: 702-891-1030. Internet:* www.mgmgrand.com. *Rack rates: $69 and up double. AE, DC, DISC, MC, V.*

The Mirage
$$$$$ Center Strip

I just dig this hotel. It's a true Vegas hoot *and* just a plain nice place to stay. What more could you ask for? It's now hard to believe that when **The Mirage** opened ten years ago people thought it would be a failure. An adult-oriented hotel with a theme? White tigers on display? A big volcano out front that "erupts" (smoke and colored lights only, alas, no lava) regularly? You gotta be kidding. But now, everyone is following humbly (or not so) in The Mirage's footsteps.

And while others may be doing the same thing, only bigger and splashier, I don't really think anyone's doing it better. Sniff the vanilla-scented air, soothe jangled nerves staring at the 200,000-gallon aquarium behind the reception desk, stroll through the indoor rain forest, loll by the tropical pool (complete with much foliage, waterfalls, and water slides), go play (for a price) with some dolphins, watch the tigers sleep, have a fab meal (their buffet is possibly the best in town), rejuvenate at the luxe and lovely spa and health club, or gamble in their jolly casino. And when your clock winds down, you can sleep it off in one of the nicest rooms (decorated in marble and neutral shades, though bathrooms are bit less impressive) in town for the price (see if you can get one that overlooks the volcano's action). I've done it all here and I'll do it again. What don't I like? Navigating the twisting paths through the casino to go just about anywhere, paying extra for that spa and the Dolphin Habitat, and the long lines for food. If you want to try something new, there's a free tram over to **Treasure Island** (it runs nearly around the clock, except between 4 a.m. – 6 a.m.).

3400 Las Vegas Blvd. S. (between Flamingo Rd. and Sands Ave.). ☎ *800-627-6667 or 702-791-7444. Fax: 702-791-7446. Internet:* www.themirage.com. *Rack rates: $79 – $399 double. AE, CB, DC, DISC, MC, V.*

Monte Carlo Resort & Casino
$$$$ South Strip

Now, in case you didn't know, Monte Carlo is the capital of Monaco (where Grace Kelly became Princess Grace and where her children still challenge the Windsors for gossip-page headlines) and it is the Vegas of Europe — at least, in the sense that they've also got a lot of casinos. But they go in for classy gambling there — think James Bond in his tux, playing baccarat, a beautiful girl (or ten) on his arm. And so now you have a picture of what the intention here, ambiance-wise, is. This immense hotel reproduces the opulence of its namesake with colonnades, arches, fountains, and enormous statues that are nearly in good taste. Spacious rooms have a warm European feel (created by marble and fine furnishings). Of course, you'll find the usual array of restaurants and bars, plus a showroom and casino, but more noteworthy is the hotel's 20,000-acre pool area, with lush landscaping, a wave pool, a surf pond, waterfalls, and a "river" for tubing. (Kids generally like that part but will probably be bored by the rest.) Grownups love the fabulous spa that offers all the equipment and treatments you could want.

3770 Las Vegas Blvd. S. (between Flamingo Rd. and Tropicana Ave.). ☎ *800-311-8999 or 702-730-7777. Fax: 702-730-7250. Internet:* www.monte-carlo.com. *Rack rates: $49 – $269 double. AE, CB, DC, DISC, MC, V.*

New York-New York
$$$$ South Strip

Now *this* is more like it. None of that namby-pamby, "luxury resort" quiet good taste crap. No, this is Vegas at its finest, the full tradition of taking a theme and beating it into the ground. And good golly is it fun. It's almost impossible to do this place justice in just a few sentences, but here goes. The exterior is an actual reproduction of the New York skyline, with one-third–scale replicas of the Empire State Building, the Chrysler Building, the Statue of Liberty, and the Brooklyn Bridge. Inside, you'll stroll through versions of Greenwich Village, Times Square, and Central Park. Casino change carts are in the form of Yellow Cabs, the arcade is tricked up like Coney Island, and, oh, there are cobblestone streets in the Village, and there's even (not naughty) graffiti. Hey, and just for flavor, a roller coaster runs through the whole thing. The rooms can be smallish (just like New York!) but have lovely art-deco décor and everyone who stays in them raves about them. The spa and pool aren't as great here as at other hotels. The hotel is overcrowded, and there's definitely a sensory overload factor, especially in the casino. But boy is it a hoot. If you're not in the mood to stay here, you have to at least stop by to see it.

3790 Las Vegas Blvd. S. (at Tropicana Ave.). ☎ *800-693-6763 or 702-740-6969. Fax: 702-740-6920. Internet:* www.nynyhotelcasino.com. *Rack rates: $59 and up double. AE, CB, DC, DISC, MC, V.*

Orleans
$ South Strip

This is one terrific value. As the name implies, this is the Las Vegas interpretation of New Orleans, complete with French Quarter influences, Mardi Gras beads given away just for stopping in, and Cajun and Zydeco music playing in the casino. It's actually located about a mile west of the Strip. I recommend this place primarily for the rooms: They are among the biggest in town, with comfortable Victorian parlor–style furnishings (though like a true Victorian parlor, the clutter can make matters cramped). You can often get terrific prices here — so what's a little distance? This is a medium-size hotel (for Vegas), with the usual array of bars and restaurants (including a New Orleans–theme nightclub and a very good Mexican restaurant that makes its own tortillas), plus two medium-size swimming pools, a wedding chapel, and a 70-lane bowling alley.

4500 W. Tropicana Ave. (west of I-95). ☎ *800-ORLEANS or 702-365-7111. Fax: 702-365-7505. Internet:* www.orleanscasino.com. *Rack rates: $39 and up standard double. AE, DC, DISC, MC, V.*

Paris Las Vegas Casino Resort
$$$$$ Center Strip

Ooo, la la. If the French get snippy over foreigners mangling, or just making minor errors with their language, what on earth will they think of this place? A hotel that recreates all their most cherished monuments (the Eiffel Tower — looming nearly as large as the original, Arc de Triomphe, the Louvre), by vulgar Americans no less? There are signs in somewhat dubious French ("Le Car Rental") and employees who sprinkle all transactions with various phrases ("Bonjour et merci, Madame!"). Who cares? That's the kind of devotion to theme I can really get behind. Rooms here are, sadly, perfectly nice and perfectly forgettable. The health club has pretensions of posh and the pool area is cold and sterile. There are a number of restaurants that will appeal, in varying degrees, to the francophile (I particularly love **Mon Ami Gabi**), and you can ride up to the near top of the half-size Eiffel Tower, if you have a mind, and kiss your amour. Put it that way, and *pourquoi pas?*

3655 Las Vegas Blvd. S. ☎ *888-BONJOUR or 702-964-7000. Fax: 702-964-4405. Internet:* www.paris-lv.com. *Rack rates: $119 and up standard double. AE, DC, DISC, MC, V.*

Rio Hotel & Casino
$$$$ Center Strip

While this is not at the top of my list, lots of people love this hotel for its carnival ambiance, tropical theme, and oversized rooms. The rooms are big, all right, featuring sectional sofas, small refrigerators, and very nifty floor-to-ceiling windows offering fab views, but they're not quite the "suites" the hotel touts. Downsides here include location (it's a solid 20-minute walk from the Strip) and a sometimes unfriendly staff. If you're easily overwhelmed, you may not enjoy the hectic, party-all-the-time atmosphere (it's not a good choice for families with kids).

The hotel includes a newer addition — a 41-story tower and a "European" village of shops and restaurants that is really quite nice and worth coming out to stroll through. A live-action show with a carnival theme (sort of a mock Mardi Gras parade that moves about on tracks overhead), called *Masquerade in the Sky,* runs periodically throughout the day. The **Rio** is justly proud of their array of restaurants and bars including **Napa** (perhaps the best restaurant in town), **Fiore,** a wine bar where you can indulge in tastings, and the **Voodoo Lounge.** Their three swimming pools are a bit of a bust compared to some others in town and the older parts of the casino too confining — head to the section housed in the newer expansion.

3700 W. Flamingo Rd. (just east of I-15). ☎ *800-752-9746 or 702-252-7777. Fax: 702-252-0080. Internet:* www.playrio.com. *Rack rates: $95 – $149 double. AE, CB, DC, MC, V.*

Riviera Hotel & Casino
$$$ North Strip

This 50-something-year-old Vegas institution often gets overshadowed by its bigger and more boisterous competition. To be honest, the place is really going to struggle to keep up. Once-elegant décor now seems just a touch seedy, made all the more so by the topless revues that are heavily featured (and even enshrined; it includes a bronze statue commemorating the remarkable derrieres on display in their show *Crazy Girls,* in full view of the street). The **Riviera** is definitely not a good choice for families, but the rooms are adequate, and you can choose from tons of shows and snacking places to keep you entertained. Amenities here include a vast casino, an Olympic-size pool and sundeck, a large video arcade, a well-equipped health club, two tennis courts, and a wedding chapel.

2901 Las Vegas Blvd. S. (at Riviera Blvd.). ☎ *800-634-6753 or 702-734-5110. Fax: 702-794-9451. Internet:* www.theriviera.com. *Rack rates: $59 – $99 double. AE, CB, DC, MC, V.*

Sahara Hotel & Casino
$$$ North Strip

The best days of this Vegas institution, a major player since 1952, may be behind it. It recently got a face-lift, but it already needs another one. It sports the chandeliers and marble that seem to be everywhere in

Vegas, but it also has an Arabian Nights theme, so they've thrown in onion domes and mosaic tile, trying to evoke Morocco. I'm not really sure how the new roller coaster fits in. The rooms are on the smallish side (and whoever picked out the eye-straining striped bedspreads should have their heads examined), and despite their cosmetic upgrade, are already looking a little dingy; but they can be cheap. It's located in an out-of-the-way spot on the North Strip, which is a pro or con, depending on how you look at it. There's a very attractive, Olympic-size pool with Moroccan tiles and a sundeck, plus a large casino (with $1 craps!) and several restaurants and bars (including the **Casbah Lounge,** which offers solid live entertainment). It's not a good choice for families with kids, despite the roller coaster.

2535 Las Vegas Blvd. S. (at E. Sahara Ave.). ☎ *800-634-6666 or 702-737-2111. Fax: 702-737-2027. Internet:* www.saharahotelandcasino.com/. *Rack rates: $35 and up double. AE, CB, DC, DISC, MC, V.*

Stardust Resort & Casino
$$ North Strip

If you saw the movie *Showgirls* — come on, admit it! — you will recognize the facade of this hotel, with it's oh-so-very-Vegas array of countless electric bulbs. (It plays the role of "Generic Vegas Hotel" in numerous other movies, commercials, and rock videos.) But these days, this old-timer, like its peers, seems to be in search of a personality. It's less troubling than at some of the others. Everything is bright and cheery, including the rooms, which are entirely forgettable but certainly nice enough. Try to avoid the Garden rooms, which offer terrific prices but not-so-terrific accommodations. The casino here is large, crowded, and lively. In addition to the usual array of shops and restaurants, it also offers two large, attractive pools and a few whirlpools. Guests have access to a fabulous, 24-hour health club that's located behind the hotel. Check out the nifty water-ballet fountains in the front.

3000 Las Vegas Blvd. S. (at Convention Center Dr.). ☎ *800-634-6757 or 702-732-6111. Fax: 702-732-6257. Internet:* www.stardustlv.com. *Rack rates: $36 – $200 double. AE, CB, DC, DISC, JCB, MC, V.*

Stratosphere Las Vegas
$$$ North Strip

A 106-story observation tower makes this the tallest building west of the Mississippi. Aside from really stunning views (the lights, the desert, the mountains — day or night, Vegas looks mighty fine from way above ground), the tower has the world's highest roller coaster, a thrilling free-fall ride, and a wedding chapel completes the aforementioned views. Cool! But the rest of the hotel has drawbacks: It's quite a trek to anything else on the Strip (and this end of the Strip is looking particularly desolate and seedy); the rooms aren't in the tower itself (so don't expect those tremendous views from your own windows); and, as of this writing, the place is mired in bankruptcy, although it's still open and operating. I'm including it in this listing because the incredibly nice staff and the tower views make it a good backup choice if your first preferences are full. Other extras include a casino, a huge pool, and a big shopping arcade with a World's Fair theme.

I've heard from some of the locals that the **Stratosphere** offers the best gambling odds on the Strip. I'm not sure if it's true, but it's quite possible in light of their financial woes and the resulting need to attract customers. Hey, it may be worth a shot.

2000 Las Vegas Blvd. S. (between St. Louis St. and Baltimore Ave.). ☎ *800-99-TOWER or 702-380-7777. Fax: 702-383-5334. Internet:* www.stratlv.com. *Rack rates: $39 – $139 double. AE, CB, DC, DISC, JCB, MC, V.*

Treasure Island
$$$$ Center Strip

Shiver me timbers! Ever go on the Disney parks' Pirates of the Caribbean ride and think "this would be my idea of heaven if they would just add slot machines"? Well, you got your wish. **Treasure Island** is not nearly as Disney as I would have liked — and I'm pretty sure that a remodeling job included some backpedaling from the theme in order to decrease the kid traffic (and so there are less skull-and-crossbones and chests spilling treasure, darn it) — but it's still pretty great. And still pretty kid-friendly (a blessing or a curse, depending on your outlook), thanks to the pirate-village exterior that hosts a nearly full-scale pirate battle stunt show (avast, ye scurvy British!) every 90 minutes nightly.

Rooms were just upgraded and their comforts increased (including better bathrooms) so they are much more on a par with its sister location, **The Mirage.** Try to get one that overlooks the pirate battle (or at least, bag a seat at the **Battle Bar,** which has front row, so-close-you-are-breathing-the-smoke seating). Families should be aware that despite the atmosphere, this is not a theme park, so there are whole areas (like the vast casino) more or less off limits to those under 21. Kids may be soothed by the gigantic video arcade and carnival midway (one of the few I really enjoy) or, if they are more sophisticated than much of the short-attention-span generation, by a trip to see **Cirque du Soleil's Mystère,** which is housed in a wonderful theater here. Treasure Island also has a very good spa and health club, a surprisingly run-of-the-mill pool area, and some decent dining choices.

3300 Las Vegas Blvd. S. (at Spring Mountain Rd.). ☎ *800-944-7444 or 702-894-7111. Fax: 702-894-7446. Internet:* www.treasureislandlasvegas.com. *Rack rates: $69 and up double. AE, DC, DISC, JCB, MC, V.*

Tropicana Resort & Casino
$$$$ South Strip

What the Trop has going for it: location (on the busiest corner in Vegas, across from **MGM Grand, New York-New York,** and **Excalibur**), surprisingly attractive rooms in the Paradise Tower, a decent health club, and a heck of a pool area. As a matter of fact, it has three pools — one Olympic-size — and a few whirlpools set in a beautifully landscaped garden with waterfalls and lagoons. One of the pools even has a swim-up blackjack table in the summer so that you can gamble and work on your tan at the same time. What the Trop has going against it: just about everything else. Its Island Tower rooms are tacky and the Garden Court rooms are best not discussed at all. The interior is confusing and increasingly icky looking, both on its own and in comparison to newer properties. Even the birds that used to be everywhere are gone, so the place is looking less distinctive (if less messy with guano) every minute. Pedestrian walkways link the hotel with the Luxor, the MGM Grand, and Excalibur.

3801 Las Vegas Blvd. S. (at Tropicana Ave.). ☎ *800-634-4000 or 702-739-2222. Fax: 702-739-2469. Internet:* www.tropicanalv.com. *Rack rates: $79 – $229 double. AE, CB, DC, DISC, MC, V.*

The Venetian
$$$$$ Center Strip

What a cool place this is. Normally, I get all smug and patronizing about Vegas recreations of famous locales, and feel the need to gently remind you "now, this isn't really like seeing the actual place, you know." But when I walk around the outside of **The Venetian,** through some famous portions of Venice, Italy (itself a tourist destination for 400 years), which now sit grandly on the Strip, noting the meticulous attention to detail, I think "well, actually, this *is* a great deal like the original." Except it's less smelly and decayed, and not nearly as organic and authentically beautiful. But then, you knew that much. Your jaw will drop upon seeing the sweeping grand heavily marbled galleria, its ceiling covered in hand-made recreations of noted Venetian paintings, and in the ambitious and amazing shopping area, where Venetian buildings line an actual canal, complete with singing gondoliers. You can take a ride with them, while listening to costumed strolling minstrels burst into Italian arias, or flirt with Casanova and other famous Venetians in a small-scale clone of St. Mark's Square.

And then there are the rooms, each a junior suite measuring 700 square feet (the largest and probably handsomest in Vegas), with steps leading down to a sunken living room, and with grand bathrooms. Do not expect rooms like these in the real Venice. And the restaurants rival **Bellagio** for high-quality food (and prices to match) made by celebrity chefs. The swimming pool area is a disappointment, lacking the lush greenery and style of similar hotels, while the spa area is provided courtesy of the highly touted **Canyon Ranch Spa,** and there is nothing else like it (alas, including the cost) in Vegas.

3355 Las Vegas Blvd. S. ☎ *888-2-VENICE, 702-414-1000. Fax: 702-414-1000. Internet:* www.venetian.com. *Rack rates: $125 – $399 double. AE, CB, DC, DISC, JCB, MC, V.*

No Room at the Inn?

Or at least in any of my main choices (listed in the preceding section)? It happens. All too often, frankly, which never ceases to amaze me. The good news is that there are more than 120,000 rooms in Las Vegas, so the odds are good that you will find some place to rest in between gambling sessions.

Here are some other reliable choices to call with your pleas and tales of woe:

- ✔ **Alexis Park Resort ($$$$$).** 375 E. Harmon Ave. (between Koval Lane and Paradise Rd.). ☎ **800-582-2228** or 702-796-3300.

- ✔ **Boardwalk Casino & Holiday Inn ($$).** 3750 Las Vegas Blvd. S. (between Harmon and Tropicana Aves.). ☎ **800-HOLIDAY,** 800-635-4581, or 702-735-2400.

- ✔ **Bourbon Street ($$).** 120 E. Flamingo (between the Strip and Koval Lane). ☎ **800-634-6956** or 702-737-7200.

- ✔ **Courtyard Marriott ($$$).** 3275 Paradise Rd. (between Convention Center Dr. and Desert Inn Rd.). ☎ **800-321-2211** or 702-791-3600.

- ✔ **Jackie Gaughan's Plaza Hotel/Casino ($$$).** 1 Main St. (at Fremont St.). ☎ **800-634-6575** or 702-386-2110.

- ✔ **Marriott Suites ($$$$).** 325 Convention Center Dr. ☎ **800-228-9290** or 702-650-2000.

- ✔ **Palace Station ($$$).** 2411 W. Sahara Ave. ☎ **800-634-3101** or 702-367-2411.

- ✔ **Residence Inn by Marriott ($$$$).** 3225 Paradise Rd. (between Desert Inn Rd. and Convention Center Dr.). ☎ **800-331-3131** or 702-796-9300.

- ✔ **Sam's Town Hotel & Gambling Hall ($$$).** 5111 Boulder Hwy. (at Nellis Rd.). ☎ **800-634-6371** or 702-456-7777.

Chapter 9

Taking Care of Last-Minute Details

· ·

In This Chapter

▶ Buying travel and medical insurance

▶ Dealing with illness away from home

▶ Renting a car

▶ Making reservations, ordering tickets, and getting information in advance

▶ Packing like a pro

· ·

*B*efore you leave for your vacation, you'll probably feel like you need to do a thousand things: make reservations, put the dog in the kennel, pack your bags, and so on. Trust me: If you organize everything ahead of time, you will save precious hours otherwise spent waiting in line, trying to get show tickets, buying the underwear you forgot to bring, and dealing with all the other annoyances that plague the unprepared traveler. In this chapter, I tell you how to take care of all the pesky details you need to handle before you leave on your trip, right down to packing comfortable walking shoes. This chapter is a life-saver!

Buying Travel Insurance: Good Idea or Bad?

There are three primary kinds of travel insurance: *trip cancellation, lost luggage,* and *medical.* Trip cancellation insurance is a good idea for some, but lost luggage and additional medical insurance don't make sense for most travelers. Be sure to explore your options and consider the following advice before you leave home:

✔ **Trip cancellation insurance:** Cancellation insurance is a good idea if you've paid a large portion of your vacation expenses up front. If you buy a package trip, cancellation insurance comes in handy if a member of your party becomes ill or if (heaven forbid!) you experience a death in the family and aren't able to go on vacation.

Trip cancellation insurance costs approximately 6 – 8 percent of your vacation's total value.

✔ **Lost luggage insurance:** Your homeowner's insurance should cover stolen luggage if your policy encompasses off-premises theft, so check your existing policies before you buy any additional coverage. Airlines are responsible for up to $2,500 on domestic flights, but that may not be enough to cover your sharkskin suit or wedding dress. My best advice: Either wear it on the plane or carry it on board (this goes for anything else of value, too).

✔ **Medical insurance:** Your existing health insurance should cover you if you get sick while on vacation. (However, if you belong to an HMO, check to see whether you're fully covered when away from home).

Some credit cards (American Express and certain gold and platinum Visa and MasterCards, for example) offer automatic flight insurance against death or dismemberment in case of an airplane crash. Check with your credit card company for details.

If you think you need additional insurance, make sure that you don't pay for more insurance than you need. For example, if you only need trip cancellation insurance, don't purchase coverage for lost or stolen property. It's a good idea to call around to find a good deal on insurance. Here's a list of some reputable issuers of travel insurance:

✔ **Access America:** 6600 W. Broad St., Richmond, VA 23230; ☎ **800-284-8300;** Fax: 800-346-9265; Internet: www.accessamerica.com.

✔ **Travelex Insurance Services:** 11717 Burt St., Suite 202, Omaha, NE 68154; ☎ **800-228-9792**; Internet: www.travelex-insurance.com.

✔ **Travel Guard International:** 1145 Clark St., Stevens Point, WI 54481; ☎ **800-826-1300**; Internet: www.travel-guard.com.

✔ **Travel Insured International, Inc.:** P.O. Box 280568, 52-S Oakland Ave., East Hartford, CT 06128-0568; ☎ **800-243-3174**; Internet: www.travelinsured.com.

Combating Illness Away from Home

Finding a doctor you trust when you're out of town is hard. And getting a prescription refilled is no piece of cake, either. So, here are some travel tips to help you avoid a medical dilemma while you're on vacation:

✔ If you have health insurance, carry your identification card in your wallet. Likewise, if you don't think your existing policy is sufficient, purchase medical insurance for more comprehensive coverage.

✔ Bring all of your medications with you as well as a prescription for more if you think you'll run out. Better yet, just be sure you have enough so that you don't run out!

✔ Bring an extra pair of contact lenses or glasses in case you lose your primary pair.

✔ Don't forget to bring over-the-counter medicines for common travelers' ailments like diarrhea or stomach acid. Gift shops carry these items, but you'll pay a premium (and you won't find a gift shop on the airplane!).

✔ If you suffer from a chronic illness, talk to your doctor before taking your trip. For conditions such as epilepsy, diabetes, or a heart condition, wear a Medic Alert identification tag to immediately alert any doctor about your condition and give him or her access to your medical records through Medic Alert's 24-hour hotline. Participation in the Medic Alert program costs $35, with a $15 renewal fee. Contact the **Medic Alert Foundation** (2323 Colorado Ave., Turlock, CA 95382; ☎ **800-432-5378**; Internet: www. medicalert.org).

If you do get sick, ask the concierge at your hotel to recommend a local doctor — including his or her own. This is probably a better recommendation than what you'll get from a doctor's referral number. If you can't get a doctor to help you right away, try the emergency room at the local hospital. For a list of hospitals that service the Las Vegas area, see the Quick Concierge appendix at the back of the book.

Weighing Your Rental-Car Options

Do you need to rent a car in Las Vegas? *Need?* No. But I really think you should consider it. Technically, everything on the Strip is within walking distance — it's roughly three miles from **Circus Circus** to **Mandalay Bay** — but who wants to walk that in 100-degree heat (or, in winter, in near gale-force winds)? Besides, that's time that you could spend gambling, dining, or seeing a show. Without a car, you will be less inclined to get off the Strip and go downtown or to the **Liberace Museum** (and I just can't have that). Sure, you could turn to hailing a taxi, but you may easily spend more on taxi fare than on car rental.

If you're the type of person who needs hard, cold facts, consider this: If you take a taxi from the airport to the **Stardust** hotel, for example, you wind up paying around $15, including tip. And then if you want to see the pyramid-shaped **Luxor** hotel (a solid 3 miles away), that's another $20 round trip. Suppose that later the same evening you want to go see the **Fremont Street Experience** downtown and then finish off the evening with a cocktail at the top of the **Stratosphere Tower:** You've just racked up at least another $20 — more if traffic is heavy. If you add everything up, you've spent $55 on taxis, and for that amount you could be cruising the Strip in your own convertible.

And the above scenario doesn't take into account the time you'll waste standing in line for a taxi (up to an hour on weekend nights is not unheard of). With car rentals usually available for as low as $20 a day (maybe a bit more for a convertible, but who's counting?), your best bet is obvious.

When you consider the freedom that your own wheels gives you and the fact that every hotel in town offers free parking to guests *and* non-guests, the obvious answer is "Yes, rent a car!"

The walking wounded

The biggest game of chance on the Strip may not be inside the casinos, but outside on the street. Because blocks on the Strip tend to be longer than long, pedestrians often ignore crosswalks and dash across the Strip regardless of their location. When Lady Luck is with these jaywalkers, all they have to face are angry drivers swerving — while swearing — to avoid them. But, like all other gambling in Vegas, the odds for this game do not favor the player.

When traffic conditions are favorable — and sometimes even when they aren't — drivers in Las Vegas have no compunction about flooring it. And the Strip isn't very pedestrian-friendly — stop signals at the crosswalks can be so short that an Olympic sprinter would have trouble getting across the street in time. When you combine these two factors, the end result is that traffic accidents are a fact of life on the Strip. In order to safeguard pedestrians, a few locations do have above-ground sidewalks (notably between the **MGM Grand** and **New York-New York** on the South Strip and between the **Bellagio** and **Bally's** on the Center Strip).

It may take you a little longer to get where you are going, but my advice is to cross at traffic lights, or use the above-ground sidewalks. Otherwise, you should ask yourself, "Are you feeling lucky today?" Those of you who have seen a Dirty Harry movie know you won't like the answer.

And rent your car before you get into town, especially if you're arriving during a peak period. You'll have more time to search for a good rate, and you won't have to scour the Strip looking for a rental you can afford. You also won't get stuck renting a car that isn't the type you want because all of the cars in that category were booked in advance.

If, however, you decide not to rent a car, you can hop on an airport shuttle service to get to your hotel. You don't have to arrange any of this in advance (flip to Chapter 10 for more details). After you're settled in, though, you're either going to have to hail a cab or hoof it. Okay, I guess I should mention that Vegas has a regular city bus service, but it gets mixed reviews for timeliness and convenience. I only recommend it for brave souls.

Asking the right questions before renting a car

Car-rental rates vary widely. The price depends on many factors: the size of the car, the length of time you keep it, where and when you pick it up and drop it off, where you go in it, and a host of other factors (like what kind of mood the agent happens to be in). Asking a few key questions can save you boucoup bucks. Following are some questions that may help:

✔ **Is the weekend rate lower than the weekday rate?** Ask if the rate is the same for pickup Friday morning as it is Thursday night. If you're keeping the car five or more days, a weekly rate may be cheaper than the daily rate.

✔ **Will I be charged a drop-off fee if I return the car to a location that's different from where I picked it up?** Some companies may assess a drop-off charge, others, notably **National,** do not. Ask if the rate is cheaper if you pick up the car at the airport or a location in town.

✔ **Do I get a special rate for being a member?** Don't forget to mention membership in AAA, AARP, frequent-flyer programs, and trade unions. Such a membership usually entitles you to decent discounts (ranging from 5 – 30 percent). Ask your travel agent to check any and all of these rates before booking your rental car.

✔ **May I have the price I saw advertised in the local newspaper?** Be sure to ask for that specific rate; otherwise, you may be charged the standard (higher) rate.

Adding up the cost of renting a car

On top of the standard rental prices, other optional charges apply to most car rentals. The *Collision Damage Waiver (CDW),* which requires you to pay for damage to the car in a collision, is charged on rentals in most states, but is covered by many credit card companies. Check with your credit card company before you go so you can avoid paying this hefty fee (as much as $15 a day). Face it: An extra $15 in your pocket can mean a few extra pulls on a slot machine!

Car rental companies also offer additional *liability insurance* (if you harm others in an accident), *personal accident insurance* (if you harm yourself or your passengers), and *personal effects insurance* (if your luggage is stolen from your car). If you have insurance on your car at home, you're probably covered for most of these unlikelihoods. Call your insurance company to find out exactly what you're covered for. If your own insurance doesn't cover you for rentals, or if you don't have auto insurance, consider buying additional coverage (car rental companies are liable for certain base amounts, depending on the state). But, weigh the likelihood of getting into an accident or losing your luggage against the cost of extra coverage (as much as $20 a day combined), which can significantly add to the price of your rental.

Some companies also offer *refueling packages,* which means that you pay for an entire tank of gas up front. The price is usually fairly competitive with local gas prices, but you don't get credit for any gas remaining in the tank when you drop off the vehicle. If you decide not to go with this option, you pay only for the gas you use, but you have to return it with a full tank or face charges of $3 – $4 a gallon for any shortfall. If you're worried that a stop at a gas station on the way to the airport may cause you to miss your plane, by all means take advantage of the fuel-purchase option. Otherwise, I suggest that you skip it.

Because all of these extra rental charges can quickly add up, you'll be happy to know that a local car-rental agency is offering a special deal to readers of *Las Vegas For Dummies,* 1st Edition. **Allstate Car Rental** will deduct 20 percent off your rate if you show them this book at the rental counter. Not only is that a great deal, it's a great company to deal with — a genuinely friendly staff and a large, well-maintained fleet of vehicles. You can reach them at ☎ **800-634-6186**.

And frequent fliers can cheer themselves up with the knowledge that most car rentals are worth at least 500 miles in their frequent-flyer accounts!

Booking a rental car on the Internet

As with other aspects of planning your trip, using the Internet can make comparison shopping and reserving a rental car much easier. All the major booking sites — **Travelocity** (www.travelocity.com), **Expedia** (www.expedia.com), **Yahoo! Travel** (www.travel.yahoo.com), and **Cheap Tickets** (www.cheaptickets.com), for example — offer search engines that can dig up discounted car-rental rates. Enter the size of the car you want, the pickup and return dates, and the city where you want to rent, and the server returns a price. You can then make your reservation through these sites.

Making Reservations and Getting Tickets in Advance for Restaurants, Events, and Sightseeing

Las Vegas has gotten pretty informal — oh, how I long for the good old days of getting dressed up in full glamour for dinner and a show. But the new-found relaxed attitude doesn't extend to reservations. Restaurants, particularly the newer, high-profile ones, are popular, as are the bigger shows. So as soon as you think you might be interested in attending something or dining somewhere special, you should make a call about reservations, just to be safe. Many shows take reservations at least a week, and possibly a month, in advance. This is especially good advice if you are traveling during a peak holiday or convention period. Remember, with restaurants at least, you can always cancel if you change your mind. (But please remember to do so, so others can have your place at the table.)

Las Vegas is also a major concert and sporting venue, and the big-ticket events (Bette Midler or Rolling Stones concerts, boxing matches, and so on) sell out quickly, if not immediately. After you decide what events you want to see (the next section gives you details on finding event schedules), call **TicketMaster** at ☎ **702-893-3000** to secure tickets.

Where to Get the Latest on What's Happening

Following are my picks for the best resources for finding out what's going on in Las Vegas at the time you plan to visit:

✔ **Vegas4Visitors.com** is a terrific online resource packed with unbiased reviews of hotels, attractions, shows, dining, and more. Throw in their weekly column on the latest happenings around town plus gaming tips, travel advice, a Q&A feature, and more and this is one well-rounded site. Visit them at `http://www. vegas4visitors.com`.

✔ *What's On Magazine* is a free weekly publication found everywhere around Las Vegas. It's chock-full of all the latest information on shows, attractions, hotels, and restaurants. One note of caution: It's not precisely unbiased journalism — it's all paid advertising — but at least it tells you up to the minute what's happening where. Browse this magazine to find lots of coupons and specials in the advertisements. To get a copy before you arrive in Vegas, call ☎ 800- 494-2876 or check out their Web site at `whats-on.com`; you won't find the coupons online, though.

✔ **The "Official" Las Vegas Leisure Guide** at `www.pcap.com` is another comprehensive and up-to-date Web site, with listings of concerts, shows, attractions, and restaurants. A great resource for finding out if your favorite boxer is going to be in town or to check out the latest gossip.

✔ *The Las Vegas Review-Journal* (☎ 702-383-0205) is the biggest newspaper in town, and the Friday edition has a full Entertainment section. They'll send you back copies (for a hefty fee), or you can visit their Web site at `www.lvrj.com`. *The Los Angeles Times* (☎ 800-LATIMES x75951) also has a multi-page Las Vegas advertising supplement in its Sunday Calendar section that includes upcoming concerts and ongoing shows.

✔ *Las Vegas Weekly* and *City Life* are free weekly publications that you can find at local newstands and stores. They are the place for the hip to find tips on alternative culture and the like, but they're also better detailed than other publications about who can be found at what club or lounge that week. Did I mention they are free?

✔ The **Las Vegas Convention and Visitor's Authority** (☎ 800-332-5333) and the **Las Vegas Chamber of Commerce** (☎ 702-735-1616) will send you full packets of information about what to do and where to go.

✔ **Reservations agents** at the Las Vegas hotels can tell you what is going on during your stay. They can fill you in on all the hotel restaurants, give you details and times for any resident shows or upcoming concerts, and may even be able to offer you a discount on reservations. Sure, they only tell you about their specific property, but they know their stuff!

Gearing Up: Practical Packing Advice

A certain father I am related to once told me the way to pack is to lay out everything you think you want to take, and then pack half the clothes and twice the money. That's sound advice, particularly for Vegas. The big mistake any traveler, experienced or otherwise, can make is to overpack. Not only is all that luggage hard to schlep, but airlines are really cracking down on carry-ons, strictly enforcing the two-bag limit, and sometimes even cutting that down to one. Why do carry on? It saves you time at the baggage carousel, eliminates worry over lost luggage and forces you to really be judicious about what you pack. Trust me, no one ever came back from a trip saying "Boy, I wish I had brought more stuff with me." And if you get bored with your clothes, it's a good excuse to treat yourself to something new — or, at least to pick up an "I'm With Stupid" T-shirt. (Think how much fun you can have responding to envious queries about some fab new article of clothing: "This? Oh, just a little something I picked up in Paris." I won't squeal that you meant the Vegas hotel.) Besides, with all that extra room, think of how many souvenirs you can fit in!

What to pack

As I mentioned earlier in this chapter, Las Vegas is a lot less formal than it used to be. If you want to really pare down, for a week-long trip try to get away with just two pairs of pants (or one pair plus a skirt — for the women, that is), and three or four shirts, one slightly nicer for better restaurants.

Make sure to follow these essential packing tips:

- ✔ Absolutely bring a hat or cap, no matter what the weather forecast. During especially hot and sunny days, a hat keeps you from getting sunburned (wide brims all the way around offer more protection than baseball caps), and on cold nights, a hat retains some of your body's natural warmth. A light jacket should be the most you'll need to stay warm, but if you're visiting anytime between November and March, consider bringing a heavier coat for evenings.

- ✔ Sunscreen is a must if you're going to be outside even for a short time, no matter when you're planning to visit. Even during the cooler winter months, the sun can be harsh and damaging during the day. Think of the entertainment factor: Count the number of lobsters at the casino at night and feel smug about your own caution.

- ✔ Unless you're attending a board meeting, a funeral, or one of the city's finest restaurants, you probably don't need a suit or a fancy dress. (And even then it's not essential. Most of the uppity restaurants ask only for "casual chic" or "casual elegant," which usually translates as something black and neatly pressed.) Some of the fancier clubs do have dress codes (no jeans, a collared shirt), but you still won't need to get too gussied up. See Chapter 21 for more about dress codes at the dance clubs.

✔ You get the most use out of a pair of jeans or khakis and a comfortable sweater. Swap those jeans for shorts in the summer, or better still for women, a skirt. If you go during the summer, all-cotton clothes are much better than anything else (even rayon) for keeping cool, and clothes made of loose and flowing material act as natural air conditioning. Clothing items that can be "layered" help you deal with changing weather conditions. They also help you deal with an overzealous air conditioning system in the casino.

Other items you'll need to include:

✔ Comfortable walking shoes

✔ A camera

✔ A versatile sweater and/or jacket

✔ A bathing suit

✔ Toiletries (in small travel bottles to take up less space and weight)

✔ Medications (pack these in your carry-on bag so that you'll have them if the airline loses your luggage)

✔ Something to sleep in

✔ This book, of course!

How to pack

When choosing your suitcase for Las Vegas, think wheels. Even with an abundance of bellhops, chances are you'll have to carry your suitcase at some point and that sort of thing can wear you down. A foldover garment bag helps keep dressy clothes wrinkle-free, but can be a nuisance if you need to pack and unpack a lot. Hard-sided luggage protects breakable items better, but weighs more than soft-sided bags.

When packing, start with the biggest, hardest items (usually shoes) first and then fit smaller items in and around them. Pack breakable items in between several layers of clothes or keep them in your carry-on bag. Put things that can leak, like shampoos, suntan lotions, and so on, in sealable plastic bags. If you're worried about wrinkling, "rolling" your clothes (as you would a towel) may help, and it may also save some space. Lock your suitcase with a small padlock (available at most luggage stores, if your bag doesn't already have one), and put an identification tag on the outside.

Tying a colorful scarf around your suitcase handle, so you can easily spot it on the airport baggage carousel (or in someone else's grubby little paws!) is also a good idea.

Some airlines allow two pieces of carry-on luggage per person, both of which must fit in the overhead compartment or under the seat in front of you, but others restrict passengers to one. (Ask about this restriction when making your reservation.) Use carry-ons for valuables, medications, and vital documents first. You can then add a book, breakable items you don't want to put in your suitcase, and a snack if you have room. Also, carry a sweater or light jacket with you — cabins can feel like the Arctic one minute, and a sauna the next.

Know the limits of your carry-on luggage

Because lost-luggage rates have reached an all-time high, many consumers are bringing their possessions on board to try and divert disaster. But airplanes are more crowded than ever, and overhead compartment space is at a premium. Because of these factors, some domestic airlines have started cracking down, limiting you to a single carry-on for crowded flights and imposing size restrictions to the bags that you bring on board. The dimensions vary, but the strictest airlines say carry-ons must measure no more than 22 x 14 x 9 inches, including wheels and handles, and weigh no more than 40 pounds. Many airports are already furnished with x-ray machines that literally block any carry-on bigger than the posted size restriction. These measures may sound drastic, but keep in mind that many of these regulations are enforced only at the discretion of the gate attendants. If you plan to bring more than one bag aboard a crowded flight, make sure that your medications, documents, and valuables are consolidated in one bag in case you're forced to check the second bag.

Part III
Settling In to Las Vegas

The 5th Wave   By Rich Tennant

"We heard that your final vacation was spent 'killing 'em at the craps tables' in Vegas."

In this part . . .

*L*as Vegas is truly a city that never sleeps and it can seem quite overwhelming at first. Navigating your way through the haze of neon lights, megaresorts, and the Strip's ever-present traffic can be quite intimidating. Don't worry, though — it's not as complicated as it looks. In this part, I walk you through the city's neighborhoods, tell you where to catch local transportation, and erase any confusion you may have.

Chapter 10

Orienting Yourself in Las Vegas

● ●

In This Chapter

▶ Landing at the airport

▶ Exploring Las Vegas' neighborhoods

▶ Getting information after you arrive

● ●

*N*o matter how you get here, you'll probably be dazzled at first, particularly if you've never been to Las Vegas. It's so . . . bright. Neon. Weird. You'll want to come back, just to see if you've dreamed it. Even if you've been here before, if been more than a year or two you might be shocked at how little you recognize. Vegas is rarely idle; constant tear downs and build-back-ups mean that every decade or so the landscape looks totally new. It's a mind-blowing sight, so take it in and enjoy it.

Just remember, if you are driving, to take your eyes off the buildings and put them back on the road every so often. (I know it's very distracting to drive past pyramids and lions and pirate ships!)

Arriving in Las Vegas

When you get to the Las Vegas airport, you may be wondering where exactly you are. You're certainly not in Kansas anymore! **McCarran International Airport** is located at the southern end of the city, at 5757 Wayne Newton Boulevard. You're really not too far from the action, unlike some big cities, where you have to cover many miles to get to your hotel from the airport. McCarran is only about a mile from the Strip. (On the other hand, at rush hour, it could indeed take hours to cover that mile!)

Not only is the location super-convenient, but so is the airport itself. It's busy, no doubt (it's the eighth busiest airport in the world, with over 30 million people passing through annually), but it's surprisingly simple to navigate. Big, modern, and well planned, it has three concourses and more than 60 gates. And if you come back sometime around the year 2010, you're likely to see 70 additional gates (yep, every aspect of Las Vegas is growing by leaps and bounds).

The A and B concourses, which are used for both international and domestic flights, are connected by walkways to the main terminal. The C concourse, for domestic flights only, is separate from the main terminal and has access to a monorail system. Everything is well marked with overhead signs pointing the way.

If your flight arrives in the C terminal at a high gate number (22 or higher), don't bother with the monorail. Just past gate 27, you find a moving sidewalk that leads you to the main terminal. It's much faster and less crowded than the trains.

And if you couldn't bring yourself to eat airline food (I can't say that I blame you), each satellite terminal has restaurants, food stands, and stores near just about every gate. You wind up paying more for food here than you would at a place outside the airport, but if you just can't wait, you have plenty to choose from.

For more information, you can call McCarran International Airport Information at ☎ 702-261-5211.

Ready, set, gamble!

As soon as you get off the plane, you learn the first rule of Las Vegas: Gambling is *everywhere*. Even in the airport. Yup, there are more than 1,000 slot machines and video-poker games right here at **McCarran.** These banks of machines (known as *carousels*) are in all the satellite terminals, the main terminal, and the baggage-claim area.

Most people advise avoiding these machines like the plague — supposedly, they offer lower winnings (known as *paybacks*) than hotel machines. This may be true (who *really* knows?), but I won't blame you if you drop a few coins. After all, who can resist such a quintessential Las Vegas experience as shaking hands with a one-armed bandit while waiting for your luggage?

Hit the road

Assuming you took my advice and rented a car (see Chapter 9), head just past the baggage claim area and you find the rental car counters. All the usual suspects are here: **Alamo, Allstate, Avis, Budget, Enterprise, Hertz, National,** and **Thrifty,** among others. After you finish all the paperwork at the counter, the rental agent will direct you outside, where you catch a shuttle bus to the car lots. Each company has its own buses that run regularly, but make sure to ask the counter agent to notify the driver that you're waiting. From the airport, it's only about a five-minute trip to your car.

Currently there is talk of moving the entirety of the rental car experience to another location, with one bus taking you from the airport to an off-site rental counter. The whole thing is wrapped up in lawsuits (and you know how long those can take!) but it still may change by the time you read this. Call the airport or your rental company (their numbers are listed in the Quick Concierge appendix at the back of the book) and ask about this situation before you leave.

Finding Your Way to Your Hotel

For general tips on driving around Las Vegas see Chapter 11, but here I give you some sound advice for getting into town and headed for your hotel.

Going by car

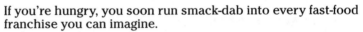

If you're driving into town (regardless of whether you are coming from the airport), you'll probably be coming in on **Interstate 15,** the major north-south freeway that runs right through the city. The following recommendations help you determine which exit to take, depending on where you're staying:

✔ **If you're staying on the South Strip** (for example, **Mandalay Bay, MGM Grand**): Traveling north on **I-15,** exit at **Tropicana Avenue** and turn right at the stoplight. The Strip is less than a half-mile to the east — trust me, you can't miss it. Southbound travelers should take the same exit but follow the signs for **Tropicana Avenue East.**

If you're hungry, you soon run smack-dab into every fast-food franchise you can imagine.

✔ **If you're staying on the Center Strip** (for example, **Bellagio, Harrah's**): North- or southbound drivers should take either the **Eastbound Flamingo Road** or **Spring Mountain Road** exit. The former puts you at the intersection populated by **Caesars Palace, Bellagio, Paris,** and more, while the latter drops you off near **Treasure Island, The Mirage,** and **The Venetian.**

✔ **If you're staying on the North Strip** (for example, the **Stratosphere, Circus Circus**): Coming from the north or south, exit at **Sahara** and head east. The Strip is about ¾ of a mile away.

✔ **If you're staying in the Paradise Road area** (for example, **Las Vegas Hilton, Hard Rock Hotel**): Take the **Flamingo Road** exit and head east. You'll cross the Strip and go about another mile to **Paradise Road.** At this intersection, you're right around the 4000 block, with higher numbers to the south (turn right) and lower numbers to the north (turn left).

✔ **If you're staying downtown** (for example, **The Golden Nugget, Main Street Station**): From **I-15,** the quickest route is to take the freeway offshoot that runs past downtown. The interchange is a bit tricky (locals call it the Spaghetti Bowl), with the freeway carrying three different numbers: **515, 95,** and **93.** Whatever you want to call it, take it south and exit at **Casino Center Boulevard.** This dumps you right into the heart of downtown, with **Fremont Street** crossing two blocks ahead and **Las Vegas Boulevard** (which eventually becomes the Strip) three blocks to the left.

When you leave the airport, follow the signs to the **215 freeway.** This is a newly completed road that makes it incredibly easy to drive to and from **McCarran.** It adds a few miles to your trip, but it's still a lot faster than going out of the airport into city-street traffic. The **215** will lead you to **I-15,** which you take north to the Strip exits or downtown.

Catching a cab

If you walk directly past the rental car counters, you find the main exit for the airport. Just outside these doors is the taxi stand. Note that, if a couple of flights have arrived at roughly the same time, the line for a cab can be daunting, with waiting times of up to 20 minutes. Basic taxi fare is $2.20 for the first mile, $1.50 for each additional mile, plus time penalties if you get stuck in traffic. The state governs these fares and so they should be the same for every company. An adequate tip for the cab driver is 10 – 15 percent, but if you're sharing a fare, you should do 10 percent per person or per small group.

All taxis can carry up to five passengers, so while you're stuck waiting on line at the taxi stand, strike up a conversation with the other people around you to see if anyone is headed in your direction and is willing to split the fare with you. Hey, cheaper is better!

Cabs are usually lined up and waiting outside the airport and all major hotels at all times. For this reason, you really should never have to phone for a cab. However, if you happen to wander into less-traveled territory, these are some of the major cab companies in town:

- ✔ ABC ☎ 702-736-8444
- ✔ Checker ☎ 702-873-2000
- ✔ Desert ☎ 702-386-9102
- ✔ Henderson ☎ 702-384-2322
- ✔ Yellow ☎ 702-873-2000

Table 10-1 shows you a few examples of what you can expect to pay for a cab from McCarran to various parts of the city. These are just estimates, so remember that your actual fare may vary a bit depending on traffic and different routes taken.

Table 10-1	Cab Prices from the Airport
Where Are You Going?	*How Much Will It Cost?*
To the South Strip area	$9.50 – $10.50
To the Center Strip area	$9.50 – $12.00
To the North Strip area	$11.00 – $13.00
To the downtown area	$16.00 – $20.00
To the Paradise Road area	$7.00 – $12.00

Going in style

If you want to try a fun alternative to cabbing it through town, why not avoid the taxi lines and consider taking a limo? You can call ahead to your hotel (most of the big ones have a limo service) and arrange to have a driver pick you up at the airport. Just give the hotel staff your flight information and the limo driver will even be waiting at your gate holding a little sign with your name on it — how posh!

Not only is it fun to pretend to be among the rich and famous, but you don't have to actually be rich to enjoy this perk: The rates are very reasonable if you're traveling with a large group. As a matter of fact, it's often less expensive than taking a cab, considering that you can fit more people into a limo. And the drivers are much more accommodating. Sit back and enjoy the sights (or watch the on-board TV) in style. And don't forget to tip the kind driver for his efforts.

Jumping on a shuttle

If you want to take a shuttle, go to the same place in the airport where you pick up a taxi or board the rental car buses. There you find shuttle buses that run regularly to and from the Strip and downtown. These buses are big and comfy and can be a bargain if you're by yourself or with one other person. They charge about $3.50 per person for a trip to the Strip or Paradise Road areas, and $4.75 per person to go downtown. And they take you right to your hotel.

If you have more than two people in your group, however, you can probably take a cab for less.

Taking a shuttle is not always a piece of cake: If the people on your bus aren't going to the same hotel as you (or one close by), you'll end up riding and waiting through a lot of extra stops. (If you share my luck, your hotel will be the last stop on the trip.) The shuttles have luggage racks though, which make these a better a bet than a city bus.

Although several companies operate these shuttle services, **Bell Trans** (☎ 702-385-5466) is the biggest and most reliable. You can usually spot these large shuttle vans with rates posted on the sides cruising the airport.

Getting on the bus

I'm going to be blunt here: For reasons I discuss further in Chapter 11, the bus should be your last resort. **Citizen's Area Transit (CAT),** ☎ 702-CAT-RIDE, runs regular service to and from the airport. The fare is $1.50 per person and 50¢ for seniors and children. Take CAT only if you have no other option. If you're lugging a heavy load, remember that even if the bus stops right in front of your hotel (which it probably won't), you may have a long walk from the bus stop to the door (distances in Vegas can be deceiving).

If you decide to take the bus (despite my advice to the contrary), remember that schedules and routes vary, so call for information. In general, though, you can catch the **no. 108** bus at the airport and take it to the **Stratosphere,** where you can transfer to the **no. 301,** which stops close to most **Strip** — and **Convention Center** — area hotels.

The **no. 109** bus goes from the airport to the **Downtown Transportation Center** at **Casino Center Boulevard** and **Stewart Avenue.**

Las Vegas by Neighborhood

Even though Las Vegas is a very spread-out city, the area you'll probably be staying in is most likely very centralized and easy to navigate.

Vegas boasts three main neighborhoods (see Chapter 6 for the pros and cons of staying in each one). There's the **Strip,** where all the big hotels and resorts are located; **downtown,** where you'll find **Glitter Gulch** and the **Fremont Street Experience;** and the **Paradise Road** area, which is home to the **Las Vegas Convention Center** and some smaller, non-casino hotels. In this section I also include a few other neighborhoods that may be of some interest to you if you're staying for more than a few days or are planning future trips.

The best analogy to help you envision the layout of Las Vegas is this: Las Vegas is shaped sort of like a crooked Santa Claus cap. The **Strip** is one side of the cap, **Paradise Road** is the other, and **downtown** is the fuzzy ball on top. Chew on that one for a moment. (And, if you're a more right-brained thinker, check out one of the many maps in this book to help you get your bearings. I labeled everything very neatly, so you won't feel lost for a minute. Just flip through the pages and you're bound to come across one that perfectly suits your needs.)

The Strip

The **Strip** (also known as **Las Vegas Boulevard South**) is the heart of Vegas. That's where first-time visitors generally spend most of their time, and with good reason — this is where most of the major attractions, hotels, and casinos (including **New York–New York, Caesars,** and **Circus Circus**) are located.

The Strip acts as the center of town, so addresses are all measured from there (100 West is a block west of the Strip, 100 East is a block east, and so on). If you're looking for the bulk of the action, keep in mind that the southern and center parts of the Strip are the most action-packed.

Las Vegas Neighborhoods

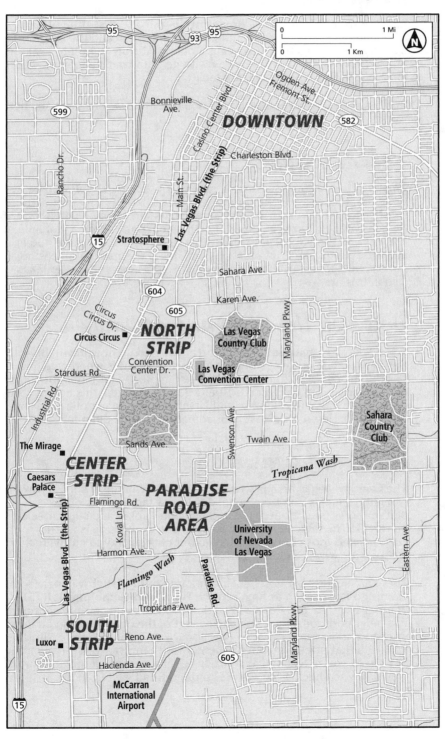

Downtown

Also known as *Glitter Gulch,* **downtown** is the oldest section of town. It's located just to the south and east of where **I-15** and the **515/95/93** freeways come together. **Las Vegas Boulevard** runs right into **Fremont Street** (now a pedestrian walkway with no auto traffic allowed), where most of the area's big hotels are located.

Bordering neighborhoods are questionable in terms of safety, so stick to the well-traveled, brightly lit parts.

Paradise Road

This area is so-named because it refers to — surprise! — **Paradise Road** and the area surrounding it. The actual road is a major north-south artery that runs from **McCarran** to its intersection with the **Strip** (which parallels **Paradise Road,** for the most part, about a half mile to the west) at the **Stratosphere Tower.** You can find a few large hotels and attractions here, but mostly it's made up of smaller, non-casino hotels and a lot of restaurants. The **Las Vegas Convention Center** is also in this area.

Between the Strip and downtown

If you take **Las Vegas Boulevard** north, you end up downtown. Between the **Strip** and **downtown** (for lack of a better term) is where you find most of the city's wedding chapels (see Chapter 17 for more about the nuptial scene). Unless you're actually getting married, this area is really only good for its high silliness and kitsch factor ("Joan Collins was married here!"). Hey, it may be fun for something a little different.

East Las Vegas

The **East Las Vegas** area is where locals go to gamble. It's less crowded and glitzy (locals don't really need the wow factor). The odds are better, too — you can actually find 9/6 video poker and single-deck blackjack! The table limits tend to be lower, everything is a little cheaper, and those hotels tend to go out of their way to cultivate a local — and loyal — clientele.

There are several big hotel/casinos along **Boulder Highway** near **Flamingo Road,** such as **Sam's Town Hotel and Gambling Hall** (5111 Boulder Hwy.; ☎ **800-634-6371**). I don't recommend getting a hotel in this neighborhood, simply because most of the other places you'll want to see are too far away — it's about 7 or 8 miles to the Strip. The upside is that prices are often much lower than what you'd pay on the Strip, so if you're feeling particularly adventuresome, it might be worth your while to check it out. Take **Flamingo Road** east from the Strip to get here.

Henderson

If you're looking for something a bit off the beaten path and want to see some fun, family-oriented attractions, check out **Henderson.** It's a small town just southeast of Las Vegas — a 20-minute car ride from the Strip if traffic is good. Specifically, you can see the **Clark County Heritage Museum** and take a tours of **Ethel M. Chocolates** factory. (I talk more about these and other attractions in Chapter 17.) To get to Henderson from the Strip, take Las Vegas Boulevard south to **Sunset Road** and head east. Most of what you'll want to see is around the intersection of **Sunset Road** and the **95 freeway.**

The **Maryland Parkway** is another major north-south artery about 2 miles west of the Strip and 1 mile west of Paradise Road. If you're look- ing for retailers or food chains, you can find just about every major (and minor) one on this road: **Sears, J.C. Penney, Toys 'Я' Us,** and all the big pharmacy/drug stores, just to mention a few.

If you need to pick up something like shaving cream or a spiffy new bathing suit and don't feel like paying the exorbitant prices charged in hotel stores, this area is a good bet.

Getting Tourist Information After You Arrive

No matter how well you prepare for your trip, you still may find your- self in need of a tidbit of information after arriving in Las Vegas. It's okay; it happens to the best of us. If you find yourself in this situation, check out the following resources to get the goods:

✔ **Major hotels:** Every major hotel has tourist information at its reception, show, or sightseeing desk. These friendly folks can tell you about special events, concerts, or shows in town that you may have missed during your research.

- Don't be shy about making show reservations at the big hotel's show desks. They'll make reservations for you at any show in town — not just the ones in that particular hotel.

- If you need detailed maps and directions (and forget to bring this book), go to the reception or sightseeing desks. They've got what you need.

- Try visiting the concierge desk if you need good information ranging from dining tips to advice on the cheapest place to have your suit dry-cleaned. (The only caveat here is that the concierge is probably prejudiced toward his personal or pro- fessional favorites, so you may not be getting an unbiased opinion.)

✔ **Las Vegas Convention and Visitors Authority:** 3150 Paradise Rd., Las Vegas, NV 89109. ☎ **800-332-5333** or 702-892-0711. Internet: www.lasvegas24hours.com.

✔ **Las Vegas Chamber of Commerce:** 711 E. Desert Inn Rd., Las Vegas, NV 89109. ☎ **702-735-1616.**

Ask the Chamber of Commerce for its *Visitor's Guide,* which contains extensive listings for accommodations, attractions, excursions, children's activities, and more. They can also answer many of your other questions (including those about quickie weddings and divorces).

Chapter 11

Getting from Here to There in Las Vegas

. . . .

In This Chapter

▶ Exploring Las Vegas' transportation options

▶ Driving in Las Vegas

▶ Strolling around the Strip and downtown

. . . .

*F*or a city of its stature, Las Vegas does not have a phenomenal public transportation network — not a surprise, considering the casinos want you to stay put. There are city buses, but no subways or rail lines. You're likely to take one of four options: driving, taking a cab, taking a bus or trolley, or hoofing it. In this chapter, I give you an idea of the pros and cons of each of these alternatives, plus some tips that may save you time and money.

Driving Around in a Car

Driving is a good option for getting around in Vegas. When you consider practicality and convenience, nothing beats your own set of wheels. Although you can walk to a lot of nearby attractions, you can get the most out of the city when you're mobile and not relying on taxis, buses, or your feet to get somewhere. Of course, as practical as having a car is, there are also some drawbacks to consider. Don't worry. I give you the lowdown on both in this section.

Considering the pros

Here are a few reasons that driving yourself around Vegas is a Good Thing:

> ✔ **Sweet freedom.** Renting a car provides you with added mobility and freedom that you don't get from other means of transportation. Unless you're a marathon walker, the Strip is too sprawling to walk its entire length, anywhere else is too far away for a cheap cab ride, and bus service is ineffective at best.

✔ **The cheap factor.** Cars are cheaper than taking cabs everywhere, especially if you want to get out and explore. Parking is not much of a concern in Vegas, as you can find lots of inexpensive (or free) garages spread throughout the city.

As I discuss later in this chapter, all the major hotels have free self-parking and most have free valet service.

Dealing with the cons

And yes, driving yourself through this wonderland of a city does have its drawbacks:

✔ **Traffic tie-ups.** Las Vegas traffic is notorious, and it's especially bad on and around the Strip. The stoplights alone can take forever to maneuver. I once took a drive from the southernmost Strip hotel, the **Luxor,** to the northernmost, the **Stratosphere.** It took almost 30 minutes to cover the 4 miles. If you do the math, that's an average of about 8 miles an hour.

✔ **Construction issues.** Vegas is not immune to the construction problems that you find in most major cities. In fact, you may find that Vegas is even more prone to these "improvements" because of its continual state of transition. Just be aware that the roads here are always ripped up for some project or another, and this only adds to traffic problems.

✔ **Gas prices.** In Las Vegas you will wax nostalgic about the cost of fuel in your own backyard. You'll pay more at the pump here than in most other American cities — as much as 15¢ per gallon higher than the U.S. average.

You can find lots of gas stations at the Tropicana Avenue exit just west of the freeway, but you should probably steer clear of them: Their prices are way higher than those at other places in town.

Although it may sound like fun to cruise around Las Vegas in a cool Porsche or convertible, you're better off sticking to something small and cheap. After all, it's just going to be sitting in a parking garage most of the time, and the parking attendants don't really care what you drive.

Parking your ride

Free valet parking — what more do you need to know? For the cheap factor alone, this has to be one of the greatest things about driving in Las Vegas. And finding parking isn't so hard either. At their main entrance, the big hotels all have signs that point you in the direction of the valet service where you can hand off your car and get a claim check. When you're ready to leave, simply turn in the claim ticket to reclaim your car and all it costs you is a $1 – $2 tip for the attendant. (In hot weather, they'll probably even turn on the air-conditioning for you so the car is cool when you get in. Nice, huh?) One small drawback to using the valet service is that the garages can fill up at night during busy times and picking up your car can take a while. Expect a 5- to 20-minute wait. But this wait is generally not much longer than the wait in the taxi line, so it's really no big deal.

If you're on a tight schedule, you may want to use the free (in most places) self-parking instead of valet parking at the major hotels. The newer hotels have parking structures that even allow you to park in the shade.

Keep in mind, however, that many times, these self-park areas are quite a hike from the casinos and showrooms. Hope you have on your walking shoes.

Parking policies vary for downtown hotels. Most charge for self-parking but offer validation in the casinos, which makes it free. Again, consider using the valet services where available to save yourself the hassle.

Steering clear of traffic jams

As I mention earlier in this chapter, driving in Las Vegas can be a nightmare when it comes to the traffic.

Because the Strip is nightmarishly crowded at all times, day or night, avoid it at all costs. Over the course of my oh-so-frequent visits (I like to call it research!), however, I have found a few alternative routes that are easier on your schedule and your blood pressure.

North-South alternatives to the Strip

If you don't want to get stuck in bumper-to-bumper traffic on the Strip, here are some alternate routes for traveling north-south:

- ✔ **I-15:** This major interstate runs parallel to the Strip and is easily accessible from **Tropicana, Flamingo, Spring Mountain,** and **Sahara Avenues.** If you need to get from one end of the Strip to the other, or especially if you are going downtown, this route is your best bet. The only exception is during morning and evening rush hours, when you can finish reading *War and Peace* in the time it takes to get from one place to another.

- ✔ **Industrial Road:** This quick-and-dirty route for getting from one Strip location to another is also a good alternative. It's located just west of the Strip and runs all the way from **Tropicana** to **Sahara Avenues.** The city has recently reconfigured and repaved what used to be a meandering two-lane road to a smooth, four-lane mini-highway that has a lot less traffic and fewer stoplights.

  Be aware though that ongoing construction means the part parallel to the northern end of the Strip is often blocked with roadwork and can be a maze of somewhat confusing detours.

- ✔ **Koval Lane:** Koval runs parallel to the Strip on the east side between **Las Vegas Boulevard** and **Paradise Road.** It only runs from **Tropicana** to **Sands,** so it isn't good for end-to-end Strip runs, but short trips are a lot faster.

Alternate Routes to Avoid Gridlock

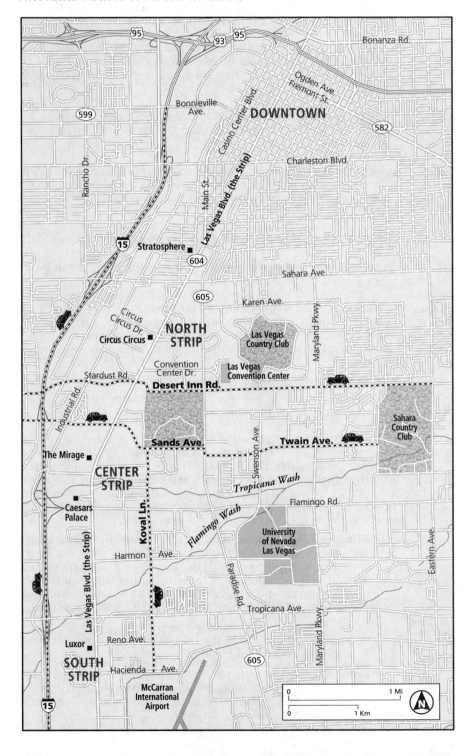

Finding your way when you're lost

The **Stratosphere** hotel may not be doing too well business-wise, but has revolutionized driving for tourists in Las Vegas. At 110 stories, this larger-than-large structure is the tallest building west of the Mississippi River and can be seen from just about every place in town (and from many places outside of town!). It's more than twice as tall as any other building in Las Vegas. If you get lost while driving, take a minute to scan the horizon and find the **Stratosphere Tower.** Head toward it and you'll eventually arrive at the northern end of the Strip and Paradise Road, only five minutes from downtown.

Lesser-known routes east-west across town

The major east-west arteries, such as **Flamingo** and **Tropicana,** can get congested, too, so here are some alternatives that generally move faster:

- **Spring Mountain/Sands/Twain:** It's one street with three different names, depending on where you are, and it crosses the Strip next to **Treasure Island** and **Paradise Road** near the **Fairfield Inn.** There are fewer stoplights and less traffic here than you'll find on other major east-west routes like **Flamingo Road** or **Tropicana Avenue.**

- **Desert Inn Road:** This is another terrific project engineered by the city. This street has been changed into a six-lane, divided freeway (with no traffic lights) that begins at **Paradise Road** on the east and ends at **Valley View** just west of **I-15.** It provides limited access to and from the Strip, so it's best used for getting from one side to the other without the hassle of **Las Vegas Boulevard, I-15,** or crosswalks filled with tourists.

Following the rules of the road

If you're counting on Vegas having loose speed limits and traffic laws, don't. Despite rumors about western states being lax, Las Vegas police and the Nevada Highway Patrol go strictly by the book. Here are a few general rules:

- You'll find that the speed limits in Vegas are comparable to those in the rest of the U.S., with 35 – 45 mph common on many major streets, 25 – 35 mph on side streets, and 55 – 70 mph on the freeways. Be sure to scope out the specific speed limits on the road you're traveling.

- Turning right on red lights is permitted in Las Vegas, and if you don't follow this convention, you're likely to hear about it from the guy behind you in the Caddy with the steer-horn hood ornament.

✔ Most of the time, you'll need to wait for the green arrow if you want to make a left turn at a major intersection. Up to three lanes of traffic can turn at the same time.

✔ U-turns are allowed at intersections where there is no sign strictly forbidding them.

Taking a Taxi

If you plan on spending all or most of your time in one general area, using the city's taxi service is a viable option. If you plan to go very far, however, be prepared to open your wallet — wide.

You can see taxis everywhere in Vegas, so finding one is usually not a problem. Even at 4 a.m., you'll find a line of them outside most major hotels and the airport. Although I can't vouch for every driver, car, and company, the taxis I've taken have all been clean, and the drivers professional and courteous.

My main issue with using taxis is that they're so darned expensive. Once, I was too tired to walk back from the southern end of the Strip to my hotel in the center section, so I hailed a cab. You guessed it: I immediately got stuck in nighttime traffic — and that meter kept on ticking even though I wasn't moving. To go about two miles cost almost $15 with tip. Now, a good cabbie does his best to avoid such nonsense (even if it means making less money), but if you do take a cab, be prepared to boss them into the swiftest route.

Taxi fares are regulated by the state of Nevada and should be the same for all companies: $2.20 for the first mile and $1.50 for each additional mile, plus time penalties (for those times when you're stuck in traffic). Be sure that the rates are prominently displayed in the cab before letting the driver start the meter.

Taking the Bus

Citizen's Area Transit (CAT) (☎ 702-CAT-RIDE) is the city bus service, and it gets really mixed reviews. You shouldn't rely on it as your major source of transportation, since the service is unreliable — like most bus services, schedules are an abstract concept — and the routes don't always make sense. Suppose that you want to get from the **airport** to the **MGM Grand,** which is less than 2 miles away. You have to take the no. 108 bus all the way up **Paradise Road** to the **Stratosphere Tower,** transfer to the no. 301, and ride that all the way back down the Strip. The bus makes you travel more than 8 miles, and if you get there in less than two hours, consider it a miracle. And, of course, many people rely on the bus services, and they can fill it so much you will not only stand through much of your endless journey, but a packed bus can simply pass by those folks who are patiently waiting at stops.

Nevertheless, it is cheap. At $1.50 for adults and 50¢ for kids and seniors, this is a pretty good bargain. The no. 301 runs right down the Strip, so if it's not a busy time of day — remember, buses get stuck in traffic just like cars and taxis — it's an economical and simple way of scooting down the Strip.

Trying the Trolley

A little less aggravating and even cheaper than the bus system is the **Las Vegas Strip Trolley** (☎ 702-382-1404), which runs from 9:30 a.m. – 2 a.m. It's really just a bus designed to look like a trolley car, but it's cheaper and cooler looking than the bus. Plus you get to hear interesting Vegas facts from the driver during your journey. The trolleys go up and down the Strip, stopping in front of every major hotel and casino. There's also a special trolley that runs from the **Stratosphere** into downtown. The fare is $1.30 per ride; children under five years old ride free. Exact change is required.

On the downside, trolleys, like city buses, are often full, full, full and will pass right by stops if they're too crowded. Even though several of them run simultaneously, because they have no definable schedule to speak of, your wait time can be interminable.

Walking Your Way Around Town

After you get into a centralized neighborhood (Center Strip, downtown, and so on), you won't have a problem walking from one hotel to the next. It's certainly easier than retrieving a car every time. However, if you want to get out of one area and into another neighborhood, walking becomes a bigger deal.

Distances are deceiving

Maybe it's the desert that makes distances here so deceiving, or the fact that the buildings are so darned big it makes them seem closer, but getting from point A to point B always seems to take much longer in Las Vegas than you think it will. I can't count the number of times I've said, "Here I am at The Mirage/Treasure Island/ Bellagio and I have dinner/business/show tickets for next door at Caesars/ The Mirage/the Monte Carlo. I'll leave about 15 minutes before I need to be there." Thirty-five minutes later, after negotiating the casino crowds at our hotel, trekking through to the exit, using the moving sidewalk or tram or my feet to get to the entrance next door, finding the entrance, negotiating the crowds there and getting lost . . . I finally arrive. Barely. The moral of the story is to *always* give yourself extra time, even if you're just going next door.

Obviously, the biggest plus to walking is that it is free and it's a good way to walk off your steak and shrimp dinner. All it's going to cost you is the price of a pair of comfortable shoes. If you're okay with staying in one basic area, why not make the hike?

A major negative is the weather, which can be brutally hot during the day and exceptionally chilly at night. This is something to consider when you're looking down the street and saying, "Oh, it's not that far!" (and remember that distances are deceiving in Las Vegas, where everything is larger than life and, therefore, seems closer than it is). Another thing to keep in mind is that the pedestrian traffic is often as congested and frustrating as the street traffic. This is especially true during peak holidays or convention times.

If you have the kids with you, keep this in mind: Sex is a big industry in Las Vegas. To promote their enterprises, many strip clubs and escort services place people on the sidewalks to hand out flyers and magazines that you may not want your children to see (they're pretty graphic). Of course you can just say "no," but remember that many people take the brochures and then discard them on the ground where anyone, including your little angel, can get an eye-popping peek at them.

If you do decide on hoofin' it, remember the following:

✔ For comfort's sake, be sure to bring some good walking shoes to Las Vegas — even if you have a rental car, you'll be doing a lot of walking. If you opt for sandals, don't forget to put sunscreen on your feet, and watch out for sidewalks cluttered with trash, broken glass, or the equivalent.

✔ When walking long distances in Vegas, be sure to carry plenty of water (the casinos allow you to bring it in). Buy yours at a convenience store; it's cheaper than the bottles sold in casinos.

✔ If you get a bit tired, several of the casino hotels have free monorail systems or moving sidewalks to help you rest your sore feet (and to guide you, lemming-like, to their casinos). See the following section for details on these transportation options.

Using People Movers to Get Around Town

When you're dead tired and you don't feel like you can move another inch, have hope! Vegas is full of monorails, trams, and moving sidewalks underfoot to help you get from one spot to another without moving a muscle. Naturally, these conveniences are there to lure you into the hotels that operate them, but one tends to overlook that sort of thing when the alternative means adding a few blisters to already sore feet.

The monorails in the following list are totally free of charge — take advantage of them and enjoy the ride!

- ✔ **MGM Grand to Bally's monorail:** Adjacent to the main entrance at the **MGM Grand** is the boarding platform for a monorail that takes you up the street to **Bally's** shopping arcade, directly adjacent to **Paris.** It's a great trick for getting from the **South Strip** to the **Central Strip.** If it can ever get out of the lawsuits that it's currently wrapped up in, the monorail will eventually extend north past the **Flamingo,** east to the **Convention Center,** and end up the street by **The Sahara.** Don't expect it before 2005 though.

- ✔ **Treasure Island to The Mirage tram:** Even though these two hotels are right next to each other, you won't find a quicker way to get from one to the other. Pick up the tram at the back of **Treasure Island** between the hotel and its parking deck, and it will deliver you practically to the front door of **The Mirage.** Convenient, huh?

- ✔ **The Mirage/Caesars Palace people movers:** If you exit **The Mirage** past the white tigers, you find a moving sidewalk that takes you out to the Strip. Walk a few steps, and you can jump on the **Caesars Palace** moving sidewalk that takes you inside the **Forum Shops** or casino. It works the other way around, too!

- ✔ **Mandalay Bay/Luxor/Excalibur monorail/people movers:** Shortly after **Mandalay Bay** opened in 1999 the Mandalay Resort Group christened an all new, high-capacity monorail that takes you from the corner of **Tropicana** and the Strip south to **Mandalay Bay.** The northbound trip features stops at **Luxor** and **Excalibur.** An air-conditioned, moving sidewalk covers the same journey.

- ✔ **Bellagio/Monte Carlo monorail:** Since MGM/The Mirage owns all or a part of both resorts, it seemed natural to put in a monorail that runs from the food court of **Monte Carlo** to the casino area of **Bellagio.** So they did.

Even more of these people movers are in the works, with proposed monorails between **The Mirage** and **Bellagio,** plus a link from **The Venetian** to the **Las Vegas Convention Center.** Those Las Vegas engineers are so thoughtful, aren't they?

Chapter 12

Keeping Your Cash in Check

· ·

In This Chapter

▶ Accessing cash in Las Vegas

▶ Handling and avoiding a stolen-wallet situation

▶ Getting a handle on the local taxes

· ·

*I*f you think you're going to get through your Vegas vacation without spending a little of the green stuff, think again. Las Vegas is built on tourist dollars and, yes, some of yours will likely go into the fund. You can hardly turn around without bumping into a cash machine, and when you turn back the other way, you'll find an infinite number of ways to spend that money. (They're called slot machines.) In this chapter, I tell you all about your different options for keeping yourself funded while making sure you don't go bankrupt in the process. Unless, of course, you insist on dropping it all in a Double Diamond slot.

Finding Funds in Las Vegas

Pardon me while I snicker. It's really not hard to get cash in Vegas. You can twitch your nose like Samantha on *Bewitched* and cash magically appears. Okay, it's not *that* easy, but really, assuming you are in Vegas as you read this, turn around. Look behind you. There is probably an ATM machine there. Really. Oh, maybe not in your room, but just about everywhere else. Whether you have money in your account, well, that's another matter, particularly if it's the end of your trip.

In other words, you don't need to seek out a bank to withdraw money, get checks cashed, get credit card advances, or make just about any other kind of financial transaction. What the machines don't do, the cashiers at the cages in the casinos do.

However, if you are dead set on using a bank — using one may help you avoid the average casino ATM fee of $2 per transaction, and that's above your own bank's charge for using an outside machine — **Bank of America, Citibank, Cal Fed** and **Wells Fargo** all have branches in Vegas, and all have ATMs.

Keeping Your Money Safe (And What to Do If It's Stolen)

 Vast amounts of money are always on display in Vegas, and crooks find lots of easy marks. Don't be one of them. Here are some tips to help you avoid this agonizing situation (or at least ease the pain if it happens anyway):

✔ At gaming tables and slot machines, men should keep their wallets well-concealed and out of the reach of pickpockets (the front pants pocket is a good place to stash it), and women should keep purses in view (preferably on their laps) at all times. Don't depend on hotel security to look out for your property. It is quite easy for a thief to swipe a purse that is sitting at your feet, whether you are at a bar or at a slot machine. Thieves are just waiting for you to become so entranced with your game that you let your guard down, so don't let it happen.

✔ Whether they're inside the casinos or strolling the Strip, women should always keep their purses slung diagonally across their chests, preferably under a jacket. The best kind of purse to take is one that folds over, rather than one that just has a zipper on top. Do not sling your purse or camera over your chair when in a restaurant. Men should ideally use a money belt or a fanny pack to store cash, credit cards, and traveler's checks in.

✔ If your hotel has an in-room safe, use it. Stash excess cash, traveler's checks, and any other valuables that you don't need for immediate use. If your hotel room doesn't have a safe, put your valuables and cash inside the hotel's safety deposit box. In general, I would say the best policy is to use an ATM machine and only withdraw the amount of money you'll need to cover your expenses for about two days at a time.

✔ If you do win a big jackpot in the casinos, ask the pit boss or slot person to cut you a check rather than give you your winnings in cash. The cash may look cool, but flashing it around sends the wrong signals to the wrong kind of people.

✔ Almost every credit-card company has a toll-free emergency number that you can call if your cards are lost or stolen. The credit-card company may be able to wire you a cash advance off your credit card immediately, and often can get you an emergency credit card within a day or two.

The issuing bank's toll-free number is usually printed on the back of the credit card. Make note of this number before you leave on your trip and stash it somewhere other than your wallet. If you forget to write down the number, you can call ☎ **800-555-1212** — that's 800 directory assistance — to get the number. And because thieves may not swipe this guidebook — though it's worth its weight in gold — **Citicorp Visa**'s U.S. emergency number is ☎ **800-336-8472. American Express** cardholders and traveler's-check carriers need to call ☎ **800-221-7282** for all money emergencies. **MasterCard** holders must call ☎ **800-307-7309.**

✔ If you opt to carry traveler's checks, make sure that you keep a record of their serial numbers in a safe location so you can handle an emergency. Traveler's checks can be somewhat cumbersome, and considering the number of ATM machines in Vegas, they're probably unnecessary. Nevertheless, they are the safest way to carry large amounts of cash (which I don't recommend). Once you buy them, record the checks' serial numbers and keep that list in a separate location from the checks. It's also a good idea to leave the serial numbers with a relative back home. Should your checks be stolen, call the issuer, give the serial numbers, and ask for instructions on getting your checks replaced.

If your wallet disappears despite your best efforts, you're not likely to recover it. The police, while having the best of intentions, probably can't help either. However, after you realize that your wallet is gone and you cancel your credit cards, you should still call the police. You may need their report number for credit card or insurance purposes later.

For more monetary information, see Chapter 3.

Taxing Matters

The casinos may do a number on your wallet or you may actually luck out at the tables, but if there is one sure thing in Vegas, it's that the city is going to get its fair share of cash regardless. You will pay a 7 percent sales tax in Las Vegas. And when you settle up your hotel bill, you'll need to ante up a 9 percent room tax if you stay anywhere in Clark County but downtown. Downtown hotels currently assess an 11 percent room tax; the city is using the extra revenue to pay off the expenses for the *Fremont Street Experience.*

Part IV
Dining in
Las Vegas

The 5th Wave   By Rich Tennant

The buffet at this place is incredible, isn't it?!

In this part . . .

*I*n the last decade or so, Las Vegas has risen out of its
culinary doldrums to become one of the greatest foodie
meccas in America. If gluttony is your sin of choice, you'll
find plenty of fine restaurants — almost every star chef in
the U.S. has at least one restaurant here — to indulge
yourself in. And, because Las Vegas attracts visitors from
every corner of the planet, you're assured of finding literally any kind of cuisine that tickles your taste buds.

In this part, I explore the vast array of dining options
Las Vegas offers, including those Vegas institutions —
the buffets.

Chapter 13

Dining — Las Vegas Style

● ●

In This Chapter

▶ Exploring the Las Vegas dining scene

▶ Making reservations

▶ Dressing to dine

▶ Cutting costs on good eats

● ●

*L*as Vegas is not only about gambling and having fun. You may be tempted to spend all your time in front of a slot machine, but you want to be sure to get a real taste of the dining scene, too. Gotta keep that blood sugar up, you know. In some of the larger hotels, you could hang out for a week and never eat in the same place twice. But there's more to Las Vegas dining than what you find adjacent to a casino. In this chapter I tell you what to expect when you go out to dine in Las Vegas; for information on specific restaurants, see Chapter 14.

What's Hot Now

It used to be that food snobs — *foodies,* we call ourselves — or simply anyone with well-developed taste buds never put the words "good," "food," and "Vegas" in the same sentence. But in the last year alone, that has changed dramatically. All kinds of celebrity chefs — you know, the ones who have very famous (and expensive) restaurants often written about in glossy magazines, or their own line of frozen foods, or their own show on the Food Network — have opened restaurants in Vegas. You can thank the owners of those fancy new luxury resort hotels. Apparently, they figured that budget travelers will eat anything put before them, but if they wanted the well-heeled to come to Vegas, they had to feed them in the manner to which they were accustomed. It's rather snobby, but no matter. I am just mighty glad. You should be, too.

If you really want to eat well in Vegas, and you don't have a trust fund, hit that jackpot and feel free to start in at the top. Alas, that's probably the only way to afford it all. If it's some consolation, you wouldn't have time to eat at all the amazing places now open, so ease your wallet's strain a little by having just two blow-out meals. That is, if you can narrow your decision down to just two. I certainly couldn't. Just look at this partial (and mouth-watering) list: Aside from Wolfgang Puck's half dozen or so places (including **Spago,** the famous Beverly Hills restaurant haunted by celebrities), and those of Emeril Lagasse (the New Orleans chef who seems to account for half the Food Network's programming), Vegas has branches of such NYC favorites as **Le Cirque, Lutece, Aureole,** and **Circo;** branches of such LA favorites as **Pinot, Nobu, Border Grill,** and **Valentino;** a branch of San Francisco favorite **Aqua;** and restaurants by famed chefs such as Julian Serrano, Jean-Louis Palladion, and Todd English. Whew! By the time you got through all that, you might well be a foodie yourself.

Not all the good news is strictly at the top end of the scale, just most of it. "But I thought Vegas was supposed to have such cheap food?" Well, Vegas is not such a budget vacation any longer. You can try the more affordable dining options, but a slide down in price generally brings a drop in quality as well.

Eat to the beat

Before bringing out the name-brand chefs, Vegas first jumped on the theme restaurant bandwagon. Name just about any hobby or passion — rock music, motorcycles, sports — and there's a restaurant for you. The **Hard Rock Café, Planet Hollywood,** and **Dive!** are just a few of the names here.

Now, I have to admit that I just loathe these places. I have my reasons. I see them as tourist traps of the highest order. And I hate it when they take business away from local restaurants that serve real local cuisine. But here's the thing — Vegas has no *real* local cuisine. Just like it has no skyline of its own — it imports it all from other cities. So, with that complaint out of the way, I step down from my soapbox.

No, wait, let me get back up for a second. Just remember that a **Planet Hollywood** in Vegas is just like a Planet Hollywood in Miami, or Chicago, or Croatia (no kidding; there's one in Zagreb). Every theme restaurant is part of a chain. You might just as well be eating at a Denny's. Except Denny's is a whole lot cheaper — you wouldn't catch them charging eight bucks for a hamburger.

Still, you may have never been to Zagreb, and so you've never seen a **Planet Hollywood,** or a **Hard Rock,** or an **All-Star Café.** And so it seems reasonable to want to do so. Kids inevitably love the places, though adults tend to wince at the loud music and prices. The "memorabilia" collected in these joints is generally not nearly as valuable as they would like you to think (it's mostly bargain-basement celebrity castoffs). But the food can be, well, okay.

All theme restaurants have adjoining gift shops where you can buy logo items or memorabilia. If you're looking for souvenirs or gifts for the folks at home, look elsewhere. Prices are often high at these shops, and the merchandise is not exactly unique.

Las Vegas Dining Overview

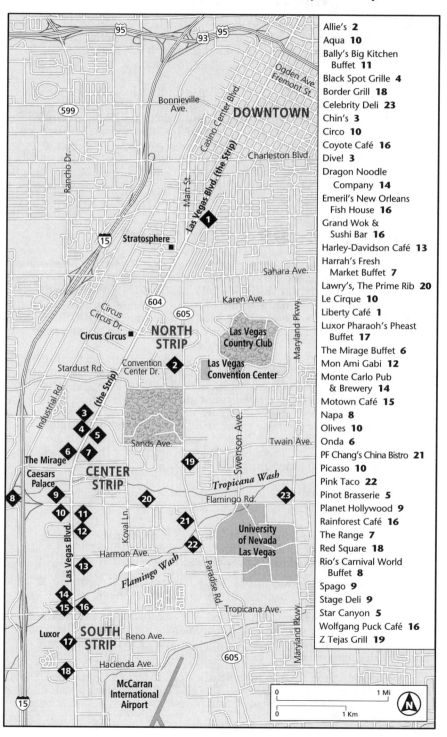

Allie's **2**
Aqua **10**
Bally's Big Kitchen
  Buffet **11**
Black Spot Grille **4**
Border Grill **18**
Celebrity Deli **23**
Chin's **3**
Circo **10**
Coyote Café **16**
Dive! **3**
Dragon Noodle
  Company **14**
Emeril's New Orleans
  Fish House **16**
Grand Wok &
  Sushi Bar **16**
Harley-Davidson Café **13**
Harrah's Fresh
  Market Buffet **7**
Lawry's, The Prime Rib **20**
Le Cirque **10**
Liberty Café **1**
Luxor Pharaoh's Pheast
  Buffet **17**
The Mirage Buffet **6**
Mon Ami Gabi **12**
Monte Carlo Pub
  & Brewery **14**
Motown Café **15**
Napa **8**
Olives **10**
Onda **6**
PF Chang's China Bistro **21**
Picasso **10**
Pink Taco **22**
Pinot Brasserie **5**
Planet Hollywood **9**
Rainforest Café **16**
The Range **7**
Red Square **18**
Rio's Carnival World
  Buffet **8**
Spago **9**
Stage Deli **9**
Star Canyon **5**
Wolfgang Puck Café **16**
Z Tejas Grill **19**

A smorgasbord of buffets

Buffets used to be *the* way to eat in Vegas. They have been an institution in Vegas since the 1940s, when the **El Rancho Hotel** offered an all-you-can-eat spread for a buck! Unlimited prime rib and shrimp — $1.00! Wa-hoo! Heck, nothing says "vacation" like that.

But along with everything else in Vegas, buffets have gone upscale. They are still everywhere — every major hotel (and some minor ones) seems to have one. Unfortunately, they aren't really such a bargain anymore, particularly the good ones where it's hard to eat $20 worth of food in one sitting (though heaven knows, you feel compelled to try). You can find a few inexpensive ones in town ($5 – $8), but the quality of those . . . well, sometimes it just doesn't bear thinking about. Still, a Las Vegas vacation isn't really complete without at least one visit to a buffet.

Eating Where the Locals Eat

This is pretty much where you are going to eat if you don't have that trust fund. Many a local has sworn to me that they don't bother cooking, since eating out in Vegas is so cheap. Obviously, they don't mean those celebrity-chef, name-brand places — though you will find them there, to be sure, on special occasions. Nevertheless, with all the great meal deals offered by the hotels, it's more affordable to eat out anyway.

Now "great" refers to price, not quality. I'm not prepared to commit to the quality. Oh, don't worry, that 69¢ shrimp cocktail is safe enough. People chow down on these bargain meals all the time, happy to save a few bucks that may have been spent at the blackjack table, and they all seem to live to tell about it. Actually, I have a brother who loves the meal deals simply because they are often offered in the middle of the night. When he can't sleep, he just tromps downstairs and munches on a steak. All the same, I recommend steering clear of the 69¢ cup of stew specials offered on the north end of the Strip.

It's almost impossible to list specifics, since they change weekly, but here are a few places that offer bargain-basement food prices:

- ✔ **Binion's Horseshoe Snack Bar** (128 E. Fremont St.; ☎ 800-237-6537) offers burgers and sandwiches in the $2.50 – $4.00 range. And the food is pretty good.

- ✔ **El Cortez Emerald Room** (600 E. Fremont St., downtown; ☎ 702-385-5200). A $1 bacon-and-egg breakfast. I kid you not.

- ✔ **The Gold Spike** (400 E. Ogden Ave.; ☎ 702-384-8444) features $2.50 roast beef dinners; full breakfasts set you back 99¢ if you arrive before 10:30 a.m. (Use your change in the casino's penny slot machines.)

- ✔ **Holiday Inn Casino Boardwalk Deli** (3750 Las Vegas Blvd. S., on the South Strip at Harmon; ☎ 702-735-2400). Here's your chance to eat three quarter-sized hamburgers or a half-pound hot dog for $1.49.

✔ **Imperial Palace Coffee Shop** (3535 Las Vegas Blvd. S., on the Center Strip just north of Flamingo Ave.; ☎ 702-731-3311). A nighttime prime-rib special for $2.95. Get outta here!

✔ **The Riviera's Nickeltown Deli** (2901 Las Vegas Blvd. S.; ☎ 702-734-5110). Located in the nickels-only section of the resort's casino, it offers 50¢ hot dogs and beers.

✔ **The Stardust's Toucan Harry's** (3000 Las Vegas Blvd. S.; ☎ 702-732-6111). The food isn't fantastic, but you can get steak and eggs from midnight to 7 a.m. for a mere $3.89.

✔ **Westward Ho Snack Bar** (2900 Las Vegas Blvd. S., on the North Strip next to Circus Circus; ☎ 702-796-3300). Have they got a deal for you: full breakfasts from $1.99. You can also get half a rack of ribs for less than $4.

These places may not always serve what I've listed here, but they usually offer some sort of special. The best way to find others is to read the signs in front of the various casinos and to check for free coupons inside the many free magazines that are available inside Vegas hotel rooms and on the Strip. They always advertise current meal deals. For more information on dining bargains, see "Bargain Bingeing" later in this chapter.

Dressing to Dine

For the most part, Las Vegas is a very informal town. You'll see people in jeans at even the best restaurants. A few places require jackets and forbid all-American denim, so bring at least one nice outfit. A general rule is *if you have to call to make a reservation, ask about a dress code while you're on the phone.* If you don't have to make reservations, don't worry about what you're wearing.

Bargain Bingeing

You can easily feed a family of four for under $20 (though not in a nutritionally sound way) in Las Vegas; on the other hand you can quickly blow $200 on dinner for two. I've discussed the latter; the former can be achieved through careful application of those famous Vegas meal specials: all-you-can-eat pasta $2.95, complete prime-rib dinners $4.95, steak and eggs $3.95, shrimp cocktail 99¢. They are easy to find, thanks to advertisements in the giveaway magazines in the rooms, and on billboards and hotel marquees. Sometimes they are only offered late at night (as late as midnight to dawn), and of course, any great bargain attracts lots of other thrifty types. You aren't going to find these specials at many of the name-brand hotels, but check the hotels in downtown, on the northern end of the Strip and just off the Strip. But are they any good? What do you want for nothing? For more on meal deals, see "Eating Where the Locals Eat," earlier in this chapter.

You'll also find a slew of national chain restaurants in Las Vegas — **Denny's, Tony Roma's, Olive Garden,** and so on — but they aren't the great bargains that they are in other cities. Obviously, the amount of money you spend on food depends on whether you can be satisfied with eating on the chain gang or the hotel's spiritual equivalent. If you avoid the celeb joints, food generally sets you back around $30 to $50 per person, per day. You can do it for less if you want to pinch pennies (fill up at one buffet — even cram your pockets and purse with transportable leftovers, though you didn't hear that from me — and the rest of the day can be handled with light snacking).

The farther away from tourist areas you are, the better the food bargains.

If you want to try all these mouth-watering, foodie-heaven, critically acclaimed restaurants, but your budget doesn't allow for it, note which ones are open for lunch, and go then. The menu offerings aren't shockingly different, and the prices are much more affordable.

On the Lighter Side: Munchies and Meals to Go

If you're not in the mood for a major meal, or are just looking for something to nibble on before you head off to a show, you have a number of options to choose from. A lot of the big hotels have food courts similar to what you find in your local mall, although prices are slightly higher than what you're used to paying for similar fare at home. And there are also some alternatives to the brand-name generic sameness these places mostly offer.

Food courts

The best of the hotel food courts is **La Piazza Food Court,** in **Caesars Palace** (3570 Las Vegas Blvd. S.; ☎ **702-731-7110**), which has a **Haagen-Dazs** and a number of non-chain offerings. Stands offer a wide variety of cuisines, a salad bar, and a fresh bakery. The food quality is leaps and bounds above that of the typical food court and has prices to reflect it ($7 – $15, which is still a reasonable deal). Hours vary at each place, but collectively, the food court is open from 8:30 a.m. – 11:00 p.m. Sun – Thurs, and from 9 a.m. – 12 a.m. on Fridays and Saturdays. It's opposite the entrance to the **Forum Shops** at the northern end of the casino.

On the South Strip, the **Monte Carlo Resort & Casino** (3770 Las Vegas Blvd. S.; ☎ **702-730-7777**) has a food court featuring **Haagen-Dazs, McDonald's, Nathan's Hot Dogs, Sbarro,** and the **Golden Bagel** (a first-class bagel bakery). It's open (varying from stand to stand) from 6 a.m. – 3 a.m. Look for it between the lobby (which is at the back of the hotel's first floor) and casino (at the front).

New York-New York (3790 Las Vegas Blvd. S.; ☎ **702-740-6969**) doesn't have a food court per se, but a bunch of (surprise!) New York–theme eateries — **Nathan's Hot Dogs,** and **Schraft's Ice Cream** (yippee!) to name a couple — are scattered throughout the Greenwich Village and Times Square re-creations.

If you're casino-hopping at the northern end of the Strip, your best bet is to check out the **Mardi Gras Food Court** at the **Riviera** (2901 Las Vegas Blvd. S.; ☎ **702-734-5110**). It's adjacent to the main casino entrance. You'll find a **Burger King, Panda Express, Pizza Hut,** and other stands that sell everything from Mexican to Philippine food. Hours at each outlet vary, but generally fall between 8 a.m. – 2 a.m.

For the sweet tooth

Harrah's (3475 Las Vegas Blvd. S.; ☎ **702-369-5000**) has a **Ghirardelli Chocolate Shop and Soda Fountain.** You can't watch the chocolate being mixed in vats (darn!) like at their flagship store in San Francisco, but this is where I like to spend time on a hot Vegas day.

You can also find cinnamon rolls and **Ben & Jerry's** on the second floor of the Masquerade Village at the **Rio** (3700 W. Flamingo Rd; ☎ **702-252-7777**).

And then there are chocolate shakes at a gen-u-ine soda fountain like they don't make anymore — or, actually, do make but as copies of the real thing, whereas this *is* the real thing — the 24-hour **Liberty Café,** (1700 Las Vegas Blvd. S.; ☎ **702-383-0101**).

If you want **Krispy Kreme** donuts — and trust me, you do — make the 15-minute drive from the Strip to the chain's outlet; it's worth it. Skip all the tempting, crème-filled varieties and go right to their specialty: the basic glazed. To say it is just a donut is to say the Grand Canyon is just a big ditch. The first time I tried one, I ate two before I cleared the drive-thru. Krispy Kreme is at 7010 Spring Mountain, at Rainbow (☎ **702-222-2320**). It has a 24-hour drive-thru and the best time to go for hot donuts is 5 a.m. – 11 a.m., and 5 p.m. – 11 p.m. I make a trip here every time I'm in town. Sometimes twice. Krispy Kreme also has a branch in **Excalibur** (3850 Las Vegas Blvd. S.; ☎ **702-597-7777**), but it's higher priced than the outlet.

If you poop out along the way, you can always try **Ronald's Donuts,** at 4600 Spring Mountain (☎ **702-873-1032**), whose glazed have been called celestial. It's open Mon – Sat 5 a.m. – 5 p.m., Sun 5 a.m. – 2 p.m. Other sweets worth checking out include the frozen custard (softer than regular ice cream but harder than soft serve) at **Luv-It Frozen Custard** (505 E. Oakley; ☎ **702-384-6554**). The hours vary, so call ahead.

You can find some great baked goods served up by **Freed's Bakery** (4780 S. Eastern Ave.; ☎ **702-456-7762**), where it smells just like a heavenly Grandma's kitchen.

Man cannot live by cake alone (I've tried), so vary your diet with bagels from either **Einstein Bros. Bagels** (4624 S. Maryland Parkway; ☎ 702-795-7800) or **Bagelmania** (855 Twain Ave.; ☎ 702-369-3322), both of which provide good alternatives to expensive hotel breakfasts.

Coffeehouses and cafés

If you're headed for downtown, swing by the **Enigma Café** (918½ S. Fourth St; ☎ 702-386-0999). It can be tricky to find, but worth it for their vast number of smoothies, coffees, and other frothy drinks, plus some fine healthy (and not-so) sandwiches, and lighter fare like a plate of hummus, feta cheese, pita, and cucumbers. Their not-so-Vegas menu, along with their charming little outside courtyard seating makes this one of my favorite spots in Vegas. It's open most days from 7 a.m. – 12 a.m.

The **Jazzed Café and Vinoteca** (2055 E. Tropicana, at Eastern; ☎ 702-798-5995) serves not only authentic Italian espresso and coffee, but also such marvelous plates of pasta, you might call it a small (very small) trattoria. The café is open from 6 p.m. – 3 a.m., making it a perfect late-night snacking (or light-dining) option.

Making Reservations

If you plan on going to any of the high-profile, fancy-schmancy places, make your reservations as far in advance as possible. Unless you're a high roller, it's unlikely that you'll get a table at the best hotel restaurants without making a reservation beforehand. If you didn't reserve ahead, try to go on off-hours — 6 p.m. or 10 p.m. — when the restaurant is less likely to be full.

Chapter 14

Getting Your Fill at Las Vegas' Best Restaurants

. . . .

In This Chapter

▶ Checking out Las Vegas' restaurants by location, price, and cuisine

▶ Reading full reviews of Las Vegas' best restaurants

. . . .

*A*fter you've exhausted yourself pulling slot machine handles and shooting craps, it's time to refuel. To help you pick a place that suits your particular tastes, consult the indexes in this chapter. Restaurants are indexed by location, so you can find a good restaurant in the area that's most convenient for you; by price, so you can budget yourself; and by cuisine, so you can satisfy your cravings.

After that, it's on to my picks for the most noteworthy restaurants in town, listed alphabetically so you can easily refer to them. Each name is followed by its price range, the part of town it's in, and the type of cuisine you'll find there. You may notice that the picks are a bit heavy on the expensive food; that's because, as I sadly explain at length in Chapter 13, there just aren't as many recommendable places at more reasonable prices. The good news is that you can often enjoy a more affordable meal at expensive restaurants, and I'll let you know if this is an option (usually, all you have to do is eat there at lunch, when the menu is cheaper). You should, however, let your hotel know that it needs to work on better budget options. After all, if you don't complain, who will?

Pricing the Competition

The price categories used in this chapter are based on the average cost of a dinner entree (à la carte). The following table gives you the rundown:

$$$$$	Very Expensive	Main courses more than $20
$$$$	Expensive	Most main courses $15 – $19
$$$	Moderate	Most main courses $10 – $14
$$	Inexpensive	Most main courses $5 – $9
$	A mind-blowing deal	Most main courses less than $5

The dollar signs give you a general idea how much a place costs. Don't rely on them solely, as some restaurants offer prix-fixe meals or other deals that will affect the price rankings.

To help you figure out what to expect for your money, here's the lowdown on the restaurants in a given price category:

- ✔ **$ (Dirt Cheap):** These are the popular places that have been around for a while. You can expect plain food in simple surroundings.

- ✔ **$$ (Inexpensive):** Most buffets and decent, if not stellar, restaurants fall into this category. They're cheaper than you may expect because they're located a little out of the way or the food emphasizes quantity over quality.

- ✔ **$$$ (Medium):** Think theme restaurants and smaller hotel joints. These are good bets for a decent dinner that won't blow your budget out of the water. Expect a unique décor, good service, and better-than-average food.

- ✔ **$$$$ (Expensive):** These are among the top Vegas restaurants: tops for food, chefs, service, décor, and ambiance. You usually get what you pay for in this life, so be prepared to fork over a bundle.

- ✔ **$$$$$ (Very Expensive):** We're talking foodie nirvana here. These restaurants deserve respect. Here's where the well-heeled come for dinner. The food is above reproach and the décor may include priceless artworks. One thing's for certain: People come here because the restaurant is well-known, usually for its chef, atmosphere, and high-rolling clientele.

Restaurant Index by Price

$$$$$
Andre's — Downtown
Aqua — Center Strip
Coyote Café — South Strip
Emeril's New Orleans Fish House — South Strip
Lawry's The Prime Rib — Paradise Road
Le Cirque — Center Strip
Napa — Center Strip
Onda — Center Strip
Picasso — Center Strip
The Range — Center Strip
Second Street Grille — Downtown
Star Canyon — Center Strip

$$$$
Border Grill — South Strip
Chin's — North Strip

Circo — Center Strip
Limericks — Downtown
Olives — Center Strip
Pinot Brasserie — Center Strip
Red Square — South Strip
Spago — Center Strip

$$$
Café Heidelberg — Off the Beaten Path
Dive! — North Strip
Grand Wok and Sushi Bar — South Strip
Hard Rock Café — Paradise Road
Harley-Davidson Café — South Strip
The Mirage Buffet — Center Strip
Mon Ami Gabi — Center Strip
Motown Café — South Strip
PF Chang's China Bistro — Paradise Road
Planet Hollywood — Center Strip
Rainforest Café — South Strip
Stage Deli — Center Strip
Viva Mercados — Off the Beaten Path

Wolfgang Puck Café — South Strip
Z Tejas Grill — Paradise Road

$$
Allie's — Paradise Road
Black Spot Grille — Center Strip
Capriotti's — Off the Beaten Path
Celebrity Deli — Paradise Road
Dragon Noodle Company — South Strip
El Sombrero Café — Downtown
Harrah's Fresh Market Buffet — Center
   Strip
The Luxor Pharoah's Pheast Buffet —
   South Strip

Main Street Station Garden Court
   Buffet — Downtown
Monte Carlo Pub & Brewery — South
   Strip
Pink Taco — Paradise Road
Rio's Carnival World Buffet — Center
   Strip

$
Enigma Café — Off the Beaten Path
Liberty Café — North Strip
Mediterranean Café & Market — Off the
   Beaten Path

Restaurant Index
by Location

South Strip

Border Grill — $$$$
Coyote Café — $$$$$
Dragon Noodle Company — $$
Emeril's New Orleans Fish House —
   $$$$$
Grand Wok and Sushi Bar — $$$
Harley-Davidson Café — $$$
The Luxor Pharoah's Pheast Buffet —
   $$
Monte Carlo Pub & Brewery — $$
Motown Café — $$$
Rainforest Café — $$$
Red Square — $$$$
Wolfgang Puck Café — $$$

Center Strip

Aqua — $$$$$
Black Spot Grille — $$
Chin's — $$$$
Circo — $$$$
Dive! — $$$
Harrah's Fresh Market Buffet — $$
Le Cirque — $$$$$
The Mirage Buffet — $$$
Mon Ami Gabi — $$$
Napa — $$$$$

Olives — $$$$
Onda — $$$$$
Picasso — $$$$$
Pinot Brasserie — $$$$
Planet Hollywood — $$$
The Range — $$$$$
Rio's Carnival World Buffet — $$
Spago — $$$$
Stage Deli — $$$
Star Canyon — $$$$$

North Strip

Chins — $$$$
Dive! — $$$
Liberty Café — $

Downtown

Andre's — $$$$$
El Sombrero Café — $$
Limericks — $$$$
Main Street Station Garden Court
   Buffet — $$
Second Street Grille — $$$$$

Paradise Road

Allie's — $$
Celebrity Deli — $$
Hard Rock Café — $$$
Lawry's The Prime Rib — $$$$$
PF Chang's China Bistro — $$$
Pink Taco — $$
Z Tejas Grill — $$$

Off the Beaten Path

Café Heidelberg — $$$
Capriotti's — $$
Enigma Café — $

Mediterranean Café & Market — $
Viva Mercados — $$$

Restaurant Index by Cuisine

American

Capriotti's — Off the Beaten Path — $$
Dive! — North Strip — $$$
Hard Rock Café — Paradise Road — $$$
Harley-Davidson Café — South Strip — $$$
Liberty Café — Off the Beaten Path — $
Monte Carlo Pub and Brewery — South Strip — $$
Planet Hollywood — Center Strip — $$$

Asian

Chin's — North Strip — $$$$
Dragon Noodle Company — South Strip — $$
Grand Wok Sushi — South Strip — $$$
PF Chang's China Bistro — Paradise Road — $$$

Buffets & Brunches

Harrah's Fresh Market Buffet — Center Strip — $$
The Luxor Pharoah's Pheast Buffet — South Strip — $$
Main Street Station Garden Court Buffet — Downtown — $$
The Mirage Buffet — Center Strip — $$$
Rio's Carnival World Buffet — Center Strip — $$

International

Andre's — Downtown — $$$$$
Café Heidelberg — Off the Beaten Path — $$$
Circo — Center Strip — $$$$
Le Cirque — Center Strip — $$$$$

Mediterranean Café — Off the Beaten Path/Greek — $
Olives — Center Strip — $$$$
Onda — Center Strip — $$$$$
Picasso — Center Strip — $$$$$
Pinot Brassiere — Center Strip — $$$$
Red Square — South Strip — $$$$

Mexican & Southwestern

Allie's — Paradise Road — $$
Border Grill — South Strip — $$$$
Coyote Café — South Strip — $$$$$
El Sombrero — Downtown — $$
Pink Taco — Paradise Road — $$
Viva Mercados — Off the Beaten Path — $$$
Z Tejas Grill — Paradise Road — $$$

Regional American

Celebrity Deli — Off the Beaten Path — $$
Emeril's New Orleans Fish House — South Strip/Cajun & Creole — $$$$$
Enigma Café — Off the Beaten Path — $
Motown Café — South Strip/Southwestern, Southern, & Cajun — $$$
Rainforest Café — South Strip — $$$
Second Street Grille — Downtown — $$$$$
Spago — Center Strip/California — $$$$
Stage Deli — Center Strip — $$$
Wolfgang Puck Café — South Strip — $$$

Steak/Seafood

Aqua — Center Strip — $$$$$
Lawry's The Prime Rib — Paradise Road — $$$$$
Limericks — Downtown — $$$$
The Range — Center Strip — $$$$$

Las Vegas Restaurants from A to Z

Allie's

$$ Paradise Road Southwestern

You wouldn't expect a dining find tucked away in a **Marriott,** but that's why you have me to advise you. A humble coffee shop at breakfast, **Allie's** transforms itself into Super Southwestern for lunch and dinner. Its delightful menu is quite affordable. Try fun variations on standards, like the chicken portobella quesadilla or the salmon BLT — a thick slab of fish with maple pepper bacon and a side of cilantro coleslaw, it's an inventive twist on a classic. And the dessert menu features a genuine root beer float!

325 Convention Center Dr. (in Marriott Suites). ☎ *702-650-2000. Main courses: $8.25 – $15, sandwiches $6 – $9.25. AE, CB, DC, DISC, MC, V. Open: Daily 6:30 a.m. – 10:30 p.m.*

Andre's

$$$$$ Downtown French

A downtown staple for many years, **Andre's** was once *the* place to go for gourmet dining. Now, with all the big boys hogging the gourmet limelight on the Strip, it runs the risk of being overlooked. It shouldn't. In addition to pampering, but not snooty, service, you might well be rubbing shoulders in this pretty, converted house with such celebs as Steven Spielberg and Tom Hanks (at least, they were here one night for a bachelor party). Presentation of the French cuisine is exquisite, with a taste to match. Let the waiters guide you through the menu and enjoy. There's an excellent wine list.

401 S. 6th St., at Lewis St. (two blocks south of Fremont St.). ☎ *702-385-5016. Reservations required. Main courses: $20 – $33. AE, CB, DC, MC, V. Open: Daily from 6 p.m.; closing hours vary.*

Aqua

$$$$$ Center Strip Seafood

I usually get a bit worried about eating fish in a place miles from the ocean — in the middle of the desert, no less — but the fresh, wonderful Asian-influenced creations served here have changed my mind. This branch of a highly regarded San Francisco restaurant serves probably the best fish dishes in town. I coo over the rather Japanese-style, delicate Chilean sea bass, but if you aren't a big fish fan you might instead try the Hawaiian-influenced swordfish, or even the lobster pot pie. Get silly with their homemade root beer float, complete with chocolate straws and homemade cookies.

3600 Las Vegas Blvd. S. (in Bellagio). ☎ *702-693-7223. Reservations recommended. Main courses: $29 – $34 (lobster and whole foie gras higher). AE, DISC, MC, V. Open: Nightly 5:30 p.m. – 10 p.m.*

South Strip Dining

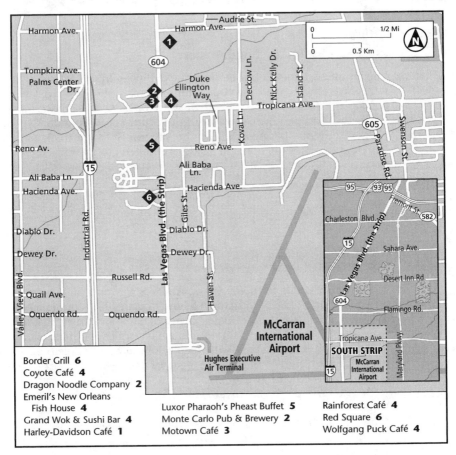

Border Grill **6**
Coyote Café **4**
Dragon Noodle Company **2**
Emeril's New Orleans
  Fish House **4**
Grand Wok & Sushi Bar **4**
Harley-Davidson Café **1**

Luxor Pharaoh's Pheast Buffet **5**
Monte Carlo Pub & Brewery **2**
Motown Café **3**

Rainforest Café **4**
Red Square **6**
Wolfgang Puck Café **4**

Black Spot Grille
$$ Center Strip Italian-American

Most Vegas hotel restaurants are kind of a bore (if they aren't part of a chain or celebrity chef deal), but this one is a bit of an exception. It serves modestly creative pastas and pizzas — not as scary adventurous as the high-profile places, but more interesting than humdrum choices, and that's good enough for me. Note that it's right outside the **Mystère** theater, which means it gets that crowd immediately before and after performances.

3300 Las Vegas Blvd. S. (in Treasure Island). ☎ 702-894-7352. No reservations. Main courses: $7.95 – $13.95. AE, DC, DISC, MC, V. Open: Sun – Thurs 11 a.m. – 11 p.m., Fri – Sat 11 a.m. – 12:30 p.m.

Border Grill

$$$ South Strip Mexican

You may think you love Mexican food, but unless you've been to Mexico, you've probably never eaten real Mexican food. You've just eaten American interpretations. You don't find cheesy combo platters in Mexico, except at places catering to tourists. Not that there's anything wrong with a cheesy combo platter, but you owe it to yourself to try the real thing. The chef/owners of this Los Angeles-based restaurant (known on the *Food Network* as "The Two Hot Tamales") went to Mexico and learned to cook at street markets and in homes. Consequently, **Border Grill** features the real home cooking of Mexico, and it bursts with flavor. I fancy anything stuffed with chicken, and a side of black beans.

Note that this visually delightful restaurant (interior colors are drawn from a slightly subdued Easter palate) has a separate "cantina" where the reasonable lunch prices stay in play even at dinner.

Hey, and if you want to try to cook your own Mexican cuisine, check out *Mexican Cooking For Dummies,* which happens to be written by The Two Hot Tomales mentioned here!

3950 Las Vegas S.(in Mandalay Bay). ☎ *702-632-7403. Reservations recommended. Main courses: Lunch $8 – 15; dinner $12 –$25, $8 – $15 in cantina. AE, DC, DISC, MC, V. Open: Sun – Thurs 11:30 a.m. – 10 p.m., Fri – Sat 11:30 a.m. – 11 p.m.*

Café Heidelberg German Deli and Restaurant

$$$ Off the Beaten Path German/Deli

This is an interesting alternative to over-priced hotel fare. While Germany is no France when it comes to food, the hearty menu options here may be a good choice if truffles are simply smelly fungus to you. You may have to battle the locals for one of the six booths, but you can also get food to go from the deli. Come for the very reasonably priced lunch, and plan on sharing the huge portions or live to regret it. Try some schnitzel, liebchen, or learn the difference between bratwurst and knockwurst, courtesy of their sausage sampler. You can wash it all down with imported beer.

610 E. Sahara. ☎ *702-731-5310. Reservations highly recommended for Friday and Saturday nights. Main courses: Lunch under $10, dinner $9.95 – $16. DISC, MC, V. Open: Mon – Sat 10 a.m. – 9 p.m., Sun 11 a.m. – 8 p.m.*

Capriotti's

$$ Off the Beaten Path Sandwiches

Actually, this is barely a block off the north part of the Strip, so it's an easy swing if you are looking for better-than-average submarine sandwiches. (FYI: They will deliver with a $10 minimum.) The monsters here come in various sizes, but even the "small" is too big and can be comfortably shared by two people, which makes this place easier on the wallet. The turkeys and beef are roasted right here, and as long as the staff takes the stuff out of the oven before it dries out, you've got the start of a great sandwich. The most popular is the Bobby; with turkey, stuffing, and cranberry sauce combined on a French roll, it's a complete Thanksgiving dinner, in handy packaging, any time of year. Remember this place also if you want to pack a lunch for a day's sightseeing out of the city.

324 W. Sahara Ave. (and Las Vegas Blvd. S.). ☎ *702-474-0229. All sandwiches under $10. No credit cards. Open: Mon – Sat 10 a.m. – 7 p.m.*

Celebrity Deli
$$ Paradise Road   Deli

Ironically, the one restaurant with the word "celebrity" in its name is not connected with a celebrity chef. Go figure. This is a basic, solid, New York-style deli, less high-profile than the **Stage Deli** in **Caesars,** but also without the crowds. Sandwiches are not those legendary, feed-a-small-country portions, but you won't leave hungry. You can dine or nosh on pastrami on rye, matzo ball soup, chopped liver, tongue, meat loaf, lox and bagel, among others. Desserts are a bit sparse for a deli, but you can't go wrong with the black-and-white cookies.

4055 S. Maryland Pkwy. (at Flamingo Rd.). ☎ *702-733-7827. Reservations not accepted. Main courses: $7 – $12. AE, MC, V. Open: Mon – Sat 9 a.m. – 8 p.m., Sun 9 a.m. – 4 p.m.*

Chin's
$$$$ North Strip   Chinese

This institution has been drawing tourists and locals alike for more than two decades (an eternity in Vegas). Not your average take-out joint, **Chin's** is gourmet all the way. The menu is not particularly daring, but old standbys such as orange chicken and barbecued pork are executed with skill. Especially notable is the strawberry chicken — think lemon chicken with a different fruit. It's intriguingly sweet. With a low-key, elegant atmosphere and terrific service, Chin's is a great place to chow down on Chinese food.

3200 Las Vegas Blvd. S. (in the Fashion Show Mall). ☎ *702-733-8899. Reservations recommended. Main courses: $10 – $12 for lunch, $12 – $29.50 for dinner. AE, MC, V. Open: Mon – Sat 11:30 a.m. – 9:30 p.m., Sun 12 p.m. – 9:30 p.m.*

Circo
$$$$ Center Strip   Tuscan Italian

Later in this section, I go on about the wonders of **Le Cirque.** This is their less expensive side project, focusing on Tuscan Italian food rather than

French cuisine. (What's "Tuscan Italian"? Think lighter, olive oil–based sauces rather than hearty tomato-based goop.) This is particularly fine Italian food (I love the playful-looking salads and the pasta with rock shrimp) made by people who know what they are doing. And, as a bonus, the restaurant overlooks the **Bellagio** water fountains.

While it ranks as "expensive," you can eat here much more cheaply than that by eating at lunch and focusing on pizzas and pastas (and ordering more-than-filling half-portions of the latter).

3600 Las Vegas Blvd. S. (in Bellagio). ☎ *702-693-8150. Reservations suggested for dinner. Main Course: Lunch $17 – $24 (pizza $12 – $19), dinner $20 – $32 (pizza and pasta $12 – $22). AE, DISC, JCB, MC, V.Open: Daily lunch 11:30 a.m. – 2:30 p.m., dinner 5:30 p.m. – 11 p.m.*

Coyote Café
$$$$$ South Strip   Southwestern

This is actually two restaurants in one: an upscale Grill Room and an informal Café. The innovative and contemporary cuisine in both spots incorporates Southwestern, Mexican, Cajun, and Creole features. The chef has a sure hand; especially good are the black bean and smoked Cheddar "painted" soup and the spicy pork chops. The lively Café area (with lighter and cheaper fare) has a fun atmosphere and offers especially good — and spicy — Southwestern breakfasts.

3799 Las Vegas Blvd. S. (in the MGM Grand Hotel/Casino). ☎ *702-891-7349. Reservations recommended for Grill Room, not accepted for Café. Main courses: Grill Room $15 – $32, Café $8 – $18. AE, CB, DC, DISC, JCB, MC, V. Open: Grill Room — daily 5:30 – 10 p.m., Café — daily 7:30 a.m. – 11 p.m.*

Dive!
$$$ North Strip   Sandwiches

Well, if you ever wondered what a submarine set on a Steven Spielberg movie would look like, here's your chance. Okay, not quite, but the director did have a hand in creating this theme restaurant, whose interior suggests the inside of a fantasy submarine. There are portholes, sonar screens, working periscopes, and a high-tech video simulation of a sub dive every hour. Kids just love it. The menu is somewhat more sophisticated than average, featuring mostly — c'mon, take a guess! — submarine sandwiches.

3200 Las Vegas Blvd. S. (in the Fashion Show Mall). ☎ *702-369-DIVE. Reservations not accepted. Sandwiches: $6.95 – $13.95. AE, CB, DC, DISC, MC, V. Open: Sun – Thurs 11:30 a.m. – 10 p.m., Fri – Sat 11:30 a.m. – 11 p.m.*

Center Strip Dining

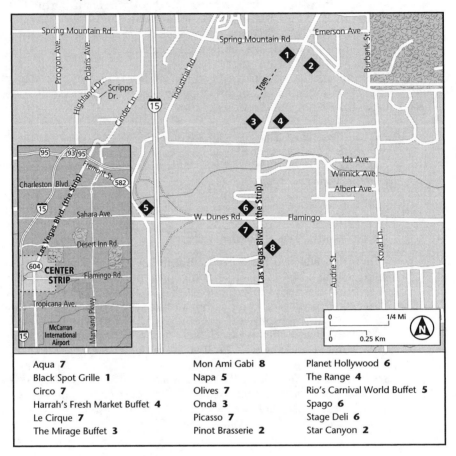

Aqua **7**	Mon Ami Gabi **8**	Planet Hollywood **6**
Black Spot Grille **1**	Napa **5**	The Range **4**
Circo **7**	Olives **7**	Rio's Carnival World Buffet **5**
Harrah's Fresh Market Buffet **4**	Onda **3**	Spago **6**
Le Cirque **7**	Picasso **7**	Stage Deli **6**
The Mirage Buffet **3**	Pinot Brasserie **2**	Star Canyon **2**

Dragon Noodle Company
$$ South Strip   Chinese

Here's a good choice for a reasonably priced meal, particularly for large groups. It's fun to let your waiter choose dishes for you (I particularly like the crispy Peking pork, the sweet pungent shrimp, the potstickers, and the generously portioned seafood soup); they're served family-style, right out of an open-air kitchen.

3770 Las Vegas Blvd. S. (in Monte Carlo Resort & Casino, between Flamingo Rd. and Tropicana Ave.). ☎ 702-730-7965. Reservations not accepted. Main courses: $5.50 – $17 (many under $10). AE, CB, DC, DISC, MC, V. Open: Sun – Thurs 11 a.m. – 10 p.m., Fri – Sat 11 a.m. – 11 p.m.

El Sombrero Café

$$ **Downtown** **Mexican**

I want you to go here simply because it's the kind of Mom-and-Pop joint that is fast disappearing in Vegas — what's more, it's been around since 1950, which for Vegas makes it practically prehistoric. You will want to go here if you like real Mexican food (well, what Americans perceive as real Mexican food). It's not in the nicest part of town, but you will find the inside quite a bit friendlier than its neighborhood. Portions (such as the large enchilada and taco combo) are generous, reliably good, and nicely spicy; and they won't mind if you ask for the beef burrito to be made with chicken.

807 S. Main St. ☎ 702-382-9234. Everything under $10. AE, MC, V. Open: Mon – Sat 11 a.m. – 10 p.m.

Emeril's New Orleans Fish House

$$$$$ **South Strip** **Seafood/Cajun**

Bam! New Orleans–based celebrity chef Emeril Lagasse loves his spices, as you know if you've ever watched him "kick it up a notch" on one of his many *Food Network* shows. Here he brings his spicy enthusiasm and creative touches to fish. Dishes, all possessing just a hint of The Big Easy, are guaranteed to wow you. There's a Cajun spin on everything from ahi steak to the freshest mussels, clams, and oysters. Try the legendary lobster "cheesecake" or barbecued shrimp. If you're not a fish fan, check out the equally tasty poultry, beef, and vegetarian selections. The banana cream pie is the star of a sinful dessert menu.

If you prefer your food on the hoof rather than the fin, Emeril just opened **Delmonico's Steakhouse** up the street at **The Venetian.**

3799 Las Vegas Blvd. S. (in the MGM Grand Hotel/Casino). ☎ 702-891-7374. Reservations required. Main courses: $12 – $18 for lunch, $18 – $38 for dinner. AE, CB, DC, DISC, MC, V. Open: Daily 11 a.m. – 2:30 p.m. and 5:30 – 10:30 p.m.

Enigma Café

$ **Downtown** **Sandwiches and Salads**

This charming café is one of my favorite places in all of Vegas, one of the few where you can have honestly good food for a reasonable sum of money. It's a sweet little coffeehouse with an outdoor courtyard, more California than Nevada desert. The menu is surprisingly large, featuring some intriguing sandwiches, many of which are downright healthy (how'd that happen here?) — except for the Elvis-dedicated peanut butter and banana job. Even lighter fare is possible thanks to a hummus/feta cheese/tomato/cuke/pita plate and a bunch of smoothies and coffee drinks. Poetry readings and other boho events occur at night, when the place is lit by candles. Here's the place to truly escape casino madness.

918 ½ S. Fourth St., at Charleston Blvd. ☎ *702-386-0999. Reservations not accepted. Main course: No items over $6. No credit cards. Open: Mon 7 a.m. – 3 p.m., Tues – Fri 7 a.m. – 12 a.m., Sat – Sun 9 a.m. – 12 a.m.*

Golden Nugget Buffet
$$$ Downtown Buffet

The fanciest of the downtown buffets by far, and one of the only two down here (the other is **Main Street Station,** also reviewed in this chapter) where I can guarantee quality. The salad bar is loaded with extra good-ies, former owner Steve Wynn's mom's bread pudding is featured among the desserts, there's fresh seafood every night, and the Sunday brunches are what that meal should be — even more decadent and indulgent. It's all set in a very plush space.

129 E. Fremont St. (in the Golden Nugget). ☎ *702-385-7111. Reservations not accepted. Buffet prices: Breakfast $5.75, lunch $7.50, dinner $10.50, Sun brunch $11. AE, CB, DC, DISC, MC, V. Open: Mon – Sat 7 a.m. – 3 p.m. and 4 p.m. – 10 p.m., Sun 8 a.m. – 10 p.m.*

Grand Wok and Sushi Bar
$$$ South Strip Pan-Asian

Does your family love Asian food but can't choose between Chinese, Japanese, Vietnamese, or Korean? (Hey, my family has that problem, why wouldn't yours?) Well, here you don't have to, because they serve it all, and surprisingly, it's all done quite well and even better than that. In addi-tion to the fine sushi, note that the soups come in huge portions and can easily feed four for a bargain price.

3799 Las Vegas Blvd. S. (in the MGM Grand). ☎ *702-891-7777. No reservations. Main courses: $8.95 – $13.95, sushi $4.50 – $9.50. AE, DC, DISC, MC, V. Open: Daily 11 a.m. – 11:30 p.m.*

Hard Rock Café
$$$ Paradise Road American

The music is the message at this theme restaurant, a shrine to all things rock 'n' roll. Here you can check out all sorts of memorabilia featuring rock's greatest legends — Elvis, Jimi Hendrix, and Kurt Cobain to name a few — including guitars, gold records, and costumes galore. It's not much different from any of the other Hard Rocks around the world, so if you've seen one, this won't come as much of a surprise. Expensive but respectable burgers rule here, but there are a few tasty salads to lighten the fare. Kids can't get enough.

North Strip Dining

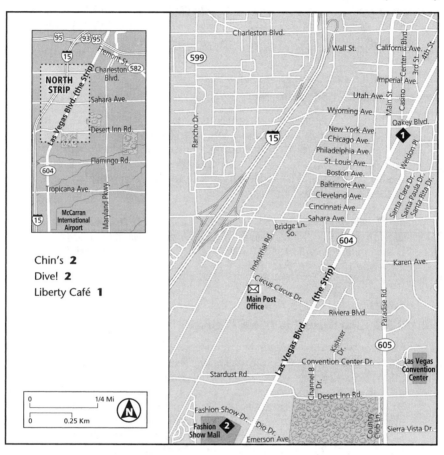

Chin's **2**

Dive! **2**

Liberty Café **1**

4475 Paradise Rd. (at Harmon Ave.). ☎ ***702-733-7625.*** *Reservations accepted. Main courses: $7 – $18. AE, DC, DISC, JCB, MC, V. Open: Sun – Thurs 11 a.m. – 12 a.m., Fri – Sat 11 a.m. – 1 a.m.*

Harley-Davidson Café
$$$ South Strip   American

Another theme restaurant enterprise, this one's dedicated to all things Harley. It features motorcycle memorabilia, gift items, and an all-American menu with everything from burgers, sandwiches, and hot dogs to barbecue and pasta. It does have a few unique items, and the desserts are all-out decadent (chocolate-chip Toll House–cookie pie). The prices are on the high side for what you get, and the music's blaring, but that's no different from the deal at any of the other theme restaurants in town.

3725 Las Vegas Blvd. S. (at Harmon). ☎ *702-740-4555. Internet:* www.harley-davidsoncafe.com. *Reservations accepted only for parties of ten or more. Main courses: $6 – $18. AE, DC, DISC, MC, V. Open: Sun – Thurs 11:30 a.m. – 12 a.m. (bar open until 1 a.m.), Fri – Sat 11:30 a.m. – 1 a.m. (bar open until 2 a.m.).*

Harrah's Fresh Market Buffet
$$ Center Strip   Buffet

Designed to resemble a farmer's market, this buffet features individual serving stations instead of one long line. (They make up for this with the endless wait to get into the buffet.) Selections include seafood, pastas, and Asian, Mexican, and American dishes (ranging from Cajun specialties to meatloaf). With a friendly staff and above-average food, this is one of the better buffets in town.

3475 Las Vegas Blvd. S. (in Harrah's Las Vegas). ☎ *702-369-5000. Reservations not accepted. Buffet prices: Breakfast $8.99, lunch $9.99, dinner $14.99, Sat – Sun champagne brunch $14.99. AE, DC, DISC, MC, V. Open: Mon – Fri 7 a.m. – 10 p.m., Sat – Sun 10 a.m. – 10 p.m.*

Lawry's The Prime Rib
$$$$$ Paradise Road   Steakhouse

Okay, now, sure you can get prime rib anywhere in town for under $6. But it's not going to taste like this. **Lawry's** didn't invent prime rib, but they might as well have. Dare I say that no one does it better? Sure I do. The elaborate meal presentation includes 50 years' worth of traditional touches, like the spinning salad bowl (a production you have to see to appreciate) and the metal carving carts piled high with meat for you to select from. You can find other things on the menu these days (fresh fish, for example), but why bother? Come here for a seriously satisfying carnivorous experience.

4043 Howard Hughes Pkwy. (just west of Paradise Rd.). ☎ *702-893-2223. Reservations recommended. Main courses: $20 – $30. AE, DC, DISC, JCB, MC, V. Open: Sun – Thurs 5 – 10 p.m., Fri – Sat 5 – 11 p.m.*

Le Cirque
$$$$$ Center Strip   Nouvelle French

This is one of those places where it's really worth blowing your budget. **Le Cirque** originated in New York, and is practically legendary there (you'll be pleased to know that the Big Apple branch's snooty service is not a problem at the Vegas location). Dining here is a complete treat, and the food not as frighteningly unusual as you might consider French food to be. You may be surprised at how tiny it is and how close your neighbors are to you. Thank goodness for the somewhat surprisingly casual atmosphere; it makes one less self-conscious about pounding the table with delight over the food. The menu changes regularly, but here are some things I love: anything with truffle, particularly foie gras pate topped with same — actually, anything with foie gras, particularly when it comes on top of properly aged filet mignon — and the roasted honey-glazed duck with figs. Desserts are all playful, pretty creations, almost too good-looking to eat. Almost.

3600 Las Vegas Blvd. S. (in Bellagio). ☎ *702-693-8150. Reservations required. Jacket and tie required for gentlemen. Main courses: $29 – $39. AE, DC, DISC, MC, V. Open: Nightly 5:30 p.m. – 10 p.m.*

Liberty Café
$ North Strip   Diner

This is the Real McCoy — a 24-hour hour restaurant that has been around for more than six decades. It's small and somewhat showing its age, but it has one of the best burgers in town and serves up fantastic old-fashioned milkshakes. Take a seat in a vinyl booth or at the counter and order from a menu of traditional comfort foods — meat loaf anyone? The food is good and unbelievably cheap. And the café is a welcome change of pace from the derivative and pretentious dining that often dominates this town. Places like this are an endangered species, so go give them some business.

1700 S. Las Vegas Blvd. (inside the Blue Castle Pharmacy, just north of the Stratosphere Tower). ☎ *702-383-0101. Reservations not accepted. Main courses: Nothing over $7. No credit cards. Open: Daily 24 hours.*

Limericks
$$$$ Downtown   Steakhouse

This is a classic steakhouse: comfortable, hearty, and plush. You'll sit in luxurious booths that occupy a sort of Olde English drawing room. The portions are beyond generous, and the T-bones, prime rib, and filet mignon are so tender they melt in your mouth. No surprises here, nothing stuffy or trendy — just solid food in a comfortable atmosphere.

301 E. Fremont St. (in Fitzgeralds Casino Holiday Inn). ☎ *702-388-2400. Reservations recommended. Main courses: $18 – $40. AE, DISC, MC, V. Open: Thurs – Mon 5 – 11 p.m., closed Tues – Wed.*

The Luxor Pharaoh's Pheast Buffet
$$ South Strip   Buffet

This buffet offers great value and better-than-average food. Set inside an amusing "archaeological dig," it has all the standards (salads, fresh fruit, a carving station with turkey and ham), plus some interesting twists, such as Mexican, Chinese stir-fry, and Italian pastas. You may feel like

Paradise Road Dining

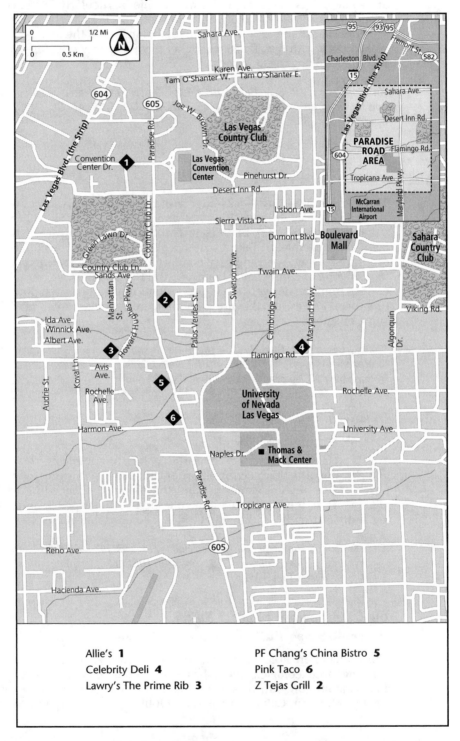

Allie's **1**

Celebrity Deli **4**

Lawry's The Prime Rib **3**

PF Chang's China Bistro **5**

Pink Taco **6**

Z Tejas Grill **2**

lying down in King Tut's tomb after negotiating the long lines at peak dining times; try to come during off-hours after the rush has died down.

3900 Las Vegas Blvd. S. (in the Luxor). ☎ *702-262-4000. Reservations not accepted. Buffet prices: Breakfast $7.49, lunch $7.99, dinner $11.49. AE, DC, DISC, MC, V. Open: Daily 6:30 a.m. – 11 p.m.*

Main Street Station Garden Court Buffet
$$ Downtown   Buffet

This is the best buffet in downtown, and possibly in the city. It has succeeded in rising above the rest with a pretty dining room (high ceilings and actual windows provide real sunlight — a rarity in Vegas) and food that is decidedly a cut above its peers. Selections are prepared at stations that dish out barbecue and soul food, Chinese and Hawaiian specialties, and wood-fired, brick-oven pizzas. On Friday nights, you can dine on a seafood buffet that features lobster and other fresh fish.

200 N. Main St. (in the Main Street Station). ☎ *702-387-1896. Reservations not accepted. Buffet prices: Breakfast $4.99, lunch $6.99, dinner $8.99, Friday seafood buffet $13.99, Sunday champagne brunch $9.99. AE, CB, DC, DISC, MC, V. Open: Daily 7 a.m. – 10:30 a.m., 11 a.m. – 3 p.m., and 4 p.m. – 10 p.m. Sunday brunch 7 a.m. – 3 p.m.*

Mediterranean Café & Market
$ Off the Beaten Path   Greek/Middle Eastern

This authentic, family-owned Middle Eastern restaurant offers great value and terrific food with no glitz and neon in sight. The *gyros* (lamb and beef in a pita) are fresh and delicious, and the menu features other favorites, such as phyllo pie served with a side of hummus, and chicken and vegetable kabobs. Eat here and then get some to take home at the adjoining market.

4147 S. Maryland Pkwy. (at Flamingo Rd.). ☎ *702-731-6030. Reservations not accepted. Main courses: $8 – $16 (sandwiches for $5 or less). AE, MC, DISC, V. Open: Mon – Sat 11 a.m. – 9 p.m.*

The Mirage Buffet
$$$ Center Strip   Buffet

The lavish spread here may cost a little more than other buffets in town, but you get what you pay for. Dine in a lovely garden setting and choose from a magnificent array of selections that are much better quality than the cheaper competition. The enormous salad bar, with more than 25 types of salads, and the dessert table, laden with sweet temptations, are especially notable. Sunday brunch adds free champagne, smoked salmon, and fruit-filled crépes for starters.

3400 Las Vegas Blvd. S. (in The Mirage). ☎ *702-791-7111. Reservations not accepted. Buffet prices: Breakfast $8.95, lunch $9.95, dinner $14.95; Sunday brunch $14.95. Children ages 4 – 10 eat for reduced prices, and children under 4 eat free. AE, CB, DC, DISC, MC, V. Open: Mon – Sat 7 a.m. – 10 p.m., Sun 8 a.m. – 10 p.m.*

Mon Ami Gabi

$$$ Center Strip   Bistro

Ooh, la la! This cute-as-a-button place is my new favorite dining spot in Vegas. You get all your classic bistro fare, from hearty onion soup to *croque monsieur* (grilled ham and cheese) to steak and pomme frites. Although you can run up a hefty tab here, note that just eating that same hearty soup or those clever sandwiches will keep the prices down while filling you up most satisfactorily. And while it's absolutely a Vegas version of a bistro, even cynics have to admit they got the décor just right. Seat your armor on the patio right on the Strip and gaze into each other's eyes, but don't get so swept up in each other you forget to order desserts; they are huge here.

3355 Las Vegas Blvd. S. (in The Venetian). ☎ *702-944-GABI. Reservations suggested. Main courses: $8.95 – $26.95. AE, CB, DC, DISC, MC, V. Open: Daily 11:30 a.m. – 3:30 p.m., Sun – Thurs 5 p.m. – 11 p.m., 5 p.m. – 12 a.m.*

Monte Carlo Pub & Brewery

$$ South Strip   Pub Fare

The food here is so cheap, generously served, and largely delicious (for its type) that you might well be better off eating here than at a buffet. This is not the place for peaceful intimate dining; it's a sort of combo sports bar and microbrewery pub, with 40-plus TVs blaring rock music along with the sound system. It's not overly stimulating, more just lively and friendly. Food is hearty and familiar — ribs, burgers, pizzas, salads — nothing frilly. Earning raves are the BBQ short ribs, the chicken fingers, the garlic pizza, the avocado and shrimp salads, and for the chocolate suicide brownie dessert. They only serve pizza after 9 p.m.

3770 Las Vegas Blvd. S. (between Flamingo Rd. and Tropicana Ave. in Monte Carlo Resort). ☎ *702-730-7777. Reservations not accepted. Main courses $6 – $8. AE, CB, DC, DISC, MC, V. Open: Sun – Thurs 11 a.m. – 1 a.m., Fri – Sat 11 a.m. – 3 a.m.*

Motown Café

$$$ South Strip   Regional American

Celebrating the Detroit music scene of the 1960s and early 1970s, this theme restaurant offers perfectly ordinary but satisfying burgers, fries, Cajun/Creole dishes, or light Southwestern fare. The classic hits of Martha Reeves & the Vandellas, Diana Ross, and The Jackson 5 — their memorabilia is also here — provide background music while you dine.

As with other theme restaurants, it's a little high-priced for what you get. After dinner, they crank up the tunes for dancing into the wee hours.

3790 Las Vegas Blvd. S. (in New York-New York). ☎ *702-895-9653. Reservations not accepted. Main courses: $6 – $17. AE, DISC, MC, V. Open: Sun – Thurs 7:30 a.m. – 11:30 p.m., Fri – Sat 7:30 a.m. – 2 a.m.*

Napa
$$$$$ Center Strip   Nouvelle French

This is another place I don't mind asking you to blow your bank account for. Hard-core foodies, who previously wouldn't be caught dead in the land of 99¢ shrimp cocktails, tend to drop everything to make a hasty pilgrimage to the restaurant of uber-celebrity chef Jean Louis Palladin. So why not join them? The menu changes seasonally, but you can expect the best of what that season has to offer (such items as cold red and yellow soup, seared foie gras with seasonal fruity glazes, a mouth-watering rack of lamb — you get the idea). It's all in a pretty, but not pretentious space, but you'll hardly notice that given how riveting your meal is.

3700 W. Flamingo Rd. (in the Rio Hotel). ☎ *702-247-7962. Reservations strongly suggested. Main courses: $28 – $42, degustation $110. AE, CB, DC, DISC, MC, V. Open: Tues – Sat. 6 p.m. – 11 p.m.*

Olives
$$$$ Center Strip   Italian/Mediterranean

The chef behind this restaurant is considered a rising young star among major chefs, so you know you are in for something special. Although the prices here can be budget busting, you can actually eat here for "moderate" cost. First of all, come when the cheaper lunch menu is in play (11 a.m. – 3 p.m.), and stick to pastas and the flatbread pizzas. The latter are a cracker-thin crust creation topped with unusual items such as Moroccan lamb and feta cheese, and prosciutto and figs. They are really quite good (I wish this place was in my neighborhood so I could eat these regularly). One pizza can feed two people, though you might want to add a salad (they are a bit pricey for what they are) or a bowl of pasta, such as the spaggetini with roasted garlic and tomatoes (wonderful, with just the right amount of richness).

3600 Las Vegas Blvd. S. (in Bellagio). ☎ *702-693-8181. Reservations recommended for parties of six or more. Lunch: $15 – $19, flatbreads $10 – $14.50, dinner main courses: $20 – $33.50. AE, DC, DISC, MC, V. Open: Daily lunch 11 a.m. – 3 p.m., dinner 5 p.m. – 11:30 p.m.*

Onda
$$$$$ Center Strip   Italian

This is the expensive version — seems like there always has to be one of those, doesn't it? — of Olives, the restaurant listed earlier, and it has quickly become very popular with Vegas locals. It's a pretty, casual but chic place, that has quite a good vibe for an expensive restaurant, and is a nice place to be during the later dining hours. Vegetables are flown in especially for **Onda,** so this is a good place to get your daily, nutritionally required servings all at once. Try the antipasta loaded with roasted veggies, a sweet baby spring pea soup, or a veggie foil packet full of mushrooms. Continue to feel virtuous with a light dessert such as a sorbet sampler.

3400 Las Vegas Blvd. S. (in The Mirage). ☎ *702-791-7223. Reservations suggested. Main courses: $16.50 – $35. AE, CB, DC, DISC, MC, V. Open: Nightly 5:30 p.m. – 11 p.m.*

PF Chang's China Bistro
$$$ Paradise Road   Chinese

Traditional Chinese food — at least as it's become a tradition in the U.S. In that context, it's terrific; but if you are looking for something more interesting or authentic, you may be disappointed. Start your meal in this lively bistro with the spiced chicken, vegetable lettuce wraps, or Peking ravioli stuffed with ground pork. Entrees run the gamut from lemon pepper shrimp to Malaysian chicken, but you'll be pleased with even such basics as Mongolian beef and sweet-and-sour pork. The portions are more than generous, and the service will cause no complaints.

4165 S. Paradise Rd. (just south of Flamingo). ☎ *702-792-2207. Reservations not accepted. Main courses: $8 – $13. AE, DC, DISC, MV, V. Open: Sun – Thurs 11 a.m. – 11 p.m., Fri – Sat 11 a.m. – 12 a.m..*

Picasso
$$$$$ Center Strip   Nouvelle French

Former Bellagio owner Steve Wynn spent nearly a year wooing superstar chef Julian Serrano —a man who works a kitchen the way Springsteen works a concert — away from his highly praised San Francisco restaurant. He succeeded, and it's your gain. Yep, the prices are what you might expect from a place with $30 million worth of genuine Picassos hanging on the wall, but Serrano's cooking produces really good food the way Picasso's painting produced really good art. The menu changes nightly, giving you a choice of two multi-course tasting menus (portions are small so you can finish everything without feeling like you are going to explode). I fell hard for the corn flan (like eating solid sunshine) with chunks of lobster, and the perfectly tender lamb crusted with black truffles. For dessert, I got silly over the molten chocolate soufflé cake with homemade chocolate ice cream — then dreamt about it all night long.

3600 Las Vegas Blvd. S. (in the Bellagio). ☎ *702-693-7111. Reservations recommended. Main courses: Four-course Prix Fixe $70, five-course degustation $80. AE, CB, DC, DISC, MC, V. Open: Sun – Tues and Thurs 6 – 10 p.m., Fri – Sat 6 – 11 p.m.; closed Wednesday.*

Pink Taco
$$ **Paradise Road   Mexican**

The folk-art bedecked interior and the deliberately ever-so-slightly-naughty name indicate that this place is hipper than hip, which is what you'd expect from any eatery in the **Hard Rock Hotel,** the epicenter of Vegas hip. But the prices are low and the portions are large. It's what you want when you want Mexican food, and even a bit better than that, so all that makes me put up with the rest of it.

4455 Paradise Rd. (in Hard Rock Hotel). ☎ *702-693-5525. No reservations. Main courses: $7.50 – $12.95. AE, CB, DC, DISC, MC, V. Open: Sun – Thus 11 a.m. – 11 p.m., 11:30 a.m. – 12 a.m.*

Pinot Brasserie
$$$$ **Center Strip   Bistro**

Here's a perfect choice if you want a really nice meal, but don't want food that is too, how shall I say, frou-frou. See, here's a secret about French food: An actual French person's favorite thing to eat is a small steak, a handful of perfect french fries, and some wine. Voilá. Sound scary? Of course not. And so while this charming bistro (I love the clubby, intimate interior here) serves "French" fare, it's going to be things you can easily recognize, and immediately love. Favorites include the roasted chicken accompanied by a heap of garlic fries, a lovely onion soup, even more lovely and crunchy salads (sometimes with toasted slices of bread topped with things like herbed goat cheese), and a sublime homemade chocolate ice cream. Simple. Delicious. Perfect. They offer some more complicated — but not outrageously so — items, if you feel inclined. Consider also coming at lunch, when prices fall into the "moderate" category.

3355 Las Vegas Blvd. S. (in The Venetian). ☎ *702-735-8888. Reservations suggested for dinner. Main course: Lunch $11.50 – $16.95, dinner $18.50 – $22.50. AE, DISC, JCB, MC, V. Open: Daily 11 a.m. – 11 p.m.*

Planet Hollywood
$$$ **Center Strip   American**

Planet Hollywood's high wattage has dimmed some thanks to its financial woes and being snotty; I can't say I'm sorry. It's a high-profile tourist trap, in my opinion. There's a lot of movie and TV memorabilia (including Barbara Eden's genie bottle!), always a boisterous young crowd, and a menu that actually offers interesting choices, such as blackened shrimp and the famous Captain Crunch Chicken (yep, it's what it sounds like). It's overpriced and overwhelming, but hey, that's Hollywood for you. Besides, your kids won't let you skip it.

3500 Las Vegas Blvd. S. (in Forum Shops at Caesars Palace). ☎ 702-791-STAR. Reservations not accepted. Main courses: $8 – $20. AE, DC, MC, V. Open: Sun – Thurs 11 a.m. – 12 a.m., Fri – Sat 11 a.m. – 1 a.m.

Rainforest Café
$$$ **South Strip   California**

I probably spent too much time on the Jungle Cruise ride at Disneyland as a kid, and that's why I rather enjoy this place, my feelings toward theme restaurants notwithstanding. Filled with fake foliage and real fish, plus animatronic animals, there is plenty, particularly for a kid, to look at while dining on some needlessly busy, but better than average (for a theme restaurant) food. In theory, your child (or you) can also learn about environmental issues, which to my way of thinking is a better use of everyone's time than gawking at used football jerseys.

3799 Las Vegas Blvd. S. (in the MGM Grand). ☎ 702-891-8580. Reservations not required. Main courses: $9 – $13 breakfast, $10 – $19 dinner. AE, DC, DISC, JCB, MC, V. Open: Mon – Thurs 8 a.m. – 11 p.m., Fri – Sat 8 a.m. – 12 a.m., Sun 8 a.m. – 10 p.m.

The Range
$$$$$ **Center Strip   Steakhouse**

This very fine steakhouse has a warm copper-and-mahogany interior that is classy and plush yet not intimidating. Panoramic windows offer incredible views of the Strip below. The kitchen does chicken, seafood, salads, and of course, wonderful, tender steaks best, so the menu naturally features these items. As an added touch, side dishes are served family style. Try not to miss the five-onion soup appetizer (baked in a large onion with cheese) or the chicken quesadillas.

3475 Las Vegas Blvd. S. (in Harrah's Las Vegas). ☎ 702-369-5000. Reservations highly recommended. AE, CB, DC, DISC, MC, V. Main courses: $19 – $27. Open: Daily 5:30 – 11 p.m.

Red Square
$$$$ **South Strip   Continental**

No one parties like the Red Party, and this restaurant sets out to prove it. No, no, no — no Communist propoganda here, quite the opposite, as symbols and artifacts from Iron Curtain days are defaced or otherwise turned into capitalist décor. Heck, when folks protested the giant statue of Lenin (like the one found in the real Red Square), the restaurant promptly decapitated it and covered it with fake pigeon poop. Enjoy the topplings of sacred cows as you dine on real cow — the Chef's Special is a terrific filet mignon topped with roquefort — or caviar (pricey ounces allow you to taste several varieties) or other Russia-meets-the-rest-of-the-world fare. Be sure to have a drink at the bar, which is partially constructed out of a block of ice, the better to keep that vodka glass nicely chilled.

3950 Las Vegas Blvd. S. (in Mandalay Bay). ☎ *702-632-7407. Reservations recommended. Main courses: $16.75 – $31. AE, DC, MC, V. Open: Sun – Wed 5:30 p.m. – 1:00 a.m., Thurs – Sat 5:30 p.m. – 2:00 a.m.*

Rio's Carnival World Buffet
$$ Center Strip   Buffet

This is an excellent buffet with cheerfully decorative food booths set up like stations in an upscale food court. And it serves up an incredible selection including barbecue and ribs, stir-fry, Mexican, Chinese, sushi and teppanyaki, Italian, and diner food (burgers and hot dogs). The desserts are especially indulgent. Everything is fresh and well prepared. The festive carnival décor (here and in the rest of the hotel), strikes me as a bit too much, but it does have its fans.

3700 W. Flamingo Rd. (in the Rio Hotel & Casino). ☎ *702-252-7777. Reservations not accepted. Buffet prices: Breakfast $7.95, lunch $9.95, dinner $12.95, weekend brunch $9.95. AE, CB, DC, MC, V. Open: Daily 8 a.m. – 10:30 a.m., and 11 a.m. – 11 p.m.*

Second Street Grill
$$$$ Downtown   International

One of the best-kept secrets in town, this lovely bit of romantic class is tucked away in downtown, where most restaurants seem stuck in a time warp. Think of it as an upscale hotel restaurant in Hawaii — no flaming whatevers, or sickly sweet-and-sour sauce. Instead, try the unusual lemon chicken potstickers and the duck comfit for starters. Entrees include lobster, ahi tuna, and filet mignon, but the whole fish (opaka paka on a recent visit), served in a bowl with a giant tea-leaf lid, is the best bet. Fun side dishes include melt-in-your-mouth sautéed mushrooms and pesto mashed potatoes. Don't forget the Chocolate Explosion: a piece of chocolate cake topped with chocolate mousse, covered with a rich chocolate shell.

200 E. Fremont St. (in the Fremont Hotel). ☎ *702-385-3232. Main courses: $17 – $23. Reservations recommended. AE, DC, DISC, MC, V. Open: Sun, Mon, and Thurs 5 p.m. – 10 p.m., Fri – Sat 5 p.m. – 11 p.m.*

Spago
$$$$ **Center Strip   California**

It's no longer the only foodie game in town — this was, after all, the restaurant that launched the Vegas dining revolution — but this branch of celebrity chef Wolfgang Puck's famed L.A. restaurant is worth a visit. Smoked salmon pizza, Chinois chicken salad, scallops, and crispy Chinese-style duck (duck doesn't get much better) are among your choices, all lovingly prepared and presented. The European-style sidewalk café out front has a more relaxed atmosphere than the somewhat snooty and high-priced dining room.

3500 Las Vegas Blvd. S. (in the Forum Shops at Caesars Palace). ☎ *702-369-6300. Reservations recommended for the dining room, not accepted for the café. Main courses: $14 – $31 in the dining room, $9.50 – $23 in the café. AE, CB, DC, DISC, MC, V. Open: Dining room — Sun – Thurs 6 p.m. – 10 p.m., Fri – Sat 5:30 p.m. – 11:00 p.m.; café — daily 11 a.m. – 12 a.m.*

Stage Deli
$$$ **Center Strip   Deli**

Yes, Las Vegas has a branch of this Big Apple legend, and it somehow retains its essence, even way out here in the desert. Fresh-baked breads, meats, bagels, lox, and pickles are flown in from New York daily, so you're getting the real deal here. This place offers a monstrous menu featuring all the standard deli offerings, such as pastrami, knishes, and matzo-ball soup. The sandwiches are similarly immense; be wise and start by splitting them. You can always order another if your stomach still needs filling. It's a great place to pick up a quick, inexpensive breakfast, too!

3500 Las Vegas Blvd. S. (in the Forum Shops at Caesars Palace). ☎ *702-893-4045. Reservations accepted for large parties only. Main courses: $6 – $14. AE, DC, DISC, MCB, MC, V. Open: Sun – Thurs 7:30 a.m. – 10:30 p.m., Fri – Sat 7:30 a.m. – 12:00 a.m.*

Star Canyon
$$$$$ **Center Strip   Southwestern**

Yee-ha! This is the place to go for fun, fancy food without any fear of frills or snooty attitude (it's a most casual, lively environment). Think all there is to Texas food is BBQ? Think again. Chef Stephen Pyles, who originated **Star Canyon** in Dallas, is here to show you how Southwestern spices and some down-home sensibilities, when applied to the concept of chi-chi food, can blow your mind as well as your taste buds. Play around with the appetizers (I love the spicy tamale pie filled with cooling roast garlic custard and crabmeat, and the foie gras paired with corn cake and pineapple salsa) to see what fun can be had, but be sure to save room for the main courses. No dainty portions here. Instead, the Cowboy steak, a bone-in ribeye with some magnificient spicing, is a monster, topped with a tower of thin fried onions. It's a heck of a piece of meat.

3355 Las Vegas Blvd. S. (in The Venetian). ☎ 702-414-3772. Reservations suggested for dinner. Main courses: Lunch $10 – $17, dinner $21 – $30. AE, MC, V. Open: Lunch daily 11:30 a.m. – 2:30 p.m.; dinner Sun – Thurs 6 p.m. – 10 p.m., Fri – Sat 6 p.m. – 11 p.m.

Viva Mercados
$$$ Off the Beaten Path   Mexican

Locals consider this the best Mexican restaurant in town, and surprisingly enough, the fare is astonishingly healthy. They cook everything in canola oil, and you can choose from lots of vegetarian and seafood selections. They serve 11 varieties of salsa, from extremely mild to call-the-fire-department hot. The food is fresh, the staff friendly, and the price is right. It's definitely worth the 10-minute drive from the Strip.

6182 W. Flamingo Rd. (about 3 miles west of the Strip on your right). ☎ 702-871-8826. Reservations not accepted. Main courses: $8 – $17. AE, DISC, MC, V. Open: Sun – Thurs 11 a.m. – 10 p.m., Fri – Sat 11 a.m. – 11 p.m.

Wolfgang Puck Café
$$$ South Strip   California

So you may notice that this guy, Wolfgang Puck, has an awful lot of restaurants in Vegas — five, at last count, though goodness knows I might have missed one or two. But since most of them are expensive or very expensive, you may have decided to give the guy a miss. You don't have to. This brightly colored café serves more moderately priced versions of Puck's influential California cuisine — in other words, fancy salads and pizzas (topped with things like sautéed chicken and the like) and pastas. Some folks practically live on his Chinese chicken salad, so you might order that to find out why. A bonus is that most of the menu is on the healthy side, although the rich desserts could ruin your waistline. Note that **EFX** plays just opposite in the casino and so you may find long lines when the show lets out.

3799 Las Vegas Blvd. S. (in the MGM Grand). ☎ 702-895-9653. Reservations not accepted. Main courses: $9 – $15. AE, DC, MC, V. Open: Daily 11 a.m. – 11 p.m.

Z Tejas Grill
$$$ Paradise Road   Tex-Mex

This lively Tex-Mex restaurant has a comfortable interior, as well as a vine-covered patio for outdoor dining (it's misted in summer). The restaurant labels its cuisine "South by Southwestern," and the wide-ranging menu focuses heavily on spicy dishes. I especially like the generous grilled fish tacos and the Jamaican jerked chicken. You can down large margaritas made from scratch at the full bar. Pop in for happy hour (4 p.m. – 7 p.m.) when they offer half-priced appetizers (which can make a fine, affordable meal) and discounted drinks.

3824 S. Paradise Rd. (between Twain Ave. and Corporate Dr.). ☎ *702-732-1660. Reservations recommended. Main courses: $7 – $17. AE, CB, DC, DISC, JCB, MC, V. Open: Daily 11 a.m. – 11 p.m.*

Part V
Exploring
Las Vegas

The 5th Wave   By Rich Tennant

"Would you mind not sitting at that machine? It throws off the feng shui in this row."

In this part . . .

Yes, it's true: You can do more in Las Vegas than drop coins into a slot machine.

Ultimately, this city is one big amusement park, with a healthy dose of resort pampering thrown in for good measure. Where else can you ride a roller coaster, play a few hands of blackjack, watch a live pirate battle, go bowling, take a simulator ride through ancient Egypt, play with a dolphin, practice your golf swing, get a massage, shop 'til you drop, and get married? In this part, I give you tips on how to gamble, cover all the top attractions, tell you where to shop, and suggest all kinds of fun stuff to do.

Chapter 15

Gambling Tips and Tricks (Or Keeping the Farm)

. . . .

In This Chapter

▶ Gambling 101

▶ Playing the slots and video poker

▶ Gaming at the tables

▶ Cruising the casinos

. . . .

*H*ey — did you know they've got gambling in Vegas?

Well, of course, you did. If you knew only one thing about Vegas before you read this book, I'd bet dollars to donuts it was that. See how quickly the gambling begins? In fact, what you may not have realized, and may not fully comprehend until you actually get there is how *much* gambling there is in Vegas. It starts at the airport, follows you to the gas station, and then hits hyper drive when you finally get to your hotel.

Clearly, it is time to ante up and get serious.

Getting Started at Gambling

If you want to try the gambling scene, but you've never done it before and you don't know all the rules, don't worry. I can get you started. It's not as fun to gamble if you aren't savvy enough to know when to "double down." The last thing you want to do in Vegas is lose your shirt. So, in this section I give you the basics (although I can't guarantee a win — you have to rely on Lady Luck for that one!).

Entire books have been written about the nuances of casino gambling, so if you're looking for an in-depth analysis, I suggest that you go grab an additional reference. *Poker For Dummies* (IDG Books Worldwide, Inc.) may be right up your alley!

Before you even walk into a casino, you need to keep some basic rules in mind:

✔ **Age:** You have to be at least 21 years old to even enter a casino area, much less play the games. If you bring your kids to Vegas and plan on spending significant time inside the casino, check into finding a baby-sitter or childcare center at your hotel. If you happen to look younger than than 21, be sure to carry a valid driver's license (or other piece of ID) with you. Casino officials and cashiers can and do card patrons.

If you're under 21 and somehow manage to make it to a table or slot machine, don't think you're home-free: Just a few years ago, a big slot winner had his jackpot taken away when the casino found out he was only 17.

✔ **Casino clubs:** Most hotels offer free enrollment in their slot and gaming clubs. All you need to do is fill out a form and you get a card (that looks kind of like a credit card) that you insert into a special reader on slot machines or turn in at gaming tables. Each time you place a bet (most of the casino hotels have 25-cent bet minimums for their club programs) or pull the handle, you rack up points on your account (just remember to take your card with you when you leave!). You can later trade these points in for discounts on meals, shopping, and accommodations. If you gamble enough, you may even get a free room.

Getting a club card is one of the best deals in Vegas. No matter what, even if you think you aren't going to gamble enough to make it worth while, sign up for as many of these as you can. After all, you never know — vows to drop only small amounts of cash on the tables often have the longevity of New Year's resolutions, so you might as well get something out of all this if you can. Signing up for the club also puts you on the hotel's mailing list, which can be a plus, since hotels often offer special deals on room rates and packages to their club members. Check at the main cashier cage in any casino to find out the details on their clubs.

✔ **Booze galore:** Almost all of the casinos offer you free drinks (alcoholic or not) if you're gambling. All you need to do is flag down one of the many cocktail servers who roam the casino floor. (The servers often pop up mere moments after you've seated yourself.) It may be a while, however, before your drink arrives. Servers blame the delay on the long trek they have to make to get from the kitchens to the casino, but the suspicious among us suspect that they just want you to keep pumping quarters into that slot machine while you wait. And suddenly, that free beer cost you $20.

✔ **Lighting up:** Smokers, who must often take to the streets in other American cities to light up, will be happy to know that the huff 'n' puff crowd rules in Las Vegas' casinos. Some casinos even offer free packs of cigarettes to gamblers. A few casinos have no-smoking sections, but you'll still be sharing the same air with the rest of the casino. Nonsmokers should take solace in the Vegas legend that casinos constantly pump in fresh oxygen to keep players from getting tired.

✔ **Cheaters really don't prosper:** Don't even think about cheating. If you don't believe me, just look up at the ceiling when you walk into any casino. Those innocuous little black domes or opaque glass panels are actually cameras poised to watch your every move. They are extremely high-tech and can cover every square inch of the casino. And somebody is always watching. Floor staff and undercover operators also roam the floors just trying to catch you doing anything out of the ordinary. They've seen every trick in the book and many not in the books. They know more than you do and they *will* catch you. And while there may no longer be goons named Guido ready to rearrange your face for your transgressions, legal punishment is pretty humiliating. Save the cheating for your Monday-night Bridge club.

✔ **Be prepared to lose:** One thing you must understand before you set out to play: Losers outnumber winners in any casino. They don't build these super-casinos on winners. After all, they have to have some way to pay for those big chandeliers, and volcanos, and Siegfried and Roy's salary. And they do, and then some. Vegas casinos rake in somewhere in the neighborhood of $6 to $7 billion dollars annually. Chew on that for a minute.

Don't budget any more gambling money than you can afford to lose. Once you set aside your bankroll for the casinos, consider it gone. If you leave the city with some jingle left in your pocket, consider yourself very lucky.

✔ **It's just a game:** You won't find the key to successful gambling in any strategy book or streak of good luck. It's a state of mind. Success means having fun without losing the farm. And so while it must be very nice (not that I would know) to bet $10,000 and win $30,000, remember that it must really hurt all the other times when that $10,000 goes bye-bye. If you remember this is just a game, for your entertainment, you can have plenty of fun playing nickel slots. Sure, you won't get rich, but you won't send your children to the poorhouse, either. If you're looking for an investment opportunity, consider the stock market.

Playing the Slot Machines

Old-timers will tell you slots were invented to give wives something to do while their husbands gambled. Slots used to be stuck on the periphery of the casinos and could be counted on one hand, maybe two. But now they *are* the casino. The casinos make more from slots than from craps, blackjack, and roulette combined. In fact, you can find more than 120,000 slot machines in Clark County!

A slot machine is actually a computer with a highly specialized program that randomly decides how much and how often you will win on any given play. Most of the time, the computer decides that you lose, but occasionally it decides that you win, and then you'll hear the coins raining down into the little bin below. The good news is that Las Vegas slot machines are the *loosest* (the house keeps less money) in the country. The bad news is that the house still holds a 3 – 25 percent advantage on the slot machines (there's a reason they're nicknamed bandits).

How they work

You put the coins in the slot and pull the handle. What, you thought there was a trick to this? Well, maybe there is a bit more to tell. In order to keep up with increasing competition, the plain old machine, where reels just spin, has become nearly obsolete. Now, they are all computerized, have fun graphics, and have added buttons to push, so you can avoid carpal tunnel syndrome yanking the handle all night. (The handles are still there on many of them so you can feel more involved in the play.) The idea is still simple: Get three (sometimes four) cherries (Elvis, sevens, dinosaurs, whatever) in a row and you win something.

Each machine has its own combination, so be sure to check the chart (included on the front of every machine) that tells you all the winning combinations. Some pay you something with just one symbol showing; on most, the more combinations there are, the more opportunities for loot. Some even pay a little if you get three blanks.

Different slots for different pots

Slot machines (see Figure 15-1 for a sample slot machine) take coins in just about any denomination. Nickel machines are usually the lowest limit (although a few penny slots still exist), followed by those that take dimes (very rare), quarters, half-dollars, dollars, and $5. The high-limit machines, usually cordoned off in their own area, can cost you anywhere from $10 – $500 or more for a single pull of the handle.

After you decide how much you want to blow (I mean, bet), you have to decide between *progressive* and so-called *flat-top* machines.

✔ **Flat-top machines** have a fixed high-end limit of how much you can win. For example, hit three gold bars and you win 1,000 coins — but never any more or less.

✔ **Progressive machines** offer unlimited high-end winnings as the jackpot grows, and the pot grows each time you put a coin in. If you play on a progressive machine, those three gold bars could win you different amounts, depending on how much money has accumulated in the jackpot. Most progressive slots are located in *carousels* — groups of machines that contribute to one central jackpot. The first person to hit the big one wins the big jackpot. These carousels are easy to find: Just look for the large electronic signs above them displaying the jackpot amount. I recently saw non-carousel machines with individual progressive jackpots. Play these, and you don't have to worry about the guy sitting next to you winning the big prize.

You can find machines that take 2 coins, 3 coins, or up to 45 coins at a time. Some even have more than one set of reels (meaning you can win on more than one "line," horizontally, vertically, or diagonally). Some include bonus wheels that spin and award you extra dough. Don't worry, though, it's not all that complicated: If you study a machine carefully for just a few moments before you play it (or watch someone else who is playing a similar machine), you get a good handle on all the rules and your possible winnings.

If you play a second coin, a winning combination will win on either the top or the center payline.

With only one coin in, you have to line the symbols up on this center payline.

When you play three coins, a winning combination on any payline wins.

Figure 15-1: A basic slot machine.

Hitting the jackpot

If you're half asleep and mindlessly pumping quarters into a machine, don't worry that you won't recognize if you hit the big one. Bells and sirens often blare, just in case you weren't paying attention (and just in case others in the casino need a little help deciding to play!). If this happens but no money rains down in the bin, relax. Most machines have *payout limits;* any jackpot that exceeds the limit is paid in cash by an attendant (who will no doubt double-time it to your frantic side).

Be aware that the casino automatically reports to the IRS any jackpot of $1,200 or more. Yes, that big win is considered income and is taxable. (You can also deduct losses, but only if you have winnings and you've kept a record of your play.) So maybe instead of trying for that one big jackpot, you should go after a bunch of smaller ones. And be sure to check with your accountant if you're unsure of how to report your winnings or losses.

Tips and tricks

There is no such thing as a slot expert (just someone whose played them a whole lot), but I still have a few hints for you to take with you to the slot machines. These are not guaranteed to make you a penny, but if you stick to them, you may do pretty well.

✔ **Be prepared to walk away:** If you sit down at a slot machine and it doesn't pay out anything within the first ten or so pulls, move your butt to the next one. Odds are that it isn't going to get any better.

✔ **For bigger pots, play bigger money:** The lower the denomination required to play a slot machine, the less likely you are to hit the jackpot. In general, nickel machines pay off less frequently than quarter machines, which pay off less frequently than dollars, and so on. Quarter slots are the most-frequently played machines (with almost 75 percent of players using them).

✔ **Play the max:** This one is a tough call; if you play the maximum number of coins, and you win, you will win much more. Of course, if you lose, you go through your money that much faster. Most machines, progressive or not, offer higher payout odds on maximum bets. Put in one quarter, get three cherries, and you get two quarters back, for example. The payout there is 2:1. However, put in three quarters, hit those same three cherries, and you get nine quarters as a payoff. This makes the payout 3:1. In addition, if you want to wint the big jackpot, you must put in the maximum number of coins. It's a hook to make you spend more money, but it's a hook that's hard to argue with. True slot junkies *always* play the maximum.

On most slot machines you find a button marked "credit." If you push this button, your winnings are credited and your spins debited electronically, as opposed to having to put your money into the machine or having it drop out into the bin. When you're ready to leave, or if you prefer to stick your money in manually, just press the "cash out" button on the machine. Using the credit feature is less noisy and somewhat more convenient, but using coins can stretch your gambling experience out, since it takes longer to feed the coins into the machine.

✔ **Look for busy carousels:** When you look for a machine to park yourself in front of, take note about whether the machine is in a carousel that is empty or teeming with players. There's a method to this madness — empty carousels likely have machines that aren't paying well. Take your time to find a carousel where lots of people have lots of money in their coin returns. Again, I'm not going to guarantee that you'll do better here, but you may have more luck.

The ins and outs of slot etiquette

You won't need to consult with Miss Manners before tackling the slots in Vegas, but you would be wise to keep a few unwritten rules in mind:

- Don't assume that a slot machine isn't in use because nobody is sitting at it. Slot fanatics often play 2 or 3 machines at a time and they can be extraordinarily territorial. If people are playing machines adjacent to the one you're thinking of using, ask before you sit down.

- If a bucket is turned down on a seat in front of a slot machine or on the handle of the machine, it's a safe bet that it is in use.

- Technically, if you're alone and you get up and walk away from a machine — even it's to go to the bathroom — you've relinquished all rights to it, even if you leave a coin bucket on the seat. In reality, unless the casino is mobbed, in which case all bets are off, etiquette holds that you don't touch a machine that is being "held." However, players can't hold slot machines indefinitely. If the "owner" doesn't show up after 10 – 15 minutes' time, sit down and start playing.

- **Investigate progressive payouts:** If you're thinking about playing at a bank of progressive slots, ask an attendant or change person what the jackpot starts at and when it usually hits. Most of the time, he will be happy to give you this "insider" information. Here's a good general rule: If you discover that a progressive slot carousel jackpot starts at $10,000, usually hits before it reaches $15,000, and is currently at $14,500, then sit down and start playing! If it's only at $10,500 (meaning that means somebody recently won), it probably won't hit again anytime soon.

- **Ask the experts:** Feel free to ask the floor or change attendants if they know of a certain area that is doing well. It sure beats wandering around from machine to machine looking for that special vibe, Technically, the attendants aren't supposed to tell you this, but many often do — especially those in the change areas above slot carousels.

Trying Your Hand at Video Poker

Rapidly coming up on slots in popularity, video poker works the same way as regular poker, except you play on a machine. This is one of the few games in Vegas where, if you play perfectly and on the right machine, you can actually break even or perhaps — gasp! — ahead of the house. It would take a lot more space than this book to expound on perfect video poker strategy and the proper machines to play on — although some books do just that — but I will give you the game's basics.

How they work

To play a round of video poker, put in your coins, press the DEAL button, and five virtual-reality cards pop up (out of a 52-card virtual deck that the machines use for each deal). Select the cards you want to keep with HOLD buttons located under each card, and press DEAL again to get replacement cards for the ones you didn't hold. You have only one chance to draw for a winning poker hand. The machine doesn't have a hand of its own, so you aren't competing *against* it. You're just trying to get a hand that's high enough to win something.

This is a bit more challenging and more active than slots because you have some control (or at least illusion of control) over your fate, and it's easier than playing actual poker with a table full of folks who probably take it very seriously. Even better, there are some video poker machines — admittedly, they're very hard to find — that actually offer favorable odds if you play perfectly.

Choosing your machine

When push comes to shove, your choice of video poker machine is affected by three factors: denomination, payout schedules, and availability. Unfortunately, you're going to have to do some footwork if you want a machine that meets your expectations for all three, since the poker machines in Vegas are in a constant state of flux.

Just like slot machines, you can play video poker in many different denominations, although quarter and dollar machines are the most played (and most available). Progressive video poker is popping up everywhere, but most are still flat, offering a fixed payout. You can also find a huge range of add-ons that may include a wild card, a *double-down feature* (where you double your money on a winning hand), or special bonuses for certain hands.

If you're a beginner, stick to the basic games that offer payouts starting with *jacks or better* until you get used to the concept. Try to get a machine that pays more than just returning your money for two pairs. If you can find it, the best machine to play on is called a *9/6 machine* because for a single coin bet, it pays out 9 coins for a full house and 6 coins for a flush. Most machines in Vegas are 8/5 machines, and those pay out less money. Check the pay schedules on the video poker machines to determine what its payout percentage is.

Knowing when you have a winner

Most video-poker machines have a minimum of *jacks or better* to win. This means that out of five cards, you have at least two jacks of any suit (the ace is always the highest card value, and the two is the lowest). Two matching cards that are higher than jacks is also a winner. If you've never played poker, consult Figure 15-2 to find out more about poker hands.

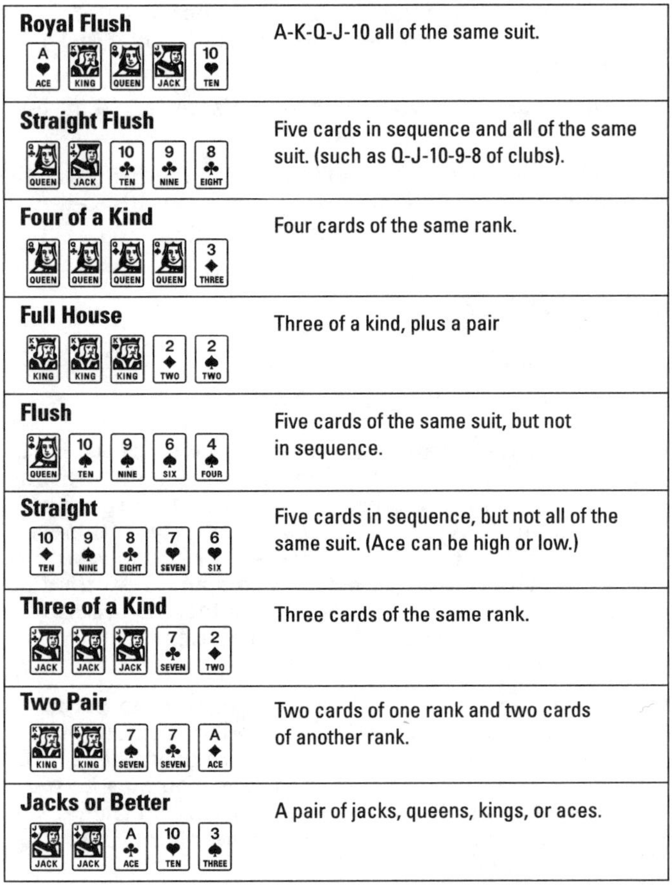

Royal Flush	A-K-Q-J-10 all of the same suit.
Straight Flush	Five cards in sequence and all of the same suit. (such as Q-J-10-9-8 of clubs).
Four of a Kind	Four cards of the same rank.
Full House	Three of a kind, plus a pair
Flush	Five cards of the same suit, but not in sequence.
Straight	Five cards in sequence, but not all of the same suit. (Ace can be high or low.)
Three of a Kind	Three cards of the same rank.
Two Pair	Two cards of one rank and two cards of another rank.
Jacks or Better	A pair of jacks, queens, kings, or aces.

Figure 15-2: The hierarchy of video poker hands.

✔ **One pair:** Out of your five cards, you have two that have the same face value. Most video-poker games require a pair of jacks as the minimum before they'll pay.

✔ **Two pair:** Two pairs have matching card values — for example, two 5s and two 8s.

✔ **Three of a kind:** Three cards out of your five have matching values (for example, three kings).

✔ **Straight:** All five of your cards are in sequential order. It doesn't matter what suit they are; they don't have to match. The lowest possible straight is 2-3-4-5-6, and the highest is 10-J-Q-K-A.

✔ **Flush:** Five cards of the same suit, regardless of value (for example, five diamonds).

✔ **Full house:** A combination of one pair and three of a kind (two aces and three 7s, for example).

✔ **Four of a kind:** Not hard to figure out but also not easy to get. Four of the five cards have the same face value (4-4-4-4-9, for example).

✔ **Straight flush:** Five cards in sequential order, all in the same suit, such as the 5-6-7-8-9 of spades.

✔ **Royal flush:** This is the ultimate poker hand and the highest possible straight flush. If you wind up with the 10-J-Q-K-A of all spades, clubs, diamonds, or hearts, you win big time.

Tips and tricks

Not enough information for you? Here are a couple of other handy tips to keep in mind when playing video poker:

✔ **Keep the rules in mind:** A pair of 3s, for example, isn't going to win you anything on a jacks-or-better machine. Drawing three cards to try to get another 3 (for a winning three of a kind) means that you only have two chances to get it right (there are only two more 3s in the deck). If you have an ace and jack with those two 3s however, you can keep the high cards and draw for a possible jacks-or-better pair. By doing so, you increase your odds of winning (you now have six chances of getting a winning hand — three more aces and three more jacks).

✔ **Don't risk a sure thing:** Unless you're bent on hitting all or nothing, consider keeping a winning hand, regardless of the potential of hitting the mother lode. Say you are dealt the A-K-10 of spades and the jacks of hearts and diamonds. You may be tempted to go for the royal flush by keeping the A-K-10, but the odds of your getting it are around 1 in 40,000. Keep your sure-thing pair of jacks and try to build on that.

Hitting Blackjack

Most casino gaming tables are devoted to the game of blackjack. It's very popular, probably because it's very simple to learn the basics and develop a strategy. You should, however, be aware of a few quirks of playing this game in a casino.

In short, you compete against the dealer — not the other players — to get as close to 21 points per hand without going over (known as *busting*). Numbered cards are worth their face value, face cards (J-Q-K) are worth 10, and the ace is worth either 1 or 11 points (your choice).

The primary differences among blackjack games are the number of decks used and the minimum bets allowed. Games range anywhere from one to six decks per game, and table minimums from $1 – $500 per hand, although $5 – $10 per hand is the most common. Most tables also have a maximum bet, so make sure you find out what the betting range for a given table is before you sit down to play.

Playing the game

The first thing you need to do is place your bet on the table. Then the dealer gives you two cards, usually face up, and then deals himself (or herself, as the case may be) two cards: one face up and one face down. If your two cards equal 21 (a 10 or face card plus an ace), the dealer calls blackjack and you win automatically.

If the dealer has a 10 or an ace showing, he will check his hidden card. If he has a blackjack, everyone sitting at the table loses.

If you don't have 21, you are allowed as many additional cards as you want to try to reach 21. You lose (or bust) if you go over.

If you didn't bust and you've gone as high as you can (or want to), the dealer reveals his hidden card and attempts to beat your score. If he does, you lose; if he doesn't, you win. If you tie, it's called a *push,* and neither of you wins or loses.

Understanding the finer points

Blackjack really isn't all that complicated, but you should know a few things before you sit down to play a hand. After you read the following tips, watch a few hands when you enter the casino and then sit down and press your luck. And if you still have any questions, ask the dealer.

✔ **Chips to play:** Casino blackjack is played with chips, not cash. You can buy chips in different denominations at the main cashier or at the table itself. And after you've placed a bet on the table and the dealer starts dealing, don't touch your bet. If you do, you're likely to get a verbal slap on the wrist (often accompanied by a stern look) from the dealer.

✔ **Dealer minimum:** Most casino blackjack games require the dealer to draw to at least 17. In other words, the dealer can't quit drawing cards until her hand totals 17 or higher. Keep this in mind when devising your own strategy.

✔ **Multi-deck versus single-deck games:** Most Vegas blackjack games use six decks of cards all mixed together in a *shoe,* which is a special card dispenser. The cards are dealt face up in front of you. *Don't touch them!* The dealer is the only one allowed to handle the cards in these multi-deck games, and you'll get scolded if you do. You can occasionally find a single-deck game, and the dealer usually deals them by hand face down in front of you. In this case, you are allowed to touch the cards (they're face down, so you have to pick them up to look at them).

No matter which type of blackjack game you play, you need to know the hand signals for *hitting* (asking for another card) or *standing* (telling the dealer you don't want another card). It's kind of like the secret handshake of blackjack players (luckily, no decoder rings are involved). You signal for an additional card by making a light scratching motion toward yourself on the table with your hand (or with your cards, if you're holding them). This is sort of a non-verbal way of saying *gimme another one*. If you don't want to draw, wave your hand once above your cards to signal *no more* (or if you're holding your cards, tuck them face down on the table gently under your bet).

Devising a basic strategy

You better your chances of winning at the blackjack table if you have a basic strategy going into the game.

If your two cards total 17 or above, don't draw. Your chances of getting a higher hand are slim (and the dealer has a decent chance of busting while trying to beat your hand). If you have a two-card total of 11 or less, draw a card — it's impossible to go over 21 with one additional card.

When you have 12 – 16 points, regardless of how many cards you have, things start to get a bit tricky. This is when you should take a long, hard look at the dealer's single upturned card. If you fall into that 12 – 16-point range and the dealer has a 7 or higher showing, you should probably draw a card. Chances are that the dealer has a 10-point card hidden, and you'll lose if you don't draw a card. If the dealer has a 6 or lower card showing, she'll probably have to draw (to reach at least 17), and there's a good chance of her going over 21 and losing. Consider staying, even with a hand as low as 12.

Insurance

When the dealer has an ace upturned, she asks if you want to take out *insurance*. When taking out insurance, you are allowed to place an additional bet of up to half your original wager (for example, if you bet $10, you can wager up to $5 on an insurance bet). If the dealer has 21, you lose your original bet but are paid 2:1 on your insurance bet. By doing so, you come out even if your insurance bet was half your original bet (you lose your $10 bet but gain an additional $5 on the insurance bet; are you following me on this?). If the dealer does not have 21, you lose your insurance bet, and the game proceeds as usual. Many gambling aficionados, including myself, consider this a sucker bet because the odds are that the dealer won't have 21. I suggest you don't bother with insurance.

Doubling down

If you want to do even more fancy stuff at the blackjack tables, you can *double down*. You place this bet after you are dealt your first two cards but before any additional cards are dealt. You must double the amount you bet by placing additional chips on the table (for example, if you bet $10 originally, you put out another $10 in chips). By doing this, you are hoping that your next card will give you a high enough hand to win — but you only get one additional card. The odds are that your one additional card will be worth 10 points (a 10 or a face card), so you should go with this option when your first two cards total 10 or 11 and the dealer has a low card showing. If you're lucky, you'll wind up with 20 or 21 and will probably win the hand and double your entire bet. If you get a low card, however you don't get another card to boost your point total and you're likely to lose it all. Hey, that's why they call it gambling!

Splitting

Splitting is another option you can try if you're feeling adventurous. Here's the deal: You are allowed to split when the first two cards you are dealt are of the same value (for example, two 7s). To split this hand, separate the two cards on the table and lay down additional chips equal to your original bet. The dealer then treats each card as a separate hand, and you can draw as many cards as you like to get as close to 21 as possible *for each hand*. Whichever hand beats the dealer wins double that bet (and you may even win with both hands). If either (or both) of your hands doesn't beat the dealer, you lose the bet.

When deciding whether to split your hand, consider this: Most people agree that two aces or two 8s should always be split into separate hands. This is generally a good bet because the odds are in your favor that you'll wind up with two better hands than the one you would have had otherwise.

Tips and tricks

Blackjack is an easy game to play and can be a lot of fun under the right conditions:

✔ **Find a fun dealer:** Before you choose your table, watch the dealer to see if she is one of the stone-faced, boring ones, or if she has some kick. A fun dealer often chats, offers advice, and generally makes the entire experience more enjoyable. On the other hand, if you're in a somber mood, maybe you'll want a no-nonsense dealer. Your choice.

✔ **Look for fun tablemates:** Same concept as in the preceding bullet, only this one has to do with the other gamblers at the table. If everyone is sitting around looking sour and concentrating might-ily on his cards, you may want to bypass the table. Scope out a table where your tablemates are whooping it up, and you'll have a better time.

✔ **Keep a stash:** Any financial planner will tell you that you should always save. And it's no different when gambling. Keep two piles of chips — one for betting and one for saving. Every time you win a hand, set aside part of your winnings (maybe half?) into the "don't touch" pile and then, well, don't touch it. If your luck takes a bad turn and you go through your betting pile, walk away. At least you'll still have money left.

✔ **Practice with video blackjack.** Most of the better casinos have nifty, computerized video blackjack games that cost a quarter a try. Because most blackjack tables on the Strip start at $5 (and even downtown, $2 tables are becoming harder to find), this is an economical way to at least get a feel for the game before you start laying down real money. It's not precisely the same as working with a real dealer, and the odds aren't the same, but the rules are, and that's what matters if you're a beginner.

✔ **Gamble downtown.** Serious gamblers — and by that I mean those who play to win, pure and simple — particularly blackjack players, always gamble downtown. They don't care about glitz and flash and themes. They want single-deck play, because they believe the odds are better and because they stand a better chance of card counting (not that they do that, nosirree — that's their story and they are sticking to it!). You might want to join them for these same reasons and also because the minimum stakes are lower — often $2 a hand as opposed to $5 and $10 on the Strip.

While playing blackjack, be sure to ask the dealer or the *pit boss* (the employee overseeing a group of tables) about restaurants, shows, and attractions in that particular hotel. If you've been betting a decent amount of money per hand (think $25 per hand for a few hours in the big hotels) and have been playing a while, you may get a *comp* (Vegas lingo for complimentary) meal, show ticket, or other discount. You have to ask for these, however, since they are rarely offered.

Taking a spin with roulette

Lots of people have seen roulette wheels, but few ever sit down to play. The game is actually quite easy to learn and can be a lot of fun to play. It does, however, have a huge house advantage, so keep that in mind.

Here's the basics of playing roulette: A ball is spun on a wheel with 38 numbers (0, 00, and 1 – 36). The 0 and 00 spaces are green, and the other numbers are either red or black but divided evenly. You place your bets on the *field,* which is a grid layout on the table showing all the numbers and a variety of different combinations (see Figure 15-3). *Inside bets* are those placed on the 0 through 36 number part of the field. *Outside bets* are placed in the boxes surrounding the numbers and include red, black, even, odd, 1 through 18, 19 through 36, 1st 12, 2nd 12, 3rd 12, and the columns bets. The object is for the ball to settle on one of the numbers (or other options) that you've placed bets on.

Note that you can win on more than one bet on a single spin, depending on the outcome. For example, if you place a bet on 8, even, and 1st 12, you can potentially win all three bets if the ball lands on 8. Pretty cool, huh?

How to bet

After you choose your table, lay cash or chips down and you are given special roulette chips. Each player at the table has a different color of chips, so it's easy to keep track of which are yours. Then you can start placing your bets on the field (see Figure 15-3). You are allowed to bet even after the ball begins spinning, but once it starts to fall toward the numbers, bets are cut off.

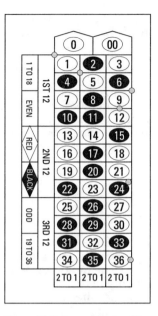

Figure 15-3: A standard roulette table.

Inside bets are complicated, so I'm going to stick to the outside bets with one exception: single-number bets (see the upcoming description). Outside bets don't pay out as much, but beginners should probably stick with them at first.

✔ **Odd-Even:** If you place a bet in the Odd field and an odd number (9, 15, and so on) comes up on the wheel, you win double your money placed on that field. If it comes up as an even number, you lose that bet. It follows, then, that if an even number comes up, you win for bets placed in the Even field. If either 0 or 00 comes up, you lose bets placed in either field.

✔ **Red-Black:** This one's really simple. Place your chips on a color, and you win if a number comes up in the color you bet. If you bet red and the ball lands on a red number, you double your bet (but you lose if black comes up). If 0 or 00 comes up — you guessed it! — you lose.

✔ **1–18, 19–36:** If you place chips in either of these boxes and the winning number falls within the range listed, you double your money for that bet. Suppose that you bet on 1–18 and the number 15 comes up on the wheel; you win. If the number 32 comes up, you lose. Either 0 or 00 causes you to lose these bets.

✔ **1st 12, 2nd 12, 3rd 12:** This is similar to the 1–18 and 19–36 bets, only a little more specific. Bet on the 1st 12 and if any number between 1 – 12 hits, you win triple your bet, but any other number is a loser. The same concept goes with 2nd 12 (numbers 13 – 24) and 3rd 12 (numbers 25 – 36).

✔ **Column bets:** At the end of the Inside fields are three boxes that are marked *2 to 1* (refer to Figure 15-3). If you place chips here, you're betting that the winning number on the wheel is one of the numbers in the column above that box. If it is, then you triple your bet. If it isn't, you lose it all.

✔ **Single-number bets:** This is the one inside bet that you may want to try. Place your chips on any single number on the field (17 or 34, for example), and if that number comes up, you win 35 times your bet. This is fun to play, and the winnings can be big, but the odds are *way* against you.

Tips and tricks

Here's some commonsense advice for first-timers:

✔ **Look for single-zero roulette:** As I mention earlier, most tables and wheels have both 0 and 00. A few have only the 0. If you can find one of these single-zero tables (The **Monte Carlo** has them), play it, because your odds are slightly better with fewer possible numbers (only 37 instead of 38) on the wheel.

✔ **Stick with the outside bets:** It's tempting to place all your money on your one single lucky number. Doing so can be exciting, but the problem is that you're much more likely to lose. The outside bets may not seem as glamorous and certainly don't pay out as as much, but your money goes farther and the odds of winning are a lot better.

Choosing Your Lucky Numbers in Keno

The ancient Chinese played a game that was very similar to your local lotto, and keno is based on the same concept. It may not be as adrenaline-filled as craps, but it's a good diversion while you're sitting in a hotel restaurant or lounge.

In the game of keno, a computer randomly draws twenty numbers from a field of 1 – 80. You place various bets on which numbers will come up, and if enough of your numbers do, you win.

Large keno boards (with the 80 numbers displayed) are scattered throughout the casino — often in the coffee shops and lounges. You can get a keno ticket from the restaurant tables or at the bar. The ticket shows the 80 numbers (called *spots*) and has boxes for the amount of your bet and the number of sequential games you want to play (see Figure 15-4). You place a bet by filling out the ticket and giving it to the *runner,* who then takes it to the keno lounge. You can find Keno runners walking around the casino floor and inside the hotel's restaurants and bars. Their uniforms usually identify them as keno runners, but they'll also announce their presence as they drift around.

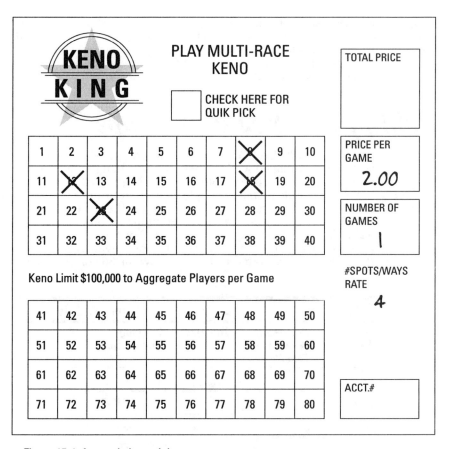

Figure 15-4: A sample keno ticket.

Casinos vary wildly regarding the possible bets you can make and the payout odds for those bets, but the most common are 6-, 7-, 8-, 9-, and 10-spot bets. If you play a 6-spot game, for example, you mark six numbers on the ticket and hand it in. Just like the lotto, if your six numbers come up, you win. If five of your six numbers are selected, you also win, but substantially less than you would have with all six numbers. Four numbers will likely pay even money, and 3 or fewer loses.

Keep in mind that you have to cash in winning tickets *before the start of the next game,* or you lose it all. If you can't find a keno runner, take your ticket to the keno cashier right away to get paid. Also, before you go dreaming about hitting the big jackpot, know this: The house advantage on keno is greater than in any other game in the casino.

In true Vegas style, you can change your betting strategy so that this fundamentally simple game takes a complex turn. For example, you can make bets involving groupings and splits. However, this is much more than you need to know if you're just looking for something to do while waiting for your drink. Just pick your lucky numbers and go. The best advice I can offer is that betting on fewer spots mean better odds of winning. It's a lot easier to get 6 out of 6 than it is to get 10 out of 10. Plus, if you get five numbers on a 6-spot ticket, you'll win something, whereas five numbers on a 10-spot will probably get you zippo. You don't win as much on a lower spot ticket, but you're likely to win more often.

Rolling the Dice with Craps

If you've ever heard that craps is really complicated — you've heard right. Oh, I struggled with it. I read books. I had people explain. My eyes always glazed over. I think I've finally gotten it, though. Despite my initial handicap, many people figure it out rather quickly (or else are faking it by randomly hurling money at the table — that works, too). Playing craps can be a little intimidating, but it is possible to play a simple game. Basically, bets are placed on what number will come up on a pair of dice thrown. You can place bets even if you're not the one throwing the dice. Table 15-1 shows how the 36 combinations stack up.

Table 15-1		Craps Combinations and Odds	
Number Rolled	**How Many Ways to Roll That Number**	**True Odds**	**Winning Combinations**
Two	1	35 to 1	
Three	2	17 to 1	
Four	3	11 to 1	
Five	4	8 to 1	
Six	5	6.2 to 1	
Seven	6	5 to 1	
Eight	5	6.2 to 1	
Nine	4	8 to 1	
Ten	3	11 to 1	
Eleven	2	17 to 1	
Twelve	1	35 to 1	

The person who is rolling the dice is called the *shooter*. When the shooter makes her first roll, it's called *coming out*. The object is for the shooter to get a 7 or 11 on the first roll in any combination (2 and 5, 5 and 6, and so on). That's an automatic winner for anyone playing the pass line (see upcoming section, "The pass-line bet"). If the shooter rolls a 2, 3, or 12, she *craps out* and is an automatic loser for anyone playing the pass line). If any other number comes up on the come-out roll (4, 5, 6, 8, 9, or 10), this number becomes the *point,* and the object of the game switches a little. After a point number has been established, the goal is for the shooter to roll the point number again before rolling a 7. If a 7 comes up before the point, then the shooter has *crapped out* and you lose your pass-line bet. Any time the shooter craps out, the dice are passed to the next shooter and the game starts over.

The following sections describe how you place bets on various parts of the gaming table (see also Figure 15-5):

There's a lot more to this game than what I describe in this section. For example, you can *play the odds* (make side bets that are placed on the point number), *Buy bets,* and *Lay bets.* If you are a beginner, I suggest that you stick with the Pass Line and Come bets at first. These are the easiest to play and offer the best odds. If you're interested in learning more about the intricacies of craps, check out the upcoming section called, "Finding Out More About Gambling."

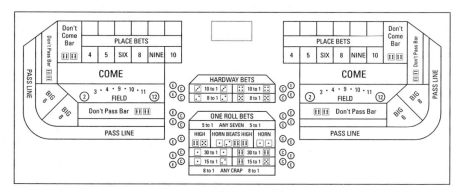

Figure 15-5: A standard craps table.

The pass-line bet

You should stick with the pass-line bet if you're a beginner. When playing this type of bet, you place your initial bet on the "pass" line, which means that you are betting that the player will not crap out. A roll of 7 or 11, or establishing a point number and rolling it before a 7, wins double your bet. Here's an example to help you out: Say you place your bet on the pass line. Once it's there, you can't touch it until you win or lose. The shooter rolls a 4. This is now the point. The next roll is a 5 and then a 10. Finally on the fourth throw, the shooter rolls a 4 and you win. If that fourth throw had turned up a 7, you would have lost.

The Don't Pass Bar bet

The *Don't Pass Bar* bet is exactly the opposite of the pass bet. You're betting that the shooter will crap out before winning. If the shooter rolls a 7 or 11, or establishes and then makes a point number, you lose a Don't Pass bet. If the shooter rolls a 2, 3, or 12, or craps out before making his point, then you win double.

The Come bet

You place a *Come* bet *after* the shooter establishes a point number. For example, say the shooter throws a 6 on his first throw. That is the point number, and placing a bet in the "Come" field is now just like a pass-line bet. You are wagering that the next throw of the dice will be 7 or 11. If it is, you win double. If the next throw is a 2, 3, or 12, you lose. If it is any other number, the bet is moved into the corresponding box (4, 5, 6, 8, 9, or 10) where it remains until the shooter either rolls the number again (you win) or rolls a 7 (you lose).

The Don't Come bet

The *Don't Come* bet is the pessimists' version of the Come bet: You win double if the throw is 2, 3, or 12 and lose if it is a 7 or 11. If any other number appears (4, 5, 6, 8, 9, or 10), you win if a 7 is thrown before that number is repeated but lose if it does not.

The place bet

To make a place bet, put your chips in this field above any number, and you are betting that the number will be rolled before a 7 is rolled. You can increase, decrease, or remove your bet entirely at any time during play.

The Hard Way, Big 6/8, Field, and Proposition bets

The Hard Way, Big 6, Big 8, Field, and Proposition bets make up the remainder of the gaming table. If you win on one of these bets, you can win big, but they are, according to most people, not worth the effort since the odds are against you in every single case.

- ✔ **The Hard Way bets** wager that 4, 6, 8, or 10 will be rolled, with one catch: The numbers must come up on the dice as double numbers (two 2s, 3s, 4s, or 5s, depending on which box you choose), and the combination has to appear *before* the number is thrown in any other combination or before a 7 appears.

- ✔ **The Big 6 and Big 8 bets** say that the shooter will throw a 6 or 8 before a 7 appears — the same as a Place bet but with lower payback odds.

- ✔ **A Field bet** wagers that the next throw of the dice will be a 2, 3, 4, 9, 10, 11, or 12 which are the seven least likely numbers that will appear. This bet is based on one single roll of the dice; avoid it if you're a beginner.

✔ **Proposition bets** say that the next roll will be either 2, 3, 7, 11, or 12 (there's a box for each) or any craps (2, 3, or 12). This bet is also based on one single roll of the dice and, again, should be avoided if you're a beginner.

Tips and tricks

I'm not a seasoned craps player, but I've managed to pick up some tips, and I'm more than happy to pass them on to you:

✔ If you can find a table with any room, just stand and watch for awhile. Even if you think you still don't understand the game, it will become a lot clearer when you see it in action. Maybe.

✔ It's definitely exciting to be the shooter, but it's a lot easier to bet and watch your money if you let someone else roll the dice. Feel free to pass when your turn as shooter comes around if you're not comfortable trying to roll and manage your bets. Alternatively, just don't bet when you're shooting.

✔ Avoid the Hard Way and one-roll bets like the plague. You'll almost always lose.

Playing Other Games

The games I mention earlier are the most popular but certainly not the only ones in town. In addition, you can find the following:

✔ **Standard poker:** This game is pretty much the same as video poker, only with real players and real cards. You don't play against the house, although the house takes a percentage of the pot, so you have a better shot at winning here than in any other game.

✔ **Baccarat:** This is a complex card game similar to blackjack; actually, the main thing that you need to know is that you bet on either the bank or the player — the dealer does all the rest of the work.

✔ **Mini-baccarat:** This is pretty much the same as baccarat, only a little simpler.

✔ **Pai-gow poker:** This is a Chinese take on seven-card stud poker.

✔ **Let-it-ride** and **Caribbean stud:** These are two more poker-based card games.

✔ **Wheel of fortune:** Basically, this game is just like it sounds, only without the puzzle or Vanna White.

✔ **Sports betting:** Yep, you can bet on just about any game in the world just by stopping in at your hotel's *Sports Book* — the area of a casino where sports betting occurs — and placing a wager.

Finding Out More About Gambling

This information I provide throughout this chapter gives you a good, basic overview on the most popular games in the casinos. If you want to know even more, check out the following valuable resources:

- ✔ **Hotel gaming lessons:** If you want some nitty-gritty details on the table game of your choice, ask if your hotel offers gaming lessons: Many of them do. These lessons are very helpful and are usually taught in an easy-to-understand manner right at the table so that you can see what's going on.

- ✔ **Computer games:** You can find tons of computer games for sale at retail stores. These games simulate live play and enable you to learn the rules of casino gambling. If you're hooked up to the Internet or any of the subscriber services like AOL, simply search for "games" or "casino games" and you're likely to find a bunch of shareware programs that you can download free.

Deciding Where to Gamble

In Las Vegas you will not lack for opportunities to gamble. I mention this earlier and you can trust me. If you're in a gambling frame of mind, you can start with the slot machines at the airport baggage carousel and keep going at restaurants, coffee shops, bars, and so on. I won't take up your time by listing every single casino in town; suffice it to say that every hotel on the Strip has a gigantic casino with all the games you could ever want to play. In many ways, a casino is a casino is a casino. They all have machines and tables and chances for joy or heartbreak. Some people may want a casino with a theme, because it's fun and gambling is fun, while others may find the themes distracting because gambling is serious business. Ultimately, let's face it; your favorite casino is one you've won at. Here are some I like (and some I don't — only because I've lost there).

Casinos for the serious gambler

The Mirage (3400 Las Vegas Blvd. S.; ☎ 702-791-7111) is my favorite place to gamble — and not even because I've won all that much there. Quite the opposite, in fact. This Polynesian-theme casino is large and surprisingly quiet, allowing for minimal distractions from your desire to win. If you want to play serious poker on the Strip, this is the place to go.

Going up the serious ladder is the **Las Vegas Hilton** (3000 Paradise Rd.; ☎ 702-732-7111). This one boasts medium-sized gambling area filled with Austrian crystal chandeliers and marble galore (and don't forget the **Spacequest Casino,** discussed in the following section).

But if you really want to gamble in high-class style, you should go to **Mandalay Bay** (3950 Las Vegas Blvd. S.; ☎ 702-632-7777), the **Monte**

Carlo (3770 Las Vegas Blvd. S; ☎ 702-730-7777), or **The Venetian** (3355 Las Vegas Blvd., S; ☎ 702-733-5000). All of these are variations on a theme; classy, European-style casinos, full of towering ceilings, marble, and glitzy lights. Tacky touches are kept at bay. I think the results are pretty interchangeable; although attractive places, once you've seen one of them, you've seen them all. On the other hand, they tend to be less noisy and chaotic than some of the others.

Outstripping even these in the hoity-toity department is the **Bellagio** (3600 Las Vegas Blvd. S.; ☎ 702-693-7111). It was built with high rollers and lovers of class in mind, as were the casinos mentioned above, only the Bellagio goes even further than its competitors. Oh, does it feel serious. I've heard the slot machines have been constructed to make less of a crash-clang than usual, but this may be a nuance too subtle for me to really notice.

Casinos for the not-so-serious gambler

Harrah's Las Vegas (3745 Las Vegas Blvd. S.; ☎ 702-369-5000), has a festive, European carnival theme. One fun aspect of Harrah's is the *party pits* — gambling-table areas where dealers are encouraged to whoop it up with the patrons by wearing funny hats and celebrating wins. This place may have the friendliest dealers in town.

The casino at **The Hard Rock Hotel & Casino** (4455 Paradise Rd.; ☎ 702-693-5000) is a masterpiece of Vegas silliness. The craps tables are shaped like grand pianos, some slot machines have guitar necks for handles, and the gaming chips have faces of famous rock stars on them. The decibel level is high — be prepared for blaring rock music — but that makes for a much looser vibe. Try to bet to the beat. And if you are staying there, don't forget to visit the pool's swim-up blackjack table. And yes, I asked — they give you little waterproof pouches to hold your money in.

Caesars Palace (3570 Las Vegas Blvd. S.; ☎ 702-731-7110) offers serious luxury for serious gamblers, but lovers of the absurd will have a great time here, too. After all, the cocktail waitresses are wearing togas, and faux marble Roman statues keep an eye on the proceedings. And that's not even counting regular appearances by Roman gladiators/soldiers, and Caesar and Cleopatra.

Hey, and speaking of silly, don't overlook the fabulous **New York-New York** casino (3790 Las Vegas Blvd. S; ☎ 702-740-6969). The change carts are tricked up to look like yellow cabs, the machines are grouped in an area called "The Pacific Slot Exchange," and the backs of the chairs at the tables are dressed in tuxedos. All this is set in areas designed to look like NYC landmarks — Central Park, Greenwich Village, and so on.

Nearly as silly — silly is a very good thing, by the way — the **Luxor** (3900 Las Vegas Blvd. S; ☎ 702-262-4000) lets you gamble inside a pyramid while surrounded by Egyptian-ephemera. Holy Moses! (Pre-Exodus, of course). And no, the talking camels do not give gaming tips.

In summer, **Tropicana Resort & Casino** (3801 Las Vegas Blvd. S.; ☎ 702-739-2222) offers swim-up blackjack in its beautiful tropical pool area. And then there's **Circus Circus** (2880 Las Vegas Blvd. S; ☎ 702-734-0410) which hits new heights — literally — in distractions with frequent live circus aerial acts over its casino. Is that trapeze artist going to miss and land on your winning poker hand? And if they do, does that count as a push?

And speaking of overhead distractions, the **Rio** (3700 W. Flamingo Rd.; ☎ 702-252-7777) interrupts play (or it would, if you find you can't pull a slot handle while looking up at the ceiling) several times each night with its "Masquerade in the Sky" Mardi Gras show. This takes place in the much more appealing part of the Rio's casino, a recent extension that has a very high ceiling (the better to accommodate said show).

The crowning achievement in gambling fun, however, is the **Spacequest Casino** at the **Las Vegas Hilton,** (3000 Paradise Rd.; ☎ 702-732-7111). It's designed as a twenty-fourth-century space station with large windows that offer a view of earth (and orbiting space shuttles, taxi cabs, and Hilton limos). Some of the slot machines here don't have handles — you pass your hand through a bar of light to trigger the mechanism instead. It's highly ridiculous in a really good way. (Be sure to visit the bathrooms, which give you an instant urinalysis while you use the facilities. Not surprisingly, it tends to predict good gaming luck for everyone.)

Casinos for the budget gambler

If you're gambling on a budget (and don't want to break the bank), make the trek downtown to make your money last the longest. (Note however that the **Sahara**, located on the Strip, often offers $1 craps.)

Binion's Horseshoe Casino (128 E. Fremont St.; ☎ 800-237-6537) is a great example of Old Las Vegas. And it has blackjack tables with a $1 minimum ($3 – $5 is the standard). **Binion's** also hosts the annual **World Series of Poker.** Because of its reputation, those people claiming to be "real" gamblers won't play anywhere but Binion's.

A few blocks down the street from Binion's is the **El Cortez Hotel & Casino** (600 E. Fremont St.; ☎ 702-385-5200) offering roulette with minimum bets as low as 10¢ and 25¢ craps. Now *that's* cheap!

One more place to try if you're a frugal soul is find the **Gold Spike** (400 E. Ogden Ave.; ☎ 702-384-8444) located one block north of Fremont at 4th Street. This casino is straight out of a 1970s time warp, complete with worn shag carpeting and fake-wood paneling. And it's the only place I know of that has penny slot machines.

Really big casinos to try your luck

The **MGM Grand** (3799 Las Vegas Blvd. S; ☎ 702-891-7777) has the largest casino in the world. And it is, needless to say, really, really big.

Four football fields would fit in here, with room left over for several basketball courts. You decide if that's a good thing or a bad thing. Learn to love emerald green, rainbows, lions and movie-related symbols. Slot-lore has it that the Majestic Lions slot machines here are always a sure thing.

Small casinos for your gambling pleasure

Or go in the completely opposite direction and head to one of my favorites, the **Main Street Station** (200 N. Main; ☎ **702-387-1896**). This is actually a sweet little place, pretty, even, with its turn-of-the-century San Francisco style. I love it.

Many of the casinos in the downtown area are small and are not affiliated with any hotel. You often see employees standing out front trying to lure you inside with the promise of free stuff. Avoid these places because, almost without exception, your free gift isn't worth it.

Chapter 16

Seeing the Crème de la Crème: Las Vegas' Top Sights

● ●

In This Chapter

▶ Indexes of Las Vegas' top sights

▶ Reviews of the best things to see and do in Las Vegas

● ●

*W*hat truly separates Sin City from other destinations is, of course, gambling — were you expecting cathedrals or something? But you can't sit at a slot machine forever. (Or maybe you can.) If there is one sure bet in Las Vegas, it's that you won't lack for things to do, regardless of your personal tastes or budget. However, Vegas being Vegas, the attractions here are not quite the same as what you'll find in other destinations. The city's most notable must-sees are those mammoth theme hotels.

However, the hotels are not all there is to Vegas — although by the time you are through investigating all the jaw-dropping architecture on the Strip, you may be too exhausted to learn otherwise. Sure, Vegas has lavish shows and Elvis impersonators, but it also has off-the-wall museums and free street-side extravaganzas. Rest assured that you'll find plenty of action-packed fun to fill your time in between poker hands.

 If you are spending a lot of time (or money) gambling in one casino, check with the dealer or casino attendant to find out if you can get a discounted (or free) admission to the hotel's attractions. A simple "How much is it to get into (fill in the blank)?" may get you a free pass if you're dumping money into their coffers via the casino.

 On a strict budget? Lost all your money in the slots? No problem. You can find lots of inexpensive diversions in town to keep you amused (and away from the casinos). Many of the free publications in town, such as *What's Up Magazine* and *Showbiz* include coupons for discount admissions to attractions. In addition, some hotels have people at the front door passing out coupons for discounted admission to the hotel's attractions. And don't forget that you can check out the free hotel shows, such as **Bellagio's** exquisite water fountains or the **Treasure Island** pirate battle.

Las Vegas Attractions Overview

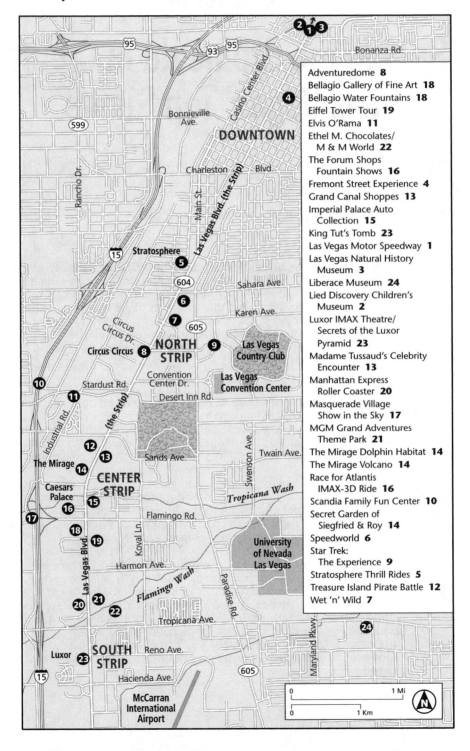

Adventuredome **8**
Bellagio Gallery of Fine Art **18**
Bellagio Water Fountains **18**
Eiffel Tower Tour **19**
Elvis O'Rama **11**
Ethel M. Chocolates/
   M & M World **22**
The Forum Shops
   Fountain Shows **16**
Fremont Street Experience **4**
Grand Canal Shoppes **13**
Imperial Palace Auto
   Collection **15**
King Tut's Tomb **23**
Las Vegas Motor Speedway **1**
Las Vegas Natural History
   Museum **3**
Liberace Museum **24**
Lied Discovery Children's
   Museum **2**
Luxor IMAX Theatre/
   Secrets of the Luxor
   Pyramid **23**
Madame Tussaud's Celebrity
   Encounter **13**
Manhattan Express
   Roller Coaster **20**
Masquerade Village
   Show in the Sky **17**
MGM Grand Adventures
   Theme Park **21**
The Mirage Dolphin Habitat **14**
The Mirage Volcano **14**
Race for Atlantis
   IMAX-3D Ride **16**
Scandia Family Fun Center **10**
Secret Garden of
   Siegfried & Roy **14**
Speedworld **6**
Star Trek:
   The Experience **9**
Stratosphere Thrill Rides **5**
Treasure Island Pirate Battle **12**
Wet 'n' Wild **7**

Las Vegas isn't Kidsville, USA, but if you have the kiddies in tow, this chapter offers some good options for entertaining them, too.

For information on the big, splashy, dare I say, Vegas-style production shows, see Chapter 20.

A Note on Practical Planning

Although I've only included Vegas' most entertaining or unusual sights in the following listings, unless you're planning on being here for a while, you're going to need to prioritize. I suggest that you whip out a pen and scribble your own interest rating in the worksheets at the back of this book.

1. **Wait till the folks at home hear about this!**

2. **Yeah, that sounds pretty cool.**

3. **Maybe if I'm not too full from the buffet.**

4. **Only if I run out of gambling money early.**

5. **Only if Elvis himself is singing there.**

For consistency's sake, I'm sticking with the South, North, and Central Strip neighborhoods which parallel those set up in the hotel and restaurant chapters. Remember that a Paradise Road designation means that an attraction is located somewhere near Paradise Road and not necessarily on it. As in other chapters, I use the Off the Beaten Path designation for places that are located outside the defined neighborhoods but are worth the extra time and mileage.

If your time in Las Vegas is limited, try to plan the attractions you want to see by neighborhood, instead of running all over town. If you stick to one area at a time, you'll maximize your sightseeing opportunities.

Unless I note otherwise, all of the following attractions offer free valet or do-it-yourself parking.

Index by Neighborhood

North Strip
Adventuredome
Speedworld
Stratosphere Tower and Thrill Rides
Wet 'n' Wild

Paradise Road
Star Trek: The Experience

Downtown
Fremont Street Experience

Off the Beaten Path
Liberace Museum
Lied Discovery Children's Museum

Index by Type

Amusement Parks/Thrill Rides
Adventuredome
Eiffel Tower
Manhattan Express Roller Coaster
MGM Grand Adventures
Stratosphere Tower and Thrill Rides
Wet 'n' Wild

Museums/Memorabilia Exhibits
Bellagio Gallery of Fine Art
Elvis O' Rama Museum
Ethel M. Chocolates/M&M World
Imperial Palace Auto Collection
King Tut's Tomb and Museum
Liberace Museum

Lied Discovery Children's Museum
The Secret Garden of Siegfried and
    Roy/Mirage Dolphin Habitat

Shows/Entertainment
Bellagio Water Fountains
Fremont Street Experience
Forum Shops at Caesars Palace
    Fountain Shows
Masquerade Village Show in the Sky
The Mirage Volcano
Treasure Island Pirate Battle

Theaters and Simulation Rides
Luxor IMAX Theater/In Search of the
    Obelisk
Race for Atlantis IMAX-3D Ride
Speedworld
Star Trek: The Experience

Las Vegas' Top Sites from A to Z

Adventuredome
North Strip

This miniature amusement park under a giant pink dome might be a good place to head on a hot day. It has a double-loop roller coaster, a water flume, laser tag, and a few other rides — plus a separate video/carnival game arcade, food stands, and a "dinosaur bone" excavation area for the smaller kids. Kids and adults alike will have their fill of this place after a couple hours.

2889 Las Vegas Blvd. S. (in Circus Circus). ☎ 702-794-3939. Admission: All-day ride pass is $15.95 if you're above 4 feet tall, $13.95 if not. Per-ride prices: $2 for

South Strip Attractions

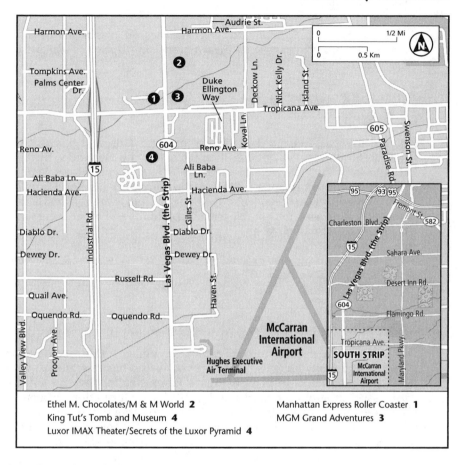

Ethel M. Chocolates/M & M World **2**

King Tut's Tomb and Museum **4**

Luxor IMAX Theater/Secrets of the Luxor Pyramid **4**

Manhattan Express Roller Coaster **1**

MGM Grand Adventures **3**

children's rides, $4 for family rides, and $5 for thrill rides. Open: Park hours vary — call ahead.

Bellagio Water Fountains
Center Strip

Okay, so we've all seen water fountains that shoot geysers into the air cued to some musical number. Ho-hum. But listen, if you trust me on anything, trust me on this: This is far, far better than what you've experienced before, and is easily the coolest, classiest free show in Vegas. Yeah, it's water geysers shooting into the air keyed to musical numbers, but I'm telling you this water shoots into the air to an impossible height, and then flirts and dances, moves like Baryshnikov, and is as witty as it is pretty. The music ranges from opera to Sinatra, with some pop and show tunes thrown in. Make a point of seeing at least one number; I bet you'll stick around for a second and third.

3600 Las Vegas Blvd. S. (at the corner of Flamingo Rd. outside the Bellagio). Admission: Free. Performances take place every 15 – 30 minutes nightly from 6 p.m. – 12 a.m.

Bellagio Gallery of Fine Art
Center Strip

Real art in Vegas? What's the world coming to? This isn't black velvet paintings or motel art — but it is hotel art, in that it was founded by then-**Bellagio** (and **The Mirage** and **Treasure Island**) owner Steve Wynn, a most respected art collector. Since **MGM** took over his hotel empire, Wynn's art collection has been moved out, but plans are for the Gallery to remain open, featuring notable traveling exhibits and other events. Get a little cultah, why don't you?

3600 Las Vegas Blvd. S. (in the Bellagio). ☎ 888-488-7111. Admission: $12 (includes audio tour). Open: Daily 9 a.m. – 12 a.m.

Eiffel Tower Tour
Center Strip

I love Paris in the springtime but I can't always make it there, so perhaps it's nice — or really hokey — that **Paris Las Vegas** has provided us with a half-scale replica of the City of Lights' famous **Eiffel Tower.** I put the word "tour" in quotation marks in the following information because in the 90 seconds or so it takes for the elevator to zoom to the observation platform, all you get are a few factoids about this tower and its more famous Parisian sister. You can get a nice view from up there, though.

3655 Las Vegas Blvd. S. (at Paris Las Vegas). ☎ 702-946-7000. Admission: $8. "Tours" leave every half hour. Open: Daily 10 a.m. – 1 a.m.

Elvis O' Rama
Center Strip

A can't-miss for Elvis-o-philes, but nothing that will convince nonbelievers he was truly The King. Less a museum than the spoils of a really cool yard sale; you've got your Elvis Army uniform, your Elvis social security card, your love letter to his girl, all sorts of singles and albums, your Elvis address book, even the contents of Pa Presley's wallet. Little of it is labeled as thoroughly as I would like, but it's certainly a collection.

3401 Industrial Rd. ☎ 702-309-7200. Admission: $9.95 adults, $7.95 seniors, kids under 12 free. (Admission includes a 20-minute Elvis impersonator show, held four times daily.) Open: Daily 10 a.m. – 6 p.m.

Center Strip Attractions

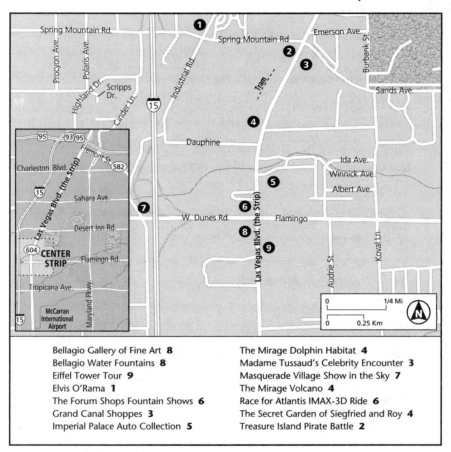

Bellagio Gallery of Fine Art **8**
Bellagio Water Fountains **8**
Eiffel Tower Tour **9**
Elvis O'Rama **1**
The Forum Shops Fountain Shows **6**
Grand Canal Shoppes **3**
Imperial Palace Auto Collection **5**

The Mirage Dolphin Habitat **4**
Madame Tussaud's Celebrity Encounter **3**
Masquerade Village Show in the Sky **7**
The Mirage Volcano **4**
Race for Atlantis IMAX-3D Ride **6**
The Secret Garden of Siegfried and Roy **4**
Treasure Island Pirate Battle **2**

Ethel M. Chocolates/M&M World
South Strip

A shrine devoted to the four basic food groups: milk chocolate, dark chocolate, white chocolate, and chocolate truffles. This four-story retail and exhibit space, brought to you by the company that makes M&Ms, Milky Way, and Snickers is more gift shop than museum, but it's still fun to wander around here — plus they give free samples! All those people exiting holding their stomachs? That's a *good* sign. (Actually, sadly, the samples usually are small. Meanies.) Check out the little film/show that runs every half hour — it's quite cute and clever. From Henderson, you can also catch a free shuttle running to the chocolate factory. It leaves every hour between 10:30 a.m. and 4:30 p.m.

3785 Las Vegas Blvd. S. (inside the Showcase Mall just north of Tropicana). ☎ *800-4-ETHELM. Admission (M&M World): $3.00. Open: Sun – Thurs 10 a.m. – 12 a.m., Fri – Sat 10 a.m. – 1 a.m.*

The Forum Shops at Caesars Palace Fountain Shows
Center Strip

Toga, toga! No, that's not a tribute to *Animal House* nor is it John Belushi springing to life in the center of two giant marble fountains in this snazzy shopping arcade. It's really Bacchus, the Roman god of wine and debauchery (and thus, if I mix religious metaphors, the patron saint of Vegas). Every hour on the hour, the faux-marble Bacchus and his buddies creakily (and creepily) move and speak to the accompaniment of lasers, water, and smoke. In the Roman Great Hall (at the end of the expansion), the Atlantis fountain uses hydraulics, projection-screen TVs, and fire effects to entertain the crowd. Another major plus — it's close to **La Salsa,** which offers some of the best and biggest margaritas in town (offerings that make the statues seem even more fun).

3500 Las Vegas Blvd. S. (at The Forum Shops at Caesars Palace). ☎ *702-893-4800. Admission: Free. Open: Shows hourly Sun – Thurs 10 a.m. – 11 p.m., Fri – Sat 10 a.m. – 12 a.m.*

Fremont Street Experience
Downtown

This high-tech light-and-laser show is Lazerium, Vegas-style. **The Fremont Street Experience** is a five-block open-air pedestrian mall, a landscaped strip of outdoor cafés, vendor carts, and colorful kiosks purveying food and merchandise. Overhead is a 90-foot-high steel-mesh "celestial vault"; at night, it is the *Sky Parade,* a high-tech light-and-laser show (the canopy is equipped with more than 2.1 million lights) enhanced by a concert hall-quality sound system, which takes place four times nightly. You're more likely to hear Ol' Blue Eyes than Pink Floyd, and it's just slightly cheesy, but still good gawking fun. Shows rotate throughout the night and seasonally (the Christmas show is a lot of fun). Aerialists and live bands perform between shows on some nights. The crowd it attracts is more upscale than in years past, and of course, downtown is a lot less crowded than the hectic Strip.

Fitzgeralds hotel has an upstairs balcony and a downstairs **McDonald's** that both offer good views of the show.

On Fremont St., between Main St. and Las Vegas Blvd. ☎ *702-678-5777. Internet:* www.vegasexperience.com. *Admission: Free. Open: Nightly, with shows every hour, on the hour, from dusk to midnight.*

Grand Canal Shoppes at The Venetian
Center Strip

If you haven't made it to Venice this year, you might try strolling through the grand shopping arcade at **The Venetian.** Oh, it's not really like being in

Venice, but between the nifty Venetian facades, the recreation of St. Mark's Square and other Venetian landmarks, the actual canal complete with singing gondoliers (who will give you a ride if you give them money), the flower girls who sing arias, and the attentions of a flirty Casanova, it's not an unacceptable substitute. Costumed characters roam the area, bursting into song or interacting with visitors, while glassblowers and other sales booths inhabit the square. As if this weren't enjoyable enough, there are over 70 brand-name stores where you can drop all your gambling winnings.

3355 Las Vegas Blvd. S. (in The Venetian). ☎ *702-414-1000. Open: Sun – Thurs 10 a.m. – 11 p.m., Fri – Sat 10 a.m. – 12 a.m.*

Imperial Palace Auto Collection
Center Strip

What did JFK, Hitler, Hirohito, Elvis, Liberace, and W.C. Fields all have in common? They all had cars. (Yes, they are also all dead. Don't be cheeky.) And some of their cars are here on display. You can long for the return of horse-and-buggy days, and still enjoy this extensive collection of classic automobiles and trucks, some of which belonged to prominent political and entertainment figures, and nearly all of which show that well-designed vehicles can be works of art. Allow one to two hours to tour the collection.

There are often people passing out free tickets to see the collection in front of the hotel, and there are often special discounts available through their Web site.

3535 Las Vegas Blvd. S. (in the Imperial Palace). ☎ *702-731-3311. Internet:* www. autocollections.com. *Admission: $6.95 adults, $3 seniors and children under 12, and free for children under 5 and AAA members. Open: Daily 9:30 a.m. – 11:30 p.m.*

King Tut's Tomb and Museum
South Strip

He was buried in his jammies. . . .Yep, Tut-O-Mania lives on here at this full-scale mock-up of the great Egyptian king's tomb, meticulously repro-duced according to historical records. ("Born in Babylonia, moved to . . . Nevada?") Everything was re-created with painstaking detail, with the replicas handcrafted in Egypt. It's hardly like seeing the real thing, but if you aren't going to Egypt any time soon, checking it out isn't a bad idea — and for a Vegas fake, it's surprisingly enjoyable. Audio tours are available in four languages.

3900 Las Vegas Blvd. S. (in the Luxor). ☎ *702-262-4000. Admission: $5. Open: Sun – Thurs 9 a.m. – 11 p.m., Fri – Sat 9 a.m. – 1 a.m.*

Liberace Museum
Off the Beaten Path

Class. Subtlety. Taste. You won't find any of that here! God love Liberace, and I wouldn't have it any other way. Whether you're a fan of the outrageous performer or not, this "museum" is a must for Vegas visitors. Costumes (bejeweled), many cars (bejeweled), many pianos (bejeweled), and many jewels (also bejeweled) fill multiple buildings, all celebrating the camp silliness that was Liberace (the patron saint of Veg — oh, no, wait, that was Bacchus). You can also see his 50-pound, $50,000 rhinestone and a gift shop with countless knickknacks of increasing tackiness. It's campy fun, so don't take it too seriously. Two hours (if you're counting rhinestones) is plenty of time to see it all.

Flash photography may result in blindness around all those stones!

1775 E. Tropicana Ave. (at Spencer St. about 3 miles west of the Strip on the right).☎ 702-798-5595. Admission: $6.95 adults, $4.95 seniors over 60 and students, free for children under 12. Open: Mon – Sat 10 a.m. – 5 p.m., Sun 1 p.m. – 5 p.m.

Lied Discovery Children's Museum
Off the Beaten Path

A hands-on science museum designed for curious kids, the bright, airy, two-story **Lied** makes an ideal outing for toddlers and young children. Clever, thought-inducing exhibits are everywhere. Learn how it feels to be disabled by playing basketball from a wheelchair. See how much sunscreen their giant stuffed mascot needs to keep from burning. Drop-in art classes are offered on weekend afternoons. Teenagers will probably find it a big yawn, but it's a terrific diversion for younger kids (as long as you don't tell them it's educational), and adults will enjoy it, too.

833 Las Vegas Blvd. N. (about 1½ miles north of Fremont). ☎ 702-382-5437. Admission: $5 adults, $4 seniors and children 2 – 17. Open: Tues – Sun 10 a.m. – 5 p.m.

Luxor IMAX Theater/In Search of the Obelisk
South Strip

The **Luxor IMAX** is a state-of-the-art theater that projects either standard two-dimensional or high-tech 3-D films onto a giant seven-story screen. You'll wear a cool 3-D headset that includes built-in speakers for total environment immersion. Movies change regularly, so call ahead to find out what's playing. If you don't like heights, request a lower-level seat.

In Search of the Obelisk is a simulator ride that mimics flight through a dangerous catacomb using video, sound, and motion technology (the seats move). If you're prone to motion sickness, you may choose a non-motion version of the ride, but even that can make you a bit queasy.

North Strip Attractions

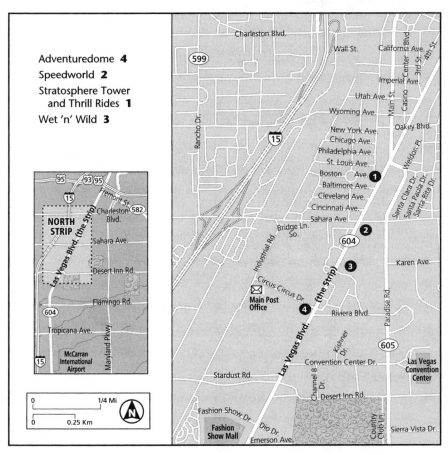

Adventuredome **4**
Speedworld **2**
Stratosphere Tower
and Thrill Rides **1**
Wet 'n' Wild **3**

3900 Las Vegas Blvd. S. (in the Luxor). ☎ *702-262-4000. Admission: $7.95 for 2-D films, $8.95 for 3-D films. In Search of the Obelisk, $6.00. Open: Sun – Thurs 9 a.m. – 11 p.m., Fri – Sat 9 a.m. – 1 a.m. IMAX show times vary, depending on the length of the film.*

Madame Tussaud's Celebrity Encounter
Center Strip

Forget any cheesy wax museum you may have previously visited — they are all amateurs compared to the genuine (though still a wee bit hokey) art created by the legendary Madame Tussaud's. (The original is still the most popular tourist attraction in London.) Waxing nostalgic? Every figure here is a noted figure in the entertainment or sports world, and you're free to get up close to take pictures with them. There is also a section where you can see the incredible, painstaking effort that goes into perfectly replicating a celebrity in wax. I miss the famously ghoulish "Chamber of Horrors," but at least this way, you don't have to worry about scaring your kids. As a bonus, think about how nicely air-conditioned this exhibit has to be!

3355 Las Vegas Blvd. S. (in The Venetian). ☎ 702-990-3530. Admission: $12.50. Open: 10 a.m. – 10 p.m. daily.

Manhattan Express Roller Coaster
South Strip

Apparently, the designers of **New York-New York** didn't think their little Big Apple looked busy enough, so they threw in a roller coaster. It's designed to look like a New York City cab, and it plummets, loops, and rolls in and around the hotel's re-created New York skyline. A unique feature of the ride is the barrel-roll drop, which turns you upside down and then drops you straight toward the ground. (And you thought nothing was as scary as a New York City cab ride.) It's not for the faint of heart. Enter through the second-level arcade and be prepared for a long line. You need to be at least 54 inches tall to ride.

3790 Las Vegas Blvd. S. (in the New York-New York). ☎ 702-740-6969. Admission: $10. Open: Sun – Thurs 10 a.m. – 11 p.m., Fri – Sat 10 a.m. – 11:30 p.m.

Masquerade Village Show in the Sky
Center Strip

Spend enough time in a casino, and you might swear you see Mardi Gras parades floating in the sky. Oh, wait, it's the **Rio's** free carnival-themed extravaganza! Phew, that had me worried there for a moment. Giant Mardi Gras–style floats filled with singers, dancers, and musicians travel on tracks in the ceiling two stories above the floor, while on an adjacent stage, you find more performers and gigantic animal puppets. If you prefer interactive entertainment, you can actually pay to get in costume and ride one of the floats.

3700 W. Flamingo Rd. (in the Rio Hotel & Casino, just east of I-15). ☎ 702-252-7777. Admission: Free to view, $12.95 to participate. Open: Shows every 2 hours, Sun – Tues 12 p.m. – 10 p.m., Thurs – Sat 1 p.m. – 11 p.m.

MGM Grand Adventures
South Strip

An amusement park on the Vegas Strip may seem redundant, but here's one of the more conventional sort. It's a nice enough spot to while away a few hours — especially if you're a teen and the weather is cooperating. Although it does have all the basics, the park seems to have more food stands and T-shirt emporiums than rides, leaving you with the impression that fun has a lot to do with the contents of one's pocketbook and/or stomach. The best thrill costs you extra: The **Sky Screamer** is a bungee jump/swing that makes you feel like you're flying.

3799 Las Vegas Blvd. S. (behind the MGM Grand Hotel/Casino). ☎ *800-929-1111. Admission: Entry plus unlimited rides $10 for everyone over 42 inches tall, free if you're not. Sky Screamer $35 for one person, $30 each for two people, $25 each for three people (includes park admission). Open: Daily; hours vary seasonally.*

The Mirage Volcano
Center Strip

After dark, this active "volcano" erupts every 15 minutes, spewing fire 100 feet above the lagoons below. To be honest, it's not very volcano-like, but it's still pretty cool. Instead of lava flow, expect a really neat light show, and you won't mind a bit. The show lasts only a few minutes, but the price is right — free!

Get there at least 10 minutes before the spewing starts for the best vantage point near the main driveway entrance.

3400 Las Vegas Blvd. S. (in front of The Mirage). ☎ *702-791-7111. Admission: Free. Open: Eruptions take place every 15 minutes from dusk – 1 a.m.*

Race for Atlantis IMAX 3-D Ride
Center Strip

The Forum Shops' contribution to the virtual-reality, motion-simulator craze is enjoyable, if not as spectacular as the **Las Vegas Hilton's Star Trek** ride (of course, that one will lighten your wallet a bit more). After you strap on your 3-D visor with built-in speakers, you're off on a four-minute wild chariot race through the lost city of Atlantis. With the 3-D glasses, the experience can get pretty intense and it's not for the weak of stomach.

If you like a bumpy ride, be sure to sit in the very front or very back.

3500 Las Vegas Blvd. S. (in The Forum Shops at Caesars Palace). ☎ *702-733-9000. Admission: $9.50 adults, $6.75 children under 12. Open: Sun – Thurs 10 a.m. – 11 p.m., Fri – Sat 10 a.m. – 12 a.m. The ride lasts 20 minutes once you get inside.*

The Secret Garden of Siegfried and Roy/The Mirage Dolphin Habitat
Center Strip

The Secret Garden is a small zoo where rare lions, tigers, leopards, and the like from **Siegfried and Roy's** show are exhibited while they aren't on stage or at home with S & R (yes, they really do live with the boys). Guests get earphones so they can listen to prerecorded facts and fun tidbits about the animals. The **Dolphin Habitat** allows you to play "catch" with and learn about our flippered friends. Playing ball with the dolphins is a thrill; see if singing the theme song to *Flipper* makes them toss it to you more often. You can also visit the gift shop and café. Allow about two hours, but you can stay as long as you like.

3400 Las Vegas Blvd. S. (behind The Mirage). ☎ 702-791-7111. Admission: $10 (except Wed, when it's $5 for the Dolphin Habitat only). Free for children under 11. Open: Secret Garden open Mon, Tues, Thurs, Fri 11 a.m. – 5 p.m., Sat – Sun 10 a.m. – 5 p.m. Dolphin Habitat open Mon – Fri 11 a.m. – 7 p.m., Sat – Sun 10 a.m. – 7 p.m. Dolphin exhibit open only on Wed, when the Secret Garden is closed; admission $5. Hours subject to change and vary by season.

Speedworld
North Strip

This wild, eight-minute motion-simulator ride puts you in replicas of NASCAR-style racers (three-fourths the size of the real cars) and lets you careen through the Las Vegas Motor Speedway or around (and even inside — whoops, there went **The Forum Shops**) the hotels on the Strip and downtown. The realistic detail — down to the wind in your hair and the required pit stops if you crash — is impressive. Adjacent 3-D-motion theaters take you on similar races as a group experience. Added to the experience in 2000, **Speed: The Ride** is a wild roller coaster that blasts you through loops and dips, even the marquee of the hotel, before you go up a tower and then do the whole thing backward.

2535 Las Vegas Blvd. S. (in the Sahara Hotel & Casino). ☎ 702-737-2111. Admission: NASCAR simulator $8 (you must be at least 48 inches tall and less than 300 pounds to ride), 3-D simulator $3, Speed: The Ride (roller coaster) $7. Open: Daily at 10 a.m.; closing hours vary seasonally but usually 10 p.m.

Star Trek: The Experience
Paradise Road

Beam me up, Scotty! It's not a five-year mission — more like a few good minutes on a state-of-the-art motion-simulator ride. Your Star Trek "Experience" kicks off with a self-guided tour of Star Trek memorabilia and clips from the TV and movie series, where Klingons and other aliens interact with you. Next, you are "beamed aboard" the *Enterprise* (wayyy cool!) and board a shuttlecraft that takes you on a virtual — and bumpy — ride through space. Gift shops and eateries (take home a Tribble) are adjacent. Die-hard Trekkies will be delighted, and others may find themselves pleasantly surprised.

If this is a must-see on your list, come early; the lines here can often stretch for light years.

3000 Paradise Rd. (in the Las Vegas Hilton). ☎ 800-GO-BOLDLY. Admission: $14.95. Open: Daily 11 a.m. – 11 p.m.

Stratosphere Tower and Thrill Rides
North Strip

If you think confronting your fears is the best way of dealing with them, come test your vertigo here. You can get a spectacular view of Vegas and the surrounding landscape from the indoor and outdoor observation decks of this 110-story tower. Adrenaline junkies (or the certifiably insane) can try the **Let It Ride** roller coaster — the world's highest, situated 1,000 feet in the air — which zooms around the outside of the tower. Or, you can send your blood pressure skyrocketing on the **Big Shot,** an open car that rockets up 160 feet to the tip of the tower before dropping back down in a bungee effect. Only for the truly adventurous. *Note:* The rides are shut down on windy days. Thank goodness.

2000 Las Vegas Blvd. S. (in Stratosphere Las Vegas). ☎ *702-380-7777. Admission: $6 for tower access, $5 for the roller coaster, $6 for the Big Shot, $14 for tower access and both rides. Minimum height to ride the rides is 48 inches. Open: Sun – Thurs 10 a.m. – 12 a.m., Fri – Sat 9 a.m. – 1 a.m. (weather permitting).*

Treasure Island Pirate Battle
Center Strip

Ahoy there maties. Here's the scuttlebutt on this star of the Strip: It's set on Buccaneer Bay — an 18th-century port village, and the show features a live-action battle (with actors and stunt people) between a full-scale British frigate and a pirate ship. Nope, I'm not kidding. If you like lots of booms and action, you'll love this! The show includes cannons and explosions, sword fights with sailors, and pirates swinging on ropes and falling into the water. Yo ho ho and a bottle of rum! It all ends with one of the ships sinking grandly into the bay — but I won't ruin the finale by telling you which one.

It's free, but get there at least 30 minutes before show time for a good viewing spot — preferably on the gangplank that leads into the casino.

3300 Las Vegas Blvd. S. (in front of Treasure Island). ☎ *702-894-7111. Admission: Free. Open: Battles every 90 minutes 4:00 p.m. – 11:30 p.m.*

Wet 'n' Wild
North Strip

The latest strip bar . . . no, no, just kidding. Unless your trunks fall off when you hit the water, this is entirely a family destination, and a particularly blessed one on hot days. The 26-acre water park is filled with a variety of thrill rides (including a 45-mph drop into a "bottomless" pool) and water slides plus a lazy river and a beach for those looking for more sedentary activities. There's even a video arcade if one kid wants to get wet and the other doesn't. What it isn't, is restful, especially if you don't appreciate the squeals and giggles of children; the noise level can make even the endless clang of a casino seem like a library.

2601 Las Vegas Blvd. S. (just south of the Sahara Hotel & Casino). ☎ *702-737-3819. Admission: $23.95 adults, $16.95 children under 10, $10.95 seniors over 55, free for children under 3. Open: April 30 – Sept 30 daily 10 a.m. – 6 or 8 p.m. Season and hours vary, so call ahead.*

Chapter 17

Getting the Full Effect: Other Cool Things to See and Do

. . . .

In This Chapter

▶ Entertaining your kids and teens

▶ Getting hitched in Las Vegas

▶ Scoping out museums and cultural activities

▶ Heading out to Henderson

▶ Working out in Las Vegas

▶ Attending sporting events

▶ Taking an organized tour

. . . .

*Y*ou really have to work at it to be bored in Las Vegas. If you like constant action and variety, then this is the place for you. Vegas is alive from dawn until, well, dawn — and I don't mean just the gambling. The attractions I list in Chapter 16 are the real biggies, but they're definitely not the only things to do. Read through this chapter and see what strikes your fancy.

All the attractions mentioned in this chapter can be found on the maps in Chapter 16 and throughout this chapter.

Especially for Kids

For a New York–minute, Vegas tried to position itself as a suitable family destination — this despite being a town built around gambling, drinking, and sex. While these are all fine pursuits if you are over the magical age of 21, for the underage crowd, the Strip is something of a drag. The great "Vegas Is Really for Families" marketing campaign failed, precisely because gambling, drinking, and sex are more profitable than thrill-park rides and kiddie shows. Nevertheless, the city recognizes that you may have occasion to bring children to town, so there are some entertainment options for the little rug rats in addition to those marked with a Kid Friendly icon in Chapter 16.

Scandia Family Fun Center
Off the Beaten Path

You know this is a good bet for families when you notice it's where the locals bring their kids. There's a very sweet miniature golf course, bumper boats, miniature-car racing, and a slightly run-down video arcade. If your young 'uns have hit double digits, you may also want to check out **GameWorks.**

2900 Sirius Ave. ☎ 702-364-0070. Take Sahara Avenue west to Rancho Drive (just past I-15), turn left, and go about one-half mile; Scandia is on your right. Admission: Free, but you pay a fee for each game or activity. Super Saver Pass $11 (includes a round of miniature golf, two rides, and five game tokens); Unlimited Wristband Package $16 (includes unlimited bumper boat and car rides, unlimited miniature golf, and ten tokens for batting cages or arcade games). Hours vary seasonally, so call ahead.

Circus Circus Midway
North Strip

Another solid, time-tested bet. Back in the pre-"Vegas Is for Families" days, this was about the only option for kids around. Your kids will enjoy carnival games (complete with prizes) and arcade games. While they are having fun, they can catch circus acts — trapeze artists, stunt cyclists, jugglers, magicians, and acrobats — that perform continuously under the big top every day from 11 a.m. – 12 a.m.

2880 Las Vegas Blvd. S. (in Circus Circus). ☎ 702-734-0410. Open: Daily, 24 hours. Admission: Free; game prices vary.

Southern Nevada Zoological and Botanical Park
Off the Beaten Path

The zoo itself is on the smallish side, but it boasts more than 250 species from around the world, plus a petting zoo for younger kids. Do remember that it can get quite hot in the desert, so if the animals are sleeping in the shade when you come by, that's just because they are smart and don't go out in the noonday sun. Try to time a visit for cooler early morning or late afternoon hours to see the most activity.

1775 N. Rancho Dr. ☎ 702-648-5955. To get there, take Charleston west from the Strip to Rancho Drive and turn right. It's up about 2½ miles on your left. Admission: $5 for adults and $3 for seniors and kids under 12. Open: Daily 9 a.m. – 5 p.m.

Keeping the kids busy at video arcades

Also of note are the video-game arcades in the **New York-New York, Excalibur,** and **Luxor** hotels. All are large and feature lots of high- (and low-) tech diversions for the kids. **New York-New York's,** in particular, is nicely done, modeled more or less on Coney Island, with plenty of non-video arcade games.

Many of the video- and carnival-game arcades offer winners of certain games tickets that can be redeemed for merchandise. Now, this could just be a way to get the little tykes introduced to the idea of gambling at an early age. But one hopes your kids will learn pretty quickly that spending $10 on Skee-Ball just to win a stuffed animal worth a buck doesn't make much sense. (On the other hand, those stuffed animals can be pretty cute.)

Especially for Teens

If Vegas is frustrating for kids, it's even more frustrating for teens, who can see the promised land, in the form of slot machines, glistening in the distance (or, more accurately, at their elbow), tantalizing them, but remaining untouchable for a few more years. If they even slow down (as they pass through the casino to the outside world) to gawk when someone hits a jackpot, security guards show up to hustle them along.

What to do? Well, send them off on the thrill rides listed in Chapter 16, to the video arcades listed in this chapter, or to your hotel pool. And there is always shopping (see Chapter 18). Following is one place that caters to the teen scene.

GameWorks
South Strip

This 47,000-square-foot facility boasts the latest interactive video games (some of them designed by Steven Spielberg's Dreamworks company), motion-simulator rides, plus a giant rock-climbing wall, and such mundane games as air hockey and pool. This is more adult arcade fun, often too sophisticated for those under ten — or at least, without parents to hover over and help, which takes precious time away from all the big fun said parents could be having themselves. It's also the perfect place for your teens to get their ya-yas out.

3785 Las Vegas Blvd. S. (located in the Showcase Mall just north of the MGM Grand Hotel/Casino). ☎ *702-432-GAME. Open: Sun – Thurs 10 a.m. – 2 a.m., Fri – Sat, 10 a.m. – 3 a.m.*

Going to the Chapel

Birds do it, bees do it, even Carmen Electra and Dennis Rodman did it — got married in Vegas, that is. (Okay, birds and bees don't bother with ceremony, but it worked as a line, all right?) And you can, too, with tremendous ease. I profoundly hope you put some more thought into this step than did Ms. Electra and Mr. Rodman, but regardless, this is a most accommodating town for impulsive lovers. All you need is a license, a couple of minutes, and someone to recite vows with you. More than 100,000 weddings are performed in Las Vegas annually. The two busiest days are Valentine's Day (some chapels perform more than 80 services in one day) and New Year's Eve.

Many of the major hotels have wedding chapels and services, but you'll find the bulk of the independent places between the Strip and downtown on Las Vegas Boulevard. In the following listings, I list a few of my favorite wedding venues, but remember that you have many to choose from. Cruise the chapels and pick the one that appeals to you the most. Note that fees vary depending on what kind of ceremony you opt for, so call the chapel ahead of time for prices. Even if you're not getting married, you may be able to watch other couples tie the knot. Just ask. You can decide for yourself whether a $100, 15-minute wedding is as likely to last as that $50,000 ceremony with its badly dressed bridesmaids.

Clark County Marriage License Bureau
Off the Beaten Path

Your first stop on your way to marital bliss has to be at the courthouse to visit the **Clark County Marriage License Bureau.** All they require is for both of you to be there and for one of you to have $35. That's it — not even a blood test.

200 S. 3rd St. ☎ 702-455-3156. Open: Daily, 8 a.m. – 12 a.m., except on legal holidays, when they are open 24 hours.

Cupid's Wedding Chapel
North Strip

This chapel offers a pretty simple and straightforward setting. It's the staff that sets this place apart; they provide genuine warmth and an infectious sense of romance. (It's probably not their fault that Axel Rose's marriage, begun here, lasted but a few turbulent months.)

827 Las Vegas Blvd. S. ☎ 800-543-2933. Internet: www.cupidswedding.com. *Open: Mon – Thurs 8 a.m. – 10 p.m., Fri – Sat 8 a.m. – 12 a.m., Sun 9 a.m. – 9 p.m.*

Las Vegas Wedding Chapels

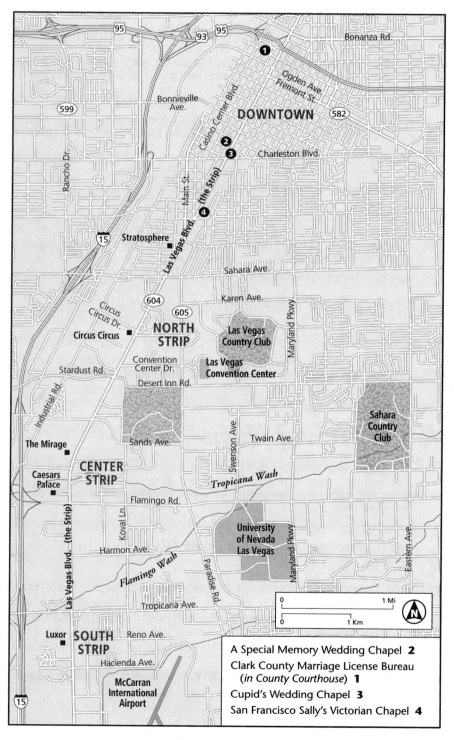

A Special Memory Wedding Chapel **2**

Clark County Marriage License Bureau
(*in County Courthouse*) **1**

Cupid's Wedding Chapel **3**

San Francisco Sally's Victorian Chapel **4**

A Special Memory Wedding Chapel
Off the Beaten Path

Here you find a more traditional style, with somewhat less of a Vegas approach to weddings. It's a clean, modern new building complete with a church-like steeple and a demi-shopping arcade for flowers, tuxes, and the like. If you're in a hurry, you can even use their drive-up window! (So much for it not being too Vegas.)

800 S. Fourth St. at Gass Ave. ☎ ***800-9-MARRYU.*** *Internet:* www.aspecialmemory. com. *Fees: $25 for drive-up service. Open: Sun – Thurs 8 a.m. – 10 p.m., Fri – Sat 8 a.m. – 12 a.m.*

San Francisco Sally's Victorian Chapel
North Strip

If you want something really small, but even more sweet, head to **San Francisco Sally's Victorian Chapel,** a tiny place that fits maybe four more guests in addition to the Couple of the Moment. But what it lacks in space, it makes up for in heart.

1304 Las Vegas Blvd. S. ☎ ***800-658-8677.*** *Internet:* www.zip2.com/klas-tv/ sfsally. *Open: Mon – Thurs 10 a.m. – 6 p.m., Fri – Sat 10 a.m. – 8 p.m., Sun 10 a.m. – 4 p.m.*

If you want to find out more about getting hitched in Vegas, make a call to **Las Vegas Weddings and Rooms** (☎ **800-488-MATE**), or surf over to the **Wedding Dreams** Web site at www.weddingdreams.com.

If You're Sick of Neon

Just about everything in Las Vegas has some neon on it — even the 7-11 and the airport parking garages. If it all gets a little much for you, there are places you can go that don't involve bright lights, marble, and concrete.

The University of Nevada Las Vegas (UNLV)
Paradise Road

Yes, it has concrete, but it also has lots of beautifully landscaped paths wandering throughout the campus. It's basically an arboretum with a wide array of plants, trees, and flowers, all of which are drought-resistant. Strolling through here is a beautiful and relaxing distraction — although, on hot days, a sweaty one.

4505 Maryland Pkwy. ☎ ***800-334-UNLV.*** *Internet:* www.unlv.edu. *Located between Paradise Road and Maryland Parkway, just east of the Strip and just north of Tropicana Avenue.*

Natural History Museum
Paradise Road

This attractive, if simplistic, display of Native American craftwork and Las Vegas history is conveniently located on the grounds of **UNLV**. It's more of a small-town than big-city museum, but it's free. They have snakes in glass cages, and air-conditioning.

At UNLV, located between Paradise Rd. and Maryland Pkwy., just east of the Strip and just north of Tropicana Ave. ☎ 702-895-3381. Open Mon – Fri 8:00 a.m. – 4:45 p.m., Sat 10 a.m. – 2 p.m.

Lorenzi Park
Off the Beaten Path

If you want to ditch the glitz and enjoy a lake, a few museums, playgrounds, jogging paths, and acres of grassy lawns and lush gardens, **Lorenzi Park** is the place for you. This, the largest park in Las Vegas, is located just west of **Rancho Drive,** northwest of the Strip.

Washington St. Take Charleston Boulevard west from the Strip, turn right on Rancho Drive, and travel about 2 miles to Washington Street and turn left. You see the park on your left in a few short blocks.

Sunset Park
Off the Beaten Path

This is another enjoyable park, if you don't mind a little airport noise (it's located just south of **McCarran International Airport**). It offers jogging paths, a swimming pool, tennis and volleyball courts, playgrounds, a lake, and lots of real plants to make up for the fake ones inside most casinos.

Corner Eastern and Sunset Rd. Head south on the Strip to Sunset Rd., turn left, and go a couple of miles to Eastern. The park is on the southeast corner.

Clark County Heritage Museum
Off the Beaten Path

Here you can go through 12,000 years of local history, including exhibits on Native American tribes, pioneer settlements, the gold-rush era, and the dawn of gambling (with old slot machines and a life-size statue of Bugsy Siegel). The 25-acre facility also has an authentic ghost town and several houses from the early to mid-1900s that have been fully restored with period furnishings.

1830 S. Boulder Hwy. ☎ 702-455-7955. Open: Daily 9 a.m. – 4:30 p.m. Admission: $1.50 for adults and $1 for seniors and kids 3 – 15. To get there, take Tropicana Avenue east to Boulder Highway and turn right. It's down about 8 miles on your left.

Las Vegas Art Museum
Off the Beaten Path

Hey, more art! Art that's not in a hotel, but in a lovely facility built just for art!

9600 W. Sahara, 5 miles west of the Strip on Sahara Ave. in a big white building. ☎ *702-360-8000. Open: Tues – Sat 10 a.m. – 5 p.m., Sun 1 p.m. – 5 p.m. Admission: $3 for adults, $2 for seniors, and $1 for students; children under 12 enter free.*

Las Vegas Natural History Museum
North Strip

Not to be confused with the snakes 'n' stuff over at the UNLV **Natural History Museum,** in this one you've got exhibits of (stuffed) bears, elk, and the like, plus a few roaring dinosaurs. There's also a hands-on activity room great for kids, and a gift shop for you. In truth, the exhibits are a bit moldy and creaky, but there's not a speck of neon anywhere in sight.

900 Las Vegas Blvd. N. ☎ *702-384-3466. Internet:* www.vegaswebworld. com/lvnahistory/. *Open: Daily, 9 a.m. – 4 p.m. Admission: $5 for adults; $4 for seniors, students, and military personnel; and $2.50 for children 4 – 12. It's a couple of miles north of downtown.*

Guinness World of Records Museum
North Strip

If the **Liberace Museum** strikes you as being too highbrow, then this museum celebrating the achievements listed in the *Guinness Book of Records* (such as the collection belonging to Louise, the Magnet Lady) in hilarious fashion will tickle your fancy. You may find some neon here though, so you have been warned.

2780 Las Vegas Blvd. S. (on the Strip just north of Circus Circus). ☎ *702-792-3766. Open: Daily, 9 a.m. – 6 p.m. Admission: $4.95 for adults, $3.95 for seniors and students, and $2.95 for children 5 – 12.*

For the Neon Lover

Face it, no matter how hard you try, it's hard to avoid neon in Las Vegas. The stuff is so much a part of the city that it should not come as a surprise that Vegas authorities have moved to preserve some of the city's neon treasures.

The Neon Museum

Downtown

Barbara Mulasky is heading up a terrific project for the city called **The Neon Museum.** The museum is helping to preserve a piece of Vegas history by rescuing classic neon signs, restoring them, and putting them on public display. Given how fast bits of Las Vegas get tossed into the wastebasket of memory, this project is a most worthy one. After all, these signs are what originally gave Vegas its unique look. They deserve better, and it's nice to know some are getting it. At the end of the *Fremont Street Experience* (see Chapter 16), you'll find the horse and rider from the **Hacienda Hotel,** the genie's lamp from the **Aladdin Hotel,** the Anderson Dairy Milkman, and the Chief Motel Motorcourt sign, among others prominently displayed. There are plans to construct an indoor facility to house smaller signs that the museum has in its collection.

Located at Fremont St. and Las Vegas Blvd. ☎ *702-229-4872. No fee.*

For the Willie Wonka Worshipper

Henderson is a community just southeast of Las Vegas, about a 20- or 25-minute drive from the Strip, where you'll find a functioning candy factory that offers tours. Next door is a clown figurine factory that is probably worth skipping, except that it's right there.

The fastest way to get to Henderson is to take the Strip south to **Sunset Road,** about a mile past the last of the big hotels. Turn left, and it's a straight shot across to **Mountain Vista,** where you'll find **Ethel M. Chocolates.**

Ethel M. Chocolates

Henderson

If you're a chocolate lover like me, come take a self-guided tour to see how chocolate and other candy is made. You even get samples in the adjoining gift shop. (Not enough samples, though, if you ask me.) By the way, out back is a surprisingly attractive, 2½-acre garden featuring rare cacti. If I wasn't such a chocoholic, I would say this is the real reason for coming here. Do not expect Oompa-Loompas.

2 Cactus Garden Dr. ☎ *702-433-2500. Open: Daily (except Christmas) from 8:30 a.m. – 7 p.m., although it's best to visit on a weekday when the business is up and running. Admission: Free. You can catch the free shuttle from M&M World on the Strip (see Chapter 16).*

For the Sports Minded

For many years, recreation in Las Vegas meant lying by the pool, and exercise came in the form of pulling handles on slot machines. But when **The Mirage** opened in the late 1980s, it signaled a change in attitude that would revolutionize the way visitors spent their time. This major resort was the first in town to offer such an unprecedented array of sporting and exercise alternatives. Sure, there were other hotels in town that had golf courses and health clubs, but nobody did it quite the way The Mirage did. Virtually every major hotel built since then has tried to imitate The Mirage's success. Odds are that your own hotel will have a huge array of options, and probably even a full-fledged spa.

Biking

If you're a biking fanatic, or just want to take a gentle cruise through the city (or outlying areas), Vegas has plenty to offer. Just be careful of the traffic — many of the Vegas drivers are tourists and may not be as careful in these unfamiliar surroundings.

Escape the City Streets

Escape the City Streets is a rental company that offers 21-speed mountain bikes for your riding pleasure. They'll even drop your bike off for you at any downtown or Strip hotel.

Consider taking a trip out to Red Rock Canyon using Charleston Boulevard. There's a nice wide bike lane starting at Rainbow Lane (in the western part of town) that runs all the way to the canyon's visitor center, about 11 challenging but not impossible miles in total. If you're really in good shape, you might consider a bike tour of the canyon itself. Contact the **Red Rock Canyon Visitors Center** (☎ 702-363-1921) or ask the bike rental agent for other options.

8221 W. Charleston Blvd. ☎ 702-596-2953. Rates: $30 for the first day, $24 for a half day or whole consecutive days, and $90 for a week (major credit card required).

Bowling

Bowlers can find a few good spots to knock down some pins, if the mood, um, strikes. And since Las Vegas hosts major Professional Bowlers Association tournaments every year, you know the city has some of the biggest and most modern facilities in the world. Here are some good recommendations:

The Showboat Hotel Bowling Center
Off the Beaten Path

One of the best bowling centers in town is **The Showboat Hotel Bowling Center,** which is southeast of downtown. With 106 lanes, it's the largest bowling center in North America. Everything is spotless and high-tech, with a variety of food stands and shops adjacent.

2800 E. Fremont St. ☎ 702-385-9153. Fees: $2.25 per game; $1.75 shoe rental. Open: Daily, 24-hours. To get there from the Strip, take Las Vegas Boulevard north to Charleston, and turn right. The hotel is at the intersection of Charleston and Fremont, about 3 miles away.

Orleans
Off the Beaten Path

Orleans has a great 70-lane facility. It's on the second floor of the hotel, which you'll see on your right as you travel west from the Strip on Tropicana Ave.

4500 W. Tropicana Ave. ☎ 702-365-7400. Fees: $2.35 per game; $1.50 shoe rental. Open: Daily, 24-hours.

Bungee jumping

If you're the thrill-seeking type, bungee jumping may be more your speed. And yes, Vegas offers this adrenaline-pumping activity for those brave enough to try it.

A.J. Hackett Bungy
North Strip

This place has a 175-foot tower where you can take a flying leap. They offer a variety of price packages, some of which include membership, T-shirts, and videotapes of your bungee jump. They swear they've never lost anyone yet. They're located next to **Circus Circus,** just west of the Strip.

810 Circus Circus Dr. ☎ 702-385-4321. Admission: $49 for first jump, $29 for second and third. Prices include membership and T-shirt. Videotapes of jumps cost $20 each. Open: Hours vary, so call ahead for more information.

Golfing

Las Vegas is a favorite destination for the PGA's annual tour, so it makes sense that the city has dozens of great golf courses for you to try.

If you're an avid golfer and intend to play the links in Las Vegas, consider bringing your own clubs. I know of more than one golfer who didn't want to haul his equipment halfway across the country but was horrified at the outrageous rental fees at the local courses.

Angel Park Golf Club
Off the Beaten Path

One notable course is the **Angel Park Golf Club,** which has a 36-hole, par-70/71 public course that was designed by Arnold Palmer. Pretty spiffy, in my humble opinion.

100 S. Rampart Blvd. ☎ 702-254-4653. Greens fees: $45 – $125. Open: Hours vary, call for times. To get here, take the Strip to Charleston Blvd. and travel west about 10 miles; then turn right on Rampart.

The Desert Inn Golf Club
North Strip

The Desert Inn Golf Club is considered by many golf pros to be one of America's best. It has an 18-hole, par-72 resort course, and everything except for the driving range is open to non-hotel guests.

Note: At press time, the closure of the Desert Inn was not expected to affect the golf course until sometime in late 2001, however, it would be wise to call ahead to make sure the course is still open.

3145 Las Vegas Blvd. S. ☎ 800-634-6906 or 702-733-4290. Greens fees: $160 – $225. Open: Daily. Reservations are required and can be booked up to 90 days in advance for a Sun – Thurs tee time and two days in advance for a Fri or Sat tee time.

Las Vegas National Golf Club
Paradise Road

Another exceptional course is located at the **Las Vegas National Golf Club,** which was formerly part of the **Las Vegas Hilton Country Club.** You can find their 18-hole, par-71 public course just past Paradise Road on your left.

1911 Desert Inn Rd. ☎ 702-796-0016. Greens fees: $50 – $175. Open: Daily; hours vary.

Health clubs

Just about every hotel in town has a health club/spa, so you'll probably find a place to work out without a problem. We especially like the outstanding facilities at **The Mirage, Bellagio,** the **Golden Nugget,** and **Caesars Palace,** which features a rock-climbing wall and Zen meditation garden. And if you feel the need to work out at 3 a.m., the Luxor has the only hotel health club that is open 24 hours a day.

Canyon Ranch Spa
Center Strip

Better still, but so costly I have trouble even typing in the numbers, is the **Canyon Ranch Spa** at **The Venetian.** This is an outpost of what is generally considered the finest spa in America. For sheer physical beauty (and I'm not even talking about the clientele) and the vast number of exotic services offered (like Subtle Energy Therapies that use Reiki healing methods), this place has no equal in town. However, the prices are virtually prohibitive. A day pass will set you back $25 and a 50-minute facial will run you $135.

3355 Las Vegas Blvd. S., (in The Venetian). ☎ ***877-220-2688*** *(toll-free); 702-414-3600. Internet:* www.canyonranch.com. *Admission: Spa packages available. Hours: Daily 5:30 a.m. – 10 p.m.*

Harrah's Las Vegas Health Club
Center Strip

If your hotel doesn't offer what you want, you can check out the health club at **Harrah's Las Vegas,** which is one of the few hotel facilities that is open to the general public. Don't miss the virtual-reality cycles and stair climbers that allow you to steer through various courses (island, snowscape, and more). They even simulate the wind blowing through your hair and have soundtracks accompanying the on-screen action. They're perfect distractions for people who hate to exercise or at least need something to keep their minds off the pain.

3475 Las Vegas Blvd. S. ☎ ***702-369-5000***. *Fees: $15. Hours: Daily 6 a.m. – 8 p.m.*

Las Vegas Sporting House
North Strip

The **Las Vegas Sporting House** boasts more than 65,000 square feet of luxurious facilities, including racquetball/handball courts, squash courts, tennis courts, a full gymnasium for basketball and volleyball, indoor and outdoors pools and jogging tracks, and a full range of free weights and Nautilus-type machines. As if that weren't enough, they also offer aerobics and spinning classes. After that hard workout, you can enjoy a sauna, steam room, Jacuzzi, massage, skin- and hair-care salon, restaurant, bar, and/or lounge (call ahead to book massages and services). Plus, you can leave the kids with the baby-sitter during your entire visit.

3205 Industrial Rd. (located right behind the Stardust Resort and Casino). ☎ ***702-733-8999***. *Fees: $15 per day; $50 per week. Open: Daily, 24 hours.*

Tennis

In addition to the tennis courts at the **Las Vegas Sporting House,** you'll also find places to play at several hotels.

Bally's Las Vegas
Center Strip

The hotel has eight, lighted hard courts that are available to both guests and non-guests. There's also a pro-shop if you forget any equipment at home.

3645 Las Vegas Blvd. S. ☎ 702-739-4598. Fees: $10 – $15 guests; $15 – $20 non-guests. Hours vary; call ahead. Reservations highly suggested.

Flamingo
Center Strip

The hotel has four outdoor hard courts (all are lit for night play) available to the public. Lessons are available.

3555 Las Vegas Blvd. S. ☎ 702-733-3444. Fees: $12 guests; $20 non-guests. Hours vary; call ahead. Reservations required.

If You Enjoy Spectator Sports

There are no major-league sporting teams in Las Vegas, so most of the local action comes from the **University of Nevada Las Vegas (UNLV).** The main campus is located just off Paradise Road between Tropicana Avenue and Flamingo Road. If you just have to get a football or basketball fix, there may be a game playing at the **Thomas and Mack Center** (☎ 702-895-3900) on campus. This 18,500-seat facility hosts the college teams and a variety of boxing tournaments, NBA exhibition games, and rodeos.

Caesars Palace (☎ 800-634-6698) and the **MGM Grand's Garden Events Arena** (☎ 800-929-1111) host major sporting events year-round, including gymnastics, figure skating, and boxing. Remember the bite that Mike Tyson took out of Evander Holyfield's ear in 1997? That happened at the MGM — how proud they must be.

Las Vegas Motor Speedway
Off the Beaten Path

The **Las Vegas Motor Speedway** is a new 107,000-seat, $100 million state-of-the-art motor-sports entertainment complex. There's a 1.5-mile oval that hosts Indy and NASCAR events, a road course, a drag strip, and a motocross course.

7000 Las Vegas Blvd. N. ☎ 702-644-4443. Admission: Ticket prices vary wildly, so call ahead to find out what's happening and how much it costs. Open: Hours vary. If you're driving, take I-15 north to the Speedway exit (#54) and follow the signs. If you're cabbing it, save your money by catching the shuttle bus that runs regularly from the **Imperial Palace.**

PBA Tournaments
Off the Beaten Path

The **PBA Classic** in January and **PBA Invitational** in March are two major stops on the Pro Bowlers Tour. Both are hosted by the **Showboat Hotel.**

Showboat Hotel, 2800 Fremont St. ☎ 702-385-9150.

Las Vegas Invitational Golf Tournament

The **Las Vegas Invitational,** a major stop on the PGA tour, is held every October on several local courses. For details, call ☎ **702-242-3000.**

National Finals Rodeo

Every December, Las Vegas hosts the **National Rodeo Finals,** considered to be the "Super Bowl of rodeos." Nearly 200,000 people attend the two-week event, which is held at the **Thomas and Mack Center** on the UNLV campus.

Tropicana Ave. and Swenson St. (located in the Thomas and Mack Center on the UNLV campus). ☎ 702-895-3900. Everything sells out quickly, so call as far in advance as possible.

If You Want to Take a Tour

There aren't many organized sightseeing tours in Vegas, but those I've uncovered are very reasonably priced. Also, a good tour guide can fill you in on entertaining and historical tidbits that you wouldn't get wandering around by yourself.

Grayline

The most reputable company around offers one of the most interesting tours: **Grayline** will take you on a 7½-hour journey around town that includes the **Strip, Fremont Street,** a visit to the top of the **Stratosphere Tower,** and a lunch buffet.

4020 E. Lone Mountain Rd. ☎ 702-384-1234. Internet: www.pcap.com/grayline. htm. *Admission: The all-inclusive price is $28 for adults, $26 for seniors and children 10 to 16, and $24 for children under 10.*

Las Vegas Tour and Travel (☎ 702-739-8975) offers similar tours and can even arrange a nighttime helicopter ride for the adventurous (and wealthy).

Char Cruze's Creative Adventures

For something really special, get a personalized tour from **Char Cruze** and her **Creative Adventures** tour company. Char's a fourth-generation Las Vegas native (yeah, people really do raise families here) and if there's a story she hasn't heard, it's not worth repeating. She also does marvelous tours of **Red Rock Canyon, Hoover Dam,** and other non-city sights. She charges a flat fee that's a bit more than the others listed, but her tour is quite a bit more personal (she can tailor any tour to your specifications and interests) — and the more people you have in your group, the more cost-effective it is. It's terrific for families and highly recommended in general.

☎ *702-361-5565. Admission: Prices vary according to size of group and method of transportation. Tours start at $100 per day per family.*

Chapter 18

Hitting the Shops and Malls

● ●

In This Chapter

▶ Checking out the malls

▶ Sniffing out a bargain

▶ Hitting the hotel shops

▶ Shopping for necessities

▶ Buying souvenirs

▶ Other cool shopping ideas

● ●

*W*ay back in the Good Ol' Days, when hotel boutiques carried merchandise that could charitably be described as taste-free, Vegas was no shopping Mecca. If you're a penny pincher, it still isn't; but as the luxury hotels have risen (and gotten better at extracting your cash at every opportunity), the shopping has escalated — in both price and quality — to the level of that found in Beverly Hills and Manhattan. Which isn't to say there aren't plenty of dubious items still available for purchase. From campy souvenir shops to ritzy designer boutiques, die-hard shoppers will find plenty of places to empty their wallets. This chapter takes a look at the basics, the bargains, and the bizarre shopping options.

Checking Out the Shopping Scene

Naturally, this being Las Vegas and all, the show must go on; the mere presence of a mall isn't enough to lure jaded shoppers. Theme malls proliferate — you can window-shop on the Appian Way or sail past stores along the Grand Canal — and many of these malls include shows and rides designed to amuse people as they spend any cash the casinos might have missed. You can find a few smaller places where you can drop a few (or considerably more) dollars, but for the most part, like the hotels here, the megajoints rule.

Las Vegas Shopping

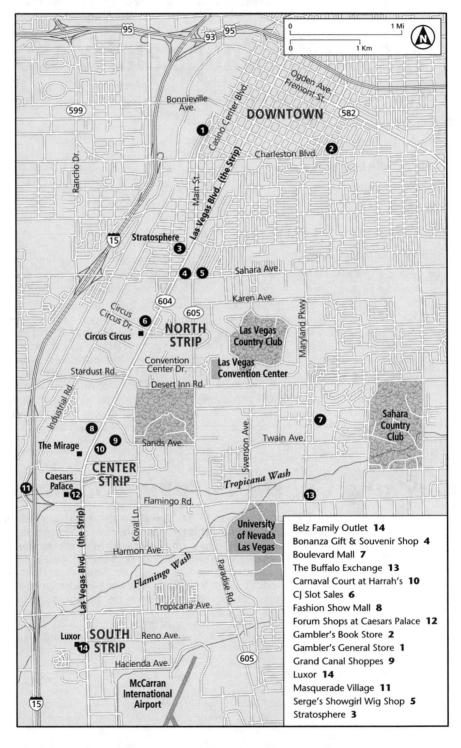

DOWNTOWN

Ogden Ave.
Fremont St.
Bonnieville Ave.
Charleston Blvd.

Casino Center Blvd.
Las Vegas Blvd. (the Strip)
Main St.
Rancho Dr.

Stratosphere ③

Sahara Ave.

Karen Ave.

Circus Circus Dr.
NORTH STRIP
Circus Circus

Las Vegas Country Club

Convention Center Dr.
Las Vegas Convention Center
Stardust Rd.
Desert Inn Rd.

Industrial Rd.

The Mirage

CENTER STRIP
Sands Ave.
Swenson Ave.
Twain Ave.

Sahara Country Club

Caesars Palace

Tropicana Wash

Flamingo Rd.

University of Nevada Las Vegas

Koval Ln.
Harmon Ave.
Paradise Rd.

Flamingo Wash

Tropicana Ave.

Las Vegas Blvd. (the Strip)

Luxor **SOUTH STRIP**
Reno Ave.
Hacienda Ave.

McCarran International Airport

Belz Family Outlet **14**
Bonanza Gift & Souvenir Shop **4**
Boulevard Mall **7**
The Buffalo Exchange **13**
Carnaval Court at Harrah's **10**
CJ Slot Sales **6**
Fashion Show Mall **8**
Forum Shops at Caesars Palace **12**
Gambler's Book Store **2**
Gambler's General Store **1**
Grand Canal Shoppes **9**
Luxor **14**
Masquerade Village **11**
Serge's Showgirl Wig Shop **5**
Stratosphere **3**

You'll find the usual assortment of sales during before- and after-school periods, and during holiday seasons, but there are no special sales periods in Las Vegas. If you like glitter and rhinestones, you'll find a good selection of flashy clothes and accessories, and if you collect gambling-related books or equipment you'll be in Nirvana. Otherwise, you really won't find that much in Las Vegas that you won't find elsewhere for a lot less money. And if you do decide to splurge here, don't forget to factor in a 7-percent sales tax to the price of whatever you buy.

Do keep in mind that, just like pricing for hotels and restaurants, shopping is more expensive on the Strip. If you're more intent on serious bargain hunting than fun browsing, head elsewhere.

Heading to the Malls

Just across the street from **Treasure Island** is the **Fashion Show Mall** (3200 Las Vegas Blvd. S.; ☎ **702-369-0704**), which is more like a classic upscale mall, with a similar range. More than 130 shops, restaurants, and services include **Nieman-Marcus, Saks Fifth Avenue, Macy's, Abercrombie & Fitch,** and **The Sharper Image,** plus your usual mall denizens, such as **The Gap, The Body Shop,** and **Victoria's Secret.** If your Caddy is looking a little dull, you can even arrange to have your car washed while you shop. Free self- and valet parking is available, and the mall is open Mon – Fri from 10 a.m. – 9 p.m., Sat from 10 a.m. – 7 p.m., and Sun from 12 p.m. – 6 p.m.

For a more traditional shopping experience, head over to the **Boulevard Mall** (3528 S. Maryland Pkwy.; ☎ **702-732-8949**). The largest mall in Las Vegas, it has 144-plus stores geared to the average traveler. Anchors here include **Sears, J.C. Penney,** and **Marshalls.** There's a wide variety of shops offering moderately priced shoes and clothing for the entire family, books and gifts, jewelry, and home furnishings, plus more than a dozen fast-food eateries. To get there, take any of the major east-west streets (**Flamingo, Tropicana,** or **Sahara**) to **Maryland Parkway,** which is about 2 miles east of the Strip. The mall is located just south of **Desert Inn Road** and north of **Flamingo.** Hours are Mon – Fri from 10 a.m. – 9 p.m., Sat from 10 a.m. – 8 p.m., and Sun from 11 a.m. – 6 p.m.

Bargain Hunting at Outlet Malls

Americans' love for factory-outlet malls has not gone unrequited in Las Vegas. If you haven't heard of them yet, outlets are where major chain stores or companies offer heavily discounted merchandise that didn't quite make the grade as regular merchandise. In most cases, I'm talking about tiny, almost invisible flaws in the material of a skirt or a small crack in some pottery. Occasionally, you find overstocked merchandise that is completely fine. No matter the reason, you can often get up to 75 percent off what you would pay for the same goods at retail stores. Of course, by the time it gets to the outlet, the stuff is often no longer first-run, but at these prices, who cares?

Before you buy something in a regular mall in Las Vegas, ask the sales staff if the store has a local outlet. You can save big bucks by exploring these alternatives.

Having said that, the indoor **Belz Factory Outlet World** (7400 Las Vegas Blvd. S.; ☎ 702-896-5599) is a bargain hunter's dream. Housed in a friendly and spacious mall-like setting are 145 outlets, including **Casual Corner, Levi's, Nike, Royal Doulton, Bugle Boy, Reebok, Oneida, Bose,** and **Waterford Crystal.** You can even find entertainment in the form of a giant indoor carousel, for kids (or bored spouses). Open Mon – Sat from 10 a.m. – 9 p.m., Sun from 10 a.m. – 6 p.m.

You can get to this mall by heading south on the Strip. It is located a few miles past the southernmost major hotel, **Mandalay Bay.**

Hitting the Hotel Shops

Just about all the big hotels offer some shopping opportunities, ranging from fancy clothing emporiums to gift shops. Avoid these places like the plague if at all possible, since the prices are astronomically higher than in the outside world. The hotels get away with this kind of price gouging because they assume hotel guests or fervent gamblers don't want to leave the property to pick up a bottle of shampoo or a pack of gum.

Most of the hotels have small gift shops (a.k.a. *logo shops*) that offer a variety of trinkets for you to bring home to friends and family. While such souvenirs are usually overpriced junk, some of what is offered in the better hotels is overpriced quality goods. In other words, expect to pay through the nose. You can try an independent souvenir shop, which will still charge too much, but without an expensive hotel overhead, may be slightly less outrageous.

The big guns

No matter what your budget, a few shopping spots inside the major hotels are attractions in their own right; put them at the top of your to-do list.

Mix equal amounts of Rodeo Drive and the Ancient Roman Empire, and then add a dash of Disney, and you may get something close to the **Forum Shops at Caesars Palace** (3570 Las Vegas Blvd. S.; ☎ 702-893-4800). And you thought I was kidding about theme malls? No matter what kind of shopper you are, make this marketplace your first stop. It's designed to look like a Roman street scene, complete with columns, marble, and animatronic statues under a "sky" that somehow transforms from day to night as time passes. You'll find mostly high-rent joints like **Louis Vuitton, Christian Dior, Armani,** and **Versace** alongside fancy restaurants like **Spago.** (Even if you don't like shopping, it's worth the stroll just to giggle.) A wing added to the arcade in 1998 houses a large aquarium, more animatronics, designer boutiques, and a three-story **FAO Schwarz** that is fronted by a gigantic Trojan horse, whose head moves while smoke comes out of its nostrils. Send the kids (or bored husbands) downstairs to the 3-D motion-simulator cinema rides simulating space flight, submarine adventures, and roller coasters (the cost is $6 – $8 for a five-minute ride). For a truly Vegas (and somewhat bizarre) experience, take in one of the every-hour-on-the-hour light-and-laser shows at the **Festival Fountain** or the **Atlantis Fountain.** The shops are open Sun – Thurs from 1 a.m. – 11 p.m., and Fri and Sat from 10 a.m. – 12 a.m.

Just up the street is gotta-see-to-believe stop #2 — the **Grand Canal Shoppes at The Venetian** (3355 Las Vegas Blvd. S; ☎ 888-488-7111). If the **Forum Shops** are a street out of Rome, this is a street out of Renaissance Venice, complete with a cloud-studded sky overhead. You can judge for yourselves the subtle nuances that differentiate the two. One big difference is the canal running down the middle of the Canal Shoppes, complete with singing gondeliers ($6 gets you a ride, a heck of lot cheaper than the real thing in Venice). The "canal" ends at a reproduction of St. Mark's Square, a stalled market where glassblowers and flower sellers ply their trades, and you can even find strolling musicians. The other big difference is that at the Canal Shoppes the entertainment is live; costumed actors, garbed as typical Venetians (flower girls, courtesans, and so on) and famous historical ones (Casanova, Marco Polo) roam the area, bursting into Italian arias, or just flirting with passersby. Will all this make you want to shop more? Who cares! But if you do, you find more than 70 retail shops — **Sephora, Kenneth Cole,** and **Donna Karan,** to name a few — to choose from. The Grand Canal Shoppes (which is accessible from the outside world via its own, casino-bypassing entrance) is open Sun – Thurs 10 a.m. – 11 p.m., and Fri – Sat 10 a.m. – 12 a.m.

If you really want a more Rodeo Drive experience, head straight for the **Via Bellagio** shops (in, where else, the **Bellagio;** 3600 Las Vegas Blvd. S.; ☎ 888-987-6667; hours for stores vary). Not one place in this mall offers prices I can afford (I can't even afford the oxygen — I make guide-book writer's wages, you know), but I sure like to browse and fantasize. **Gucci, Prada, Armani, Tiffany** — they're all here. And the setup, topped in its entirety by an overhead skylight that actually allows for — gasp! — natural lighting, is most attractive.

The rest of the pack

Two levels of shopping and dining surround a casino at **Masquerade Village** (3700 W. Flamingo Rd.; ☎ 702-252-7777), a 60,000-square-foot addition to the **Rio Hotel & Casino.** It's done up as a European village and sports mostly upscale clothing boutiques (it has the largest **Nicole Miller** in the nation) and small curio or jewelry shops. Be sure to stop by the **'Nawlins** store, which sells voodoo items, Mardi Gras masks, and the like.

Shopping is definitely no afterthought at the **Stratosphere Las Vegas** (2000 Las Vegas Blvd. S.; ☎ **702-380-7777**); you have to pass through its **Tower Shops** promenade in order to get to the tower itself. More than 40 stores are set along different international streetscapes that attempt to evoke Paris, Hong Kong, and New York City. One notable gift shop here sells functioning and decorative slot machines.

Harrah's Las Vegas (3475 Las Vegas Blvd. S.; ☎ 702-369-5000) recently completed work on an outdoor shopping promenade, the **Carnavale Court.** Among the store highlights is a branch of San Francisco's famous **Ghirardelli Chocolate** shop.

The **Giza Galleria** at the **Luxor** (3900 Las Vegas Blvd. S.; ☎ **702-262-4000**) is a shopping arcade of eight stores selling everything from men's and women's fashions to toys and upscale gifts. The **Cairo Bazaar** section features street vendors selling a variety of trinkets and doodads from carts.

Although Luxor's isn't, most of the hotel shopping arcades are adjacent to or in the middle of casinos. Perhaps they hope you'll use your shopping money on a slot machine instead? Avoid these machines if at all possible, since they are rumored to offer lower winnings than machines in other areas of the casinos.

Buying the Bare Necessities

Forgot to pack your shampoo and don't want to waste your kid's college tuition by buying it in the hotel gift shop? You might consider driving **Maryland Parkway,** which runs parallel to the Strip on the east and has just about one of everything: **Target, Toys 'Я' Us,** several major department stores, **Tower Records,** major drugstores, some alternative-culture stores (tattoo parlors and hip clothing stores), and so forth. It goes on for blocks.

If you need to fill a medical prescription, you can do it at **Walgreens** drug store at Spring Mountain (3765 Las Vegas Blvd S.; ☎ **702-895-6878**), or at **Sav-On** at Maryland Parkway (1360 E. Flamingo Rd.; ☎ **702-731-5373**). Another, more retro option is **White Cross Drugs,** just north of the Stratosphere Tower (1700 Las Vegas Blvd. S.; ☎ **702-382-1733**).

Road trippers whose cars need an emergency tune-up can try **Pep Boys** just east of Paradise (637 E. Sahara; ☎ **702-796-0600**), part of a major auto parts and service chain.

Tracking Down a Tacky Souvenir

The **Bonanza Gift and Souvenir Shop** (2460 S. Las Vegas Blvd.; ☎ **702-384-0005**), located at the northwest corner of Sahara, bills itself as the "largest souvenir shop in the world." I have no way of verifying this, but it does have a very large selection of souvenirs — your best bet in the tacky department are the earrings made out of poker chips.

Or head over to the **The Arts Factory** (101-107 E. Charleston; ☎ **702-676-1111**), which offers, in addition to several art galleries (where you can pick yourself up a really expensive souvenir, like an original painting), a very fine gift shop that caters to all camp sensibilities. Pink flamingos, fuzzy dice, and truly marvelous retro-Vegas items — they're all here and so much more.

Updating Your Wardrobe with Cool Clothes and Accessories

If you want neat hip and cool outfits, take a drive over to **The Buffalo Exchange** (4110 S. Maryland Parkway; ☎ **702-791-3960**). It's one of a chain of used-clothing stores filled with vintage and current discards — comb the racks and find something that will instantly upgrade your trendy image. Hours are Mon – Sat from 11 a.m. – 8 p.m., Sun from 12 p.m. – 6 p.m. It's in a small shopping strip at the southeast corner of Maryland Parkway and Flamingo Road (next to Tower Records). **The Attic** (1018 S. Main St; ☎ **702-388-4088**) is another vintage/used clothing store, featured for the last several years in an eye-catching, too-cool-for-words Visa ad. It also has a small coffeehouse, so you can raise your blood sugar while trying on poodle skirts.

If you crave showgirl hair (and why not?), stop in at **Serge's Showgirl Wigshop** (953 E. Sahara #A-2; ☎ **702-732-1015,** Internet: www.showgirlwigs.com), located in the Sahara Commercial Center just east of Paradise. This place has been supplying the Strip for more than 20 years and has some 2,000 wigs costing from $130 – $1,500. It has wigs by Dolly Parton and Revlon, men's and women's hairpieces, and you can customize your own special creation.

 If the prices are a little steep, **Serge's Wig Outlet** is just across the shopping center at 953 E. Sahara and offers discontinued wigs that run around $60 – $70. They are open Mon – Sat from 10:00 a.m. – 5:30 p.m. For information, call ☎ **702-732-3844.**

Finding Winning Gambling Gear

If you're not content blowing your money at the blackjack table, you can blow it on gambling-related stuff downtown at the **Gambler's General Store** (800 S. Main St.; ☎ **800-322-CHIP**), located 8 blocks south of Fremont. Another "World's largest" (who decides these things?), the store has actual gaming equipment (dice, craps tables, old slot machines, and more) and a virtual library of gambling books. The store is open daily from 9 a.m. – 5 p.m.

You can also find a wide array of used slot machines, video poker, keno, and even blackjack tables at **CJ Slot Sales** (2770 Las Vegas Blvd. S.; ☎ **702-893-0660**), located just north of **Circus Circus.** They have everything from antiques to the latest gadgets, but the prices ain't cheap! Hours are Mon – Sat from 9:00 a.m. – 5:30 p.m.

If you want to read up on strategy, try the **Gambler's Book Shop** (30 S. 11th St.; ☎ **800-522-1777**), located near Charleston Rd., whose motto is "knowledge is protection." You can browse more than 4,000 gambling-related titles here, all designed to help you beat the odds.

On request, knowledgeable clerks provide on-the-spot expert advice on handicapping the ponies and other aspects of sports betting.

Angling for Antiques

If you're an antiques hound, you'll want to poke around **East Charleston Road,** where more than 20 small, good-quality antiques stores are located within a few blocks of each other. An interior designer I know got most of her best pieces here. Go north on the Strip to Charleston Road and turn right — the stores begin at about the 1600 block. You can also stop at **Silver Horse Antiques** (1651 E. Charleston; ☎ **702-385-2700**), to pick up a map that highlights all the individual shops, complete with phone numbers and business hours.

Chapter 19

Doubling Your Odds: A Pair of Intineraries and Day Trips

● ●

In This Chapter

▶ Suggested itineraries

▶ Heading for Hoover Dam

▶ Driving through Red Rock Canyon

● ●

Arguably, there are really only two ways to spend your time in Las Vegas — gambling and looking at hotels.

Okay, that's not exactly true. But if that's all you do, unlike in most cities, you haven't missed much. These two activities, after all, are exactly what Las Vegas is all about.

But you can organize your time in Vegas to get the most out of what the city has to offer. In this chapter, I throw in a couple of day trips to give you time to recover from slot-machine elbow!

Seeing Las Vegas in Four Days

Like I said, you can just plunk yourself down at a poker table, heave yourself back off the chair four days later, and consider your time well spent. But if you want to check out the sights beyond that cute dealer, here are my suggestions.

Day one

Ignore those slot machines — oh, you can do it, and I will let you come back to them, I promise — and head right out to the Strip. This is one of the great wonders of the artificial world, as important a sight, for entirely different reasons, as the Grand Canyon. And you must take it all in, because you don't know what will be gone by your next visit. If you haven't been to Vegas in more than six years — heck, if it's been more than six *weeks* — the town will be nearly unrecognizable to you. This is a city that sheds its skin about every ten years. Things change that fast and are only changing faster. And each new construction is meant to top what has come before. So go ogle it all. A lot of people spent a lot of hours and a whole lot of money erecting these behemoths; you might as well admire their work, because after all, you are paying for it!

I give you a suggested itinerary for viewing the Strip's hotels in the upcoming section "Seeing the World-Famous Las Vegas Strip," but here's the gist: Be sure to see **The Venetian, Bellagio, The Mirage** (including the white tigers), **Treasure Island, Paris, Caesars Palace** (including the Forum Shops and the talking statues), **New York-New York,** the **MGM Grand,** the **Luxor,** and the **Excalibur.** Then at night, take a drive (if you can) down the Strip. When the street is lit up, it's even more extraordinary than it is during the day. Be sure to note the free evening entertainment: **Bellagio's** water fountains, which "perform" to various musical genres, the pirate battle at **Treasure Island** (consider watching it from the **Battle Bar**), and the volcano explosion next door at The Mirage. Have at least one meal at the quintessential Vegas dining experience, a buffet (details in Chapters 13 and 14), and have a drink at the top of the **Stratosphere,** the tallest building west of the Mississippi and, not surprisingly, the best view in town.

Oh, all right, maybe you should go gamble a little now.

This is your budget day — the buffet (depending on where you go) probably doesn't cost much, and with unlimited portions, you should eat your fill! Hotel gazing is free (but I'm not responsible for what you spend gambling).

Day two

Unless you were really energetic (and the temperatures weren't extremely hot!), you probably didn't cover the whole Strip on day one, so pick up where you left off. Then go see some smaller sights, such as the **Liberace Museum** or the significantly less bejeweled **Dolphin Habitat.** Or you can rest your feet at the **Luxor's** IMAX theater and take in one of their giant-screen films.

Because day one was your budget day, tonight it's time to kick out the jams on your wallet. First, you must take in a show. I think **Cirque du Soleil's** *O* and *Mystère* are the finest productions in Vegas — they are shows any city would be proud of — but many other choices may have greater ticket availability (not to mention cheaper prices, if you refuse to let me spend your money for you). Having done the buffet thing, take advantage of the celebrity-chef invasion and have at least one haute cuisine meal — it's as over the top as the buffets but in a different way, and, face it, mass-prepared buffet food is, shall I say, not of the same quality. **Napa** and **Picasso** are my top choices, but you can't go wrong with anything by Wolfgang Puck or Emeril Lagasse. You'll enjoy any of the following branches: **Le Cirque, Onda, Olives, Aqua, Circo, Pinot, Star Canyon,** and the **Border Grill.**

Day three

Loving this decadent thing, are you? Went into the casino "just to play for a few minutes" only to find two days have passed without your noticing?

It's time to get out into the fresh air. Get off that slot machine stool and drive out to **Red Rock Canyon.** The panoramic 13-mile **Scenic Loop Drive** is best seen early in the morning when traffic is light. If you have the time and energy, get out of your car and take a hike. You could even give your gambling budget a break by spending the whole day out. If so, have lunch at nearby **Bonnie Springs Ranch,** and afterward, take a guided trail ride into the desert wilderness or enjoy the silliness at **Old Nevada.** You can find out more about these side trips later in this chapter.

Tonight, continue to enjoy that fresh air — of a sort — and head into downtown. It's often neglected since it simply can't stand up to the over-the-top excess of the Strip, but it's far more user friendly. There are about a dozen hotels and casinos within a five-minute walk of each other, all grouped around a pedestrian mall, which at night lights up overhead with the colorful and musical *Fremont Street Experience* light show. Stick your head out of the casino to look at it and think "Look, I'm outside! I am!"

Day four

This is Culture and History Day! (No, alas the Liberace Museum did not qualify.) Go see the marvel of modern engineering that is the **Hoover Dam.** Leave early in the morning, returning to Las Vegas after lunch via **Valley of Fire State Park,** while stopping at the **Lost City Museum** in Overton en route.

Too exhausted to do that, huh? And it's kinda hot, is it? Oh, all right. Another option is to recharge your batteries by spending the day by the hotel pool, or going to the hotel spa for some detoxing and pampering. Skip another gout-inducing meal by having a healthful salad or smoothie at the **Enigma Café.**

All rested up? Then get out again to enjoy the city that never sleeps. Hit the casinos some more — you can take them down, I know you can! Catch another show — if you went with my **Cirque** suggestion, that means you haven't seen a classic Vegas topless revue, so get yourself over to *Jubilee!* (at **Bally's**) pronto. Or you can enjoy the wonderful (and reasonably priced) magic of **Lance Burton** (at the **Monte Carlo**) or the arty weirdness of **The Blue Man Group** at the **Luxor.** Get back into the decadent swing of things with another buffet orgy or worship at the shrine of a second celebrity chef.

After all, you are on vacation.

Seeing the World-Famous Las Vegas Strip

You don't exactly get architecture in Vegas — more like set design. If you're a Frank Lloyd Wright aficionado, you'll be appalled, but for the rest of us, there are a number of buildings that will make your eyes bug out. One of the main activities in town is wandering around and gawking at the gigantic, splashy, gimmick-filled hotels. This should be your first order of business and getting through them all (especially if you stop for a hand or two of blackjack at each) could take most of your trip. I describe them in detail in Chapter 8, but for sheer spectacle, here's the best way to see my favorites:

Start south on the Strip at the **Luxor** (3900 Las Vegas Blvd. S.; ☎ 702-262-4000), where you can experience the Vegas version of ancient Egypt. The Sphinx (don't worry, the real one is still in Egypt) stands guard in front of a 30-story pyramid that's big enough to house nine jumbo jets. Be sure to visit the dizzying interior of the pyramid, especially the second-floor attractions level.

Now hop on the free monorail — or the moving sidewalk; it's your call — and exit at Camelot. Oh, not really, but it is a giant medieval castle — or at least, a cartoon version of one. It's the **Excalibur** (3850 Las Vegas Blvd. S.; ☎ 702-597-7777), one of the largest hotels in the world. Check out the moat, drawbridge, and fire-breathing dragon.

Then mosey right across Tropicana Ave. (a pedestrian overhead walkway can get you there) to **New York-New York** (3790 Las Vegas Blvd. S.; ☎ 702-740-6969). Don't worry, you'll find it — it's that little place (hah!) on the corner of Trop and the Strip that looks like the New York City skyline, complete with the Empire State Building and the Statue of Liberty. Take time to really appreciate all the silly touches, such as the graffiti-covered mailboxes and the change carts dressed up like Checker cabs.

At this point, you can take the overhead pedestrian walkway to the opposite side of the Strip, for perfect photo ops of portions of New York-New York, and so you can get up close and personal with the highly impersonal **MGM Grand.** It's the second largest hotel in the world and at night, it's very, very green. Speaking of photo ops, that molten gold four-stories-high lion out front is just begging for your camera to snap away. Here, kitty, kitty, kitty!

Now take the MGM Grand's free monorail to **Bally's,** exit (it's a long walk), and use their pedestrian overhead walkway to cross back over the Strip to **Bellagio.** Outside is a 12-acre lake that features a free water fountain ballet regularly after 6 p.m.; it's one of the best free shows in town. Turn your back on the fountains (between numbers, that is) and gape at that very large replica of the Eiffel Tower back across the street at the **Paris** hotel. It costs to go up to the top, so save your dough and stay on the ground. (Though you may want to wander over there and admire all the replicas of Parisian landmarks, and get a baguette to go!) If you've come by during the day, pop inside the **Bellagio** to admire the **Conservatory,** a riot of color thanks to fresh flowers and plants that are re-landscaped every few weeks to reflect the changing seasons.

At this point, you've run out of those monorails and even the handy pedestrian walkways (some of which come with moving sidewalks) so you can either give it up for the day and pick this up tomorrow, or keep going by grabbing a cab, or just to show how tough you are, you can hoof it. In any event, your next stop is **The Mirage,** where the volcano out front explodes every ten minutes after dusk. Inside, you find a simulated (well, partially anyhow) rain forest, and some of **Siegfried and Roy's** white tigers on free display. (Not to be confused with the **Secret Garden of Siegfried and Roy,** which charges an entrance fee.)

Now proceed right next door (courtesy of a free tram) to **Treasure Island,** where you can act out your pirate fantasies (unless they are naughty ones, in which case save it for your room). A live-action pirate battle stunt show goes on after dusk. It often gets crowded, so arrive early to get a good viewing spot.

Across the Strip from **Treasure Island** is our final "must-see" destination: **The Venetian.** It's another one you are unlikely to miss, thanks to its sheer size. Unlike the appealing but off-limits exteriors of the other theme hotels, you can actually wander through the outside of this replica of Venice, that most charming of Italian cities. And with its (non-smelly) canal, tall streetlights, and promenades, it is supremely charming — for Vegas, at least. Dash inside for a cup of Gelato (stopping to admire the heavily marbled and art-covered grand entrance galleria), and bring it outside for a snack. Or head upstairs to the **Grand Canal Shoppes,** and pay a gondolier to row you about while singing an aria.

Getting Out of Town

Las Vegas can be a bit overwhelming, so if you've already blown your bankroll, or you need to take a breather from the blackjack table, a day trip may be just the thing to recharge your batteries.

Day Trip #1 — Hoover Dam, Lake Mead, and Valley of Fire State Park

A couple of thousand people visit **Hoover Dam** daily to pay homage to the engineering marvel without which, frankly, there would be no Las Vegas. A visit to the dam does not fill an entire day, but two other magnificent spots — **Lake Mead** and **Valley of Fire State Park** — are nearby that also deserve your attention.

Getting there

To get to **Lake Mead,** go east on Flamingo or Tropicana to U.S. 515 south, which automatically turns into 93 south and takes you right to the dam. This involves a rather dramatic drive, as you go through **Boulder City,** come over a rise, and Lake Mead suddenly appears spread out before you. It's a beautiful sight. At about this point, the road narrows down to two lanes and traffic can slow considerably. On busy tourist days, this means the drive can take an hour or more.

To continue on to **Hoover Dam,** go past the turnoff to **Lake Mead.** As you near the dam, you see a five-story parking structure tucked into the canyon wall on your left. Park here ($2 charge) and take the elevators or stairs to the walkway leading to the new Visitor Center.

To get to the spooky, otherworldly landscape of **Valley of Fire,** from Las Vegas take I-15 north to exit 75 (Valley of Fire turnoff). For a more scenic route, take I-15 north, and then travel Lake Mead Boulevard east to North Shore Road (Nev. 167), and proceed north to the Valley of Fire exit. The first route takes about an hour, the second 1½ hours. From **Lake Mead Lodge,** take Nev. 166 (Lakeshore Scenic Drive) north, make a right turn on Nev. 167 (North Shore Scenic Drive), turn left on Nev. 169 (Moapa Valley Boulevard) west — a spectacularly scenic drive — and follow the signs. Valley of Fire is about 65 miles from **Hoover Dam.**

Taking a tour

If you didn't rent a car or would rather go on an organized tour, **Grayline** (☎ 702-384-1234) offers several **Hoover Dam** packages, all including admission and a tour of the dam. The 4½-hour Hoover Dam **Shuttle Tour** departs daily at 7:45 a.m., 9:45 a.m., and 11 a.m. and includes pickup and drop-off and a stop at the **Ethel M. Chocolate Factory.** Most elaborate is the **Grand Hoover Dam and Lake Mead Cruise Tour,** departing daily at 9:45 a.m., which includes a 90-minute paddlewheeler cruise on **Lake Mead,** plus admission to Hoover Dam; a light lunch is available for an extra cost. You can inquire at your hotel sightseeing desk about other bus tours.

Numerous sightseeing tours also go to **Valley of Fire. Grayline** (☎ 702-384-1234) has a 7-hour tour from Las Vegas, including lunch, that costs $30 for adults, and $24.50 for children 17 and under. Inquire at your hotel tour desk. Char Cruze of **Creative Adventures** (☎ 702-361-5565) also does a fantastic tour.

 When you're in Las Vegas, look for discount coupons that offer significant savings on tours to **Hoover Dam** and **Valley of Fire State Park** in the numerous free publications available at hotels.

Seeing the sights

Obviously, you should start your day with the Dam itself, or rather, the **Hoover Dam Visitor Center,** where you can check out exhibits on the Dam, and buy tickets for a tour. Thirty-minute tours of the dam depart from the Reception Lobby every 15 minutes or so daily, except

Christmas. The Visitor Center opens at 8:30 a.m., and the first tour departs soon after. The last tour leaves at 6 p.m., and the center closes at 6:30 p.m. Admission is $8 for adults, $7 for senior citizens, and $2 for children 6 – 16; free for children under 6.

More extensive, and expensive, hard-hat tours are offered every half hour between 9:30 a.m. – 3:30 p.m.; "Survive the tour and you keep the hard hat!" Although it's not compulsory, it's not a bad idea to call in advance for the tour (☎ 702-294-3522). Both tours, by the way, are "not recommended for claustrophobics or those persons with defibrillators." Kids may be bored by the dam, unless they are budding engineers or just love big things; but your parents probably took you to things you didn't want to see for your own good when you were a kid — so why should your kids get off the hook?

After touring the dam, you can have lunch in **Boulder City** (see the upcoming section, "Where to eat") or you can go to the **Lake Mead National Recreation Area.** Start at the **Alan Bible Visitor Center,** 4 miles northeast of Boulder City on U.S. 93 at Nev. 166 (☎ 702-293-8990), which can provide information on all area activities and services. You can pick up trail maps and brochures here, view informative films, and find out about scenic drives, accommodations, ranger-guided hikes, naturalist programs and lectures, bird-watching, canoeing, camping, lakeside RV parks, and picnic facilities. The center also sells books and videotapes about the area. It's open daily 8:30 a.m. – 4:30 p.m. For information on accommodations, boat rentals, and fishing, call **Seven Crown Resorts** (☎ 800-752-9669). You can have a bite at the nautically themed restaurant, **Tale of the Whale** (☎ 702- 293-3484) at the marina (approximately a half mile away).

If you don't want to spend your post-dam time on outdoor activities, you can always drive back to Vegas via the **Valley of Fire State Park,** or you can spend a day just on the park alone. This is an awesome, foreboding desert tundra, full of flaming red fiery rocks. It looks like the setting of any number of sci-fi movies — not surprisingly, since a number of them have been filmed here.

Hoover Dam fun facts

Construction on Hoover Dam began in 1931, went around the clock, utilizing 5,200 workers, and finished in 1936, two years ahead of schedule and $15 million under budget. Surely this is one of the few examples of primo government efficiency. The dam stopped the annual floods and conserved water for irrigation, industrial, and domestic use. Equally important, it became one of the world's major electrical generating plants, providing low-cost, pollution-free hydroelectric power to a score of surrounding communities. The dam itself is a massive curved wall, 660 feet thick at the bottom and tapering to 45 feet where the road crosses it at the top. It towers 726.4 feet above bedrock (about the height of a 60-story skyscraper) and acts as a plug between the canyon walls to hold back up to 9.2 trillion gallons of water in Lake Mead — the reservoir created by its construction.

Plan on spending a minimum of an hour in the park, though you can spend a great deal of time more. It can get very hot here (there is nothing to offer relief from the sun beating down and reflecting off all that red) and there is no water, so be certain to bring a liter, if not two, with you in the summer. Without a guide, you must stay on paved roads, but don't worry if they end; you can always turn around and come back to the main road again. You can soak in a lot of the park from the car, but try one of the hiking trails if you feel up to it.

Information headquarters for **Valley of Fire** is the **Visitor Center** on Nev. 169, 6 miles west of North Shore Road (☎ **702-397-2088**). It's open daily 8:30 a.m. – 4:30 p.m. and is worth a quick stop for information and a bit of history before entering the park.

Where to eat

After touring **Hoover Dam,** you can have lunch in **Boulder City,** 7 miles northwest of the dam on U.S. 93. Feel free to check out some of the antiques and curio shops, and a number of family-style restaurants, burger and Mexican joints, including **Totos,** a reasonably priced Mexican restaurant at 806 Buchanan Blvd. (☎ **702-293-1744**) in the Von's shopping center. Or you could try the **Happy Days Diner** (512 Nevada Hwy.; ☎ **702-294-2653**), which is right on the road to and from the dam. A '50s diner in looks and menu, it has the usual burgers, shakes, and fries, plus complete breakfasts, and is quite inexpensive ($3 for a turkey burger on a recent visit). This diner is friendly and it's a good place to take the kids.

There are no food concessions or gas stations in **Valley of Fire State Park;** however, you can grab meals or gas on Nev. 167 or in nearby **Overton** (15 miles northwest on Nev. 169). I recommend eating at **Inside Scoop** (395 S. Moapa Valley Blvd.; ☎ **702-397-2055**), open daily 11 a.m. – 6 p.m. It's a sweet, old-fashioned ice-cream parlor run by extremely friendly people, with a proper menu that, in addition to the much-needed ice cream, classic sandwiches, and the like, features some surprising choices — a vegetarian sandwich and a fish salad with crab and shrimp, for example.

At the southern edge of Overton is the **Lost City Museum** (721 S. Moapa Valley Blvd.; ☎ **702-397-2193**), a sweet little museum commemorating an ancient Anasazi village that was discovered in the region in 1924. Admission is $2, free for children under 18. The museum is open daily 8:30 a.m. – 4:30 p.m. Closed Thanksgiving, Christmas, and New Year's Day.

Day Trip #2 — Red Rock Canyon and Bonnie Springs Ranch

For those of you craving a temporary escape from Vegas, but not wanting such an ambitious trip as Day Trip #1, head over to **Red Rock Canyon.** Like Valley of Fire, it's a surreal and lovely bit of outer-space-like rock formations, perfect for hiking or even just driving through while emitting cries of "oooooo!!!" It's a fine way to recharge your batteries — and it's only 19 miles west of Vegas!

Getting there

Just drive west on Charleston Boulevard, which becomes Nev. 159. Virtually as soon as you leave the city, the red rocks begin to loom around you. The **Visitor Center** will appear on your right.

You can also go on an organized tour. **Grayline** (☎ **702-384-1234**), among other companies, runs bus tours to the canyon. Inquire at your hotel tour desk.

Finally, you can go by bike. Not very far out of town (at Rainbow Boulevard), Charleston Boulevard is flanked by a bike path that continues for about 11 miles to the Visitor Center/scenic drive. The path is hilly but not difficult if you're in reasonable shape.

You should explore Red Rock Canyon by bike, however, only if you're exceptionally fit and an experienced biker.

Seeing the sights

Just off Nev. 159, you see the **Red Rock Canyon Visitor Center** (☎ **702-363-1921**), which marks the actual entrance to the park. There, you can pick up information on trails and view history exhibits on the canyon. The center is open daily 8:30 a.m. – 4:30 p.m.

The easiest thing to do is to drive the 13-mile scenic loop. It really is a loop and it only goes one way, so once you start you are committed to driving the whole thing. You can stop the car to admire any number of fabulous views and sights along the way, or have a picnic, or take a walk or hike. In fact, if you are up to it, I can't stress enough that the way to really see the canyon is by hiking. Every trail is incredible, with mini-caves and rock formations to scramble over.

You can begin from the Visitor Center or drive into the loop, park, and start from points therein. Hiking trails range from a 0.7-mile-loop stroll to a waterfall (its flow varying seasonally) at **Lost Creek** to much longer and more strenuous treks. Actually, all the hikes involve a certain amount of effort, as you have to scramble over rocks on even the shorter hikes. The unfit or the ungraceful should be cautious. Be sure to wear good shoes (the rocks can be slippery) and bring a map. As you hike, keep your eyes peeled for lizards, the occasional desert tortoise, flocks of bighorn sheep, birds, and other critters.

After Red Rock, you could keep going another 5 miles west to **Bonnie Springs Ranch** and **Old Nevada.** The latter is a kind of Wild West theme park (complete with shoot-outs and stunt shows) with accommodations and a restaurant. Okay, it's cheesy and touristy, but it's fun, honest. If you're traveling with children, a day trip to Bonnie Springs is recommended, but it is surprisingly appealing for adults, too. It could even be a romantic getaway, offering horseback riding, gorgeous mountain vistas, proximity to **Red Rock Canyon,** and temperatures 5° to 10° cooler than on the Strip.

For additional information, you can call **Bonnie Springs Ranch/ Old Nevada** at ☎ **702-875-4191.** Admission to Old Nevada is $6.50 for adults, $5.50 for seniors 62 and over, $4 for children 5 – 11, and free for children under 5. Hours vary, so call ahead.

Bonnie Springs Ranch is right next door to Old Nevada, with additional activities, including a small, and highly dated, zoo, and a less politically distressing aviary on the premises. Hours here also vary, so again, call ahead.

Riding stables offer guided trail rides into the mountain area on a continuous basis throughout the day (from 9 a.m. – 3:15 p.m. spring to fall, until 5:45 p.m. in summer). Children must be at least 6 years old to participate. Cost is $18 per hour. Scenic 20-minute stagecoach rides offered on weekends and holidays cost $5 for adults, $3 for children under 12.

Where to dine

The **Bonnie Springs Ranch Restaurant** has a lot of character and is a perfect family place. It's a bit touristy, but small-town touristy. The food is basic — steak, ribs, chicken, burgers, potato skins; pancakes and eggs for breakfast — and greasy, but good. A cozy bar is attached to the restaurant. In Old Nevada, the **Miner's Restaurant** is just a snack bar, but a large one, serving inexpensive fare (sandwiches, decent burgers, pizza, hot dogs), along with fresh-baked desserts.

Part VI

Living It Up After the Sun Goes Down: Las Vegas Nightlife

The 5ᵗʰ Wave — By Rich Tennant

FOR THE BUDGET MINDED: LAS VEGAS SHOW GOERS CAN TAKE IN "WHIP RENALDO AND HIS WILD BALLOON ANIMAL ACT."

In this part . . .

*L*as Vegas is a nonstop town, and when the sun goes down, the city really lights up. Although Vegas has a sophisticated side, it's not exactly known for symphony or theater. Nightlife in Las Vegas means dropping some of your gambling dough on big, splashy production shows and checking out the hippest clubs and bars. This part of the book helps you plan your Vegas nights.

Chapter 20

It's Showtime!

*L*as Vegas has a lot more to offer these days than the magic shows
and showgirls that helped build its reputation. Thanks to Mirage
Resorts' importation of the wildly successful (and quite avant-garde)
Canadian circus troupe **Cirque du Soleil,** you now have a wide variety
of similar big-budget shows to tickle your fancy. These days, the trend
in major production shows is toward bigger, louder, brighter, and more
expensive creations — just the right speed for Vegas audiences.

But never fear, this is still the town of Siegfried & Roy — at least until
the end of 2001, when they're set to retire — and showgirls. If you want
to see big-time magic acts or topless-dancer revues, you won't go home
disappointed. This chapter walks you through your options.

Finding Out What's On and Getting Tickets

As I discuss in Chapter 9, unless you're a pampered high roller, a reservation is a must if you want to see a show. Some shows — especially
those going on during peak periods — sell out weeks in advance. You
can often get last-minute tickets for a weekday performance, but Lady
Luck will have to be on your side to get them on weekends. You won't
have such luck for major concerts, boxing matches, and other big-
ticket performances, so reserve your tickets to these events as soon as
possible. I tell you how far in advance you can reserve a ticket for each
of the major production shows in the following listings. To order tickets
by telephone, call ☎ **702-893-3000.**

Keep your itinerary in mind when making show reservations so you're
not stuck racing through your meal to make your show of choice. If the
show you want to see is on the Strip, plan for extra time en route. You
don't want backed-up traffic to bring down your good time.

Shows on the Strip

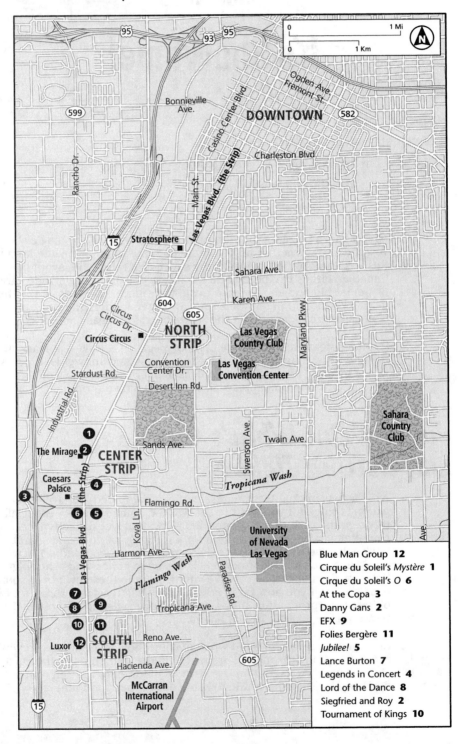

Blue Man Group **12**
Cirque du Soleil's *Mystère* **1**
Cirque du Soleil's *O* **6**
At the Copa **3**
Danny Gans **2**
EFX **9**
Folies Bergère **11**
Jubilee! **5**
Lance Burton **7**
Legends in Concert **4**
Lord of the Dance **8**
Siegfried and Roy **2**
Tournament of Kings **10**

The best way to find out what is happening in town when you're visiting is to contact the **Las Vegas Convention and Visitor's Authority** (☎ **702-892-0711**) and ask them to send you their *Showguide* brochure. The LCVA's Web site maintains a calendar of Las Vegas events at www.lasvegas24hours.com/calendar/index.html, where you can search for shows, sporting events, and more by date. Good sources for local entertainment information are the Friday edition of the local newspaper, *The Las Vegas Review Journal* (☎ **702-383-0205**), and two free weekly papers — *Scope* and *City Life* — that you can find at local newsstands and stores. For more on Las Vegas information sources, see Chapter 10.

Getting Pricing Information

I include admission prices on every listing in the following section, but use them only as guidelines. Recent show changes or special promotions may result in slightly different prices than those listed here. Tickets generally cost $40 – $100 per person.

Be sure to check if your hotel offers discounts on shows, especially shows staged on its premises. If you're gambling, ask about discounted admission or even free comp passes to shows and nightspots.

Some shows may not necessarily be obscene, but may include adult themes or skimpy costumes. If the show information doesn't list a separate price for children's admission, it's a fair bet that this show is geared toward adults. Double-check the content before taking the young 'uns to these shows.

The Inside Scoop on Las Vegas Showrooms

Most showrooms these days are nonsmoking and have pre-assigned seating. And most shows take place in the large hotels, so you'll find free self- or valet parking unless otherwise noted.

If the show you're going to see has maitre d' seating, it's likely that Old Vegas rules apply. This means that you may be able to haul out some extra cash to tip for a better seat. If you decide to take this route, plan to part with $5 – $20 per couple, depending on the original price of your ticket. One method you can try is to tip the captain who shows you to your seat rather than the maitre d'. This way, if you are lead to a satisfactory seat, you don't have to tip anything. But if you want something better, discreetly show the captain what you are prepared to tip. What can I say? Money talks.

If the venue charges extra for drinks and you plan to have a few while enjoying the show, you may want to reconsider. These shows usually charge very high prices for even the most modest cocktails. You may opt to have a couple of drinks beforehand and then a nightcap later at a more reasonably priced bar.

Las Vegas Productions A to Z

Given the spectrum of nightlife in Las Vegas, ranging all the way from glitz to sleaze, choosing what to do at night is a highly personal matter. I can point you toward the ones that are critically strong, but I've also included others to cover a spectrum. Regardless, the shows listed here are only the most noteworthy of the pack. You can find other big shows in the major hotels, but I've seen them all, so that you don't have to. Why waste your time — and money? That's what I'm here for!

At The Copa
Center Strip

At the risk of uttering blasphemy, David Cassidy may well be the Sammy Davis, Jr., of his time, in that he isn't the greatest singer, dancer, or actor, but he does all three of those things adequately, and he's mighty charming and likable on top of it. In short, he's an entertainer, and while this show is somewhat forgettable, it's a fine way to spend some vacation time. Cassidy plays Johnny Flamingo, a nightclub performer in love with fellow performer Ruby Bombay (Sheena Easton at the time of this writing), and their romantic adventures are there only to give everyone something to do in between song and dance numbers. It's cute and fluffy, shamelessly copying much from the revival of *Chicago*.

3700 W. Flamingo Rd. (in the Rio Hotel). ☎ *702-252-777. Reservations taken 45 days in advance. Admission: $58 (includes one drink, tax, and gratuity). Show times: Tues & Sat 7 p.m. and 9:30 p.m.; Sun, Wed, Thurs, Fri 8 p.m.; dark Mon. Showroom policy: Nonsmoking with pre-assigned seating.*

Blue Man Group
South Strip

Yes, there are men in this show, and yes, they are blue — not emotionally but literally, having been dipped in azure paint. This is not a typical Vegas show, having originated in New York City, where it's a still-running, highly successful performance art show for the masses. Cheese is involved, as are marshmallows, paint, and a whole lot of crepe paper. So are printed and electronic non sequitors, and some exquisite and unusual percussion music. So what's it about? Nothing. Call it slapstick Dada. It's every bit as pointless as the many revues playing around Vegas, and about 1,000 times smarter. And you'll laugh yourself silly.

3900 Las Vegas Blvd. S. (in the Luxor). ☎ *702-262-4000. Reservations accepted up to 30 days in advance. Admission: $71.50 and $60.50 (includes tax and gratuity). Show times: Sun – Mon 7 p.m., Wed – Sat 7 p.m. and 10 p.m., dark Tues. Showroom policy: Nonsmoking with pre-assigned seating.*

Cirque du Soleil's Mystère
Center Strip

It would be impossible to heap too much praise on this unforgettable and innovative spectacle, an experience like no other in Las Vegas (except, perhaps, its sister show *O* at the **Bellagio**). If you're expecting a traditional circus performance, forget it. There are no animals in this entrancing show by **Cirque du Soleil,** a Canadian circus troupe from Montreal that performs highly choreographed, imaginative acrobatics and hypnotic feats of human strength. It is true performance art: surreal, engaging, whimsical, dreamlike, and occasionally, bewildering. However, it may be a bit too sophisticated and arty for some kids' tastes. The show is presented in a huge customized showroom with state-of-the-art hydraulics, and the performers use every inch of it. Arrive early, because the hijinks usually start about 15 minutes before the actual show begins.

3300 Las Vegas Blvd. S. (in Treasure Island). ☎ *800-392-1999. Reservations accepted up to 90 days in advance (the word's out about this show, so do reserve as early as possible). Admission: $69.85 (drinks and tax extra). Show times: Wed – Sun 7:30 p.m. and 10:30 p.m. Showroom policies: Nonsmoking with pre-assigned seating.*

Cirque du Soliel's O
Center Strip

At some point when writing something like this, you run out of adjectives and superlatives. Particularly when you have to describe a second Cirque du Soleil show, one that might very well top the first, which was more or less indescribable to begin with. (If I could describe it, it wouldn't be Cirque.)

So, let's say this: Read the preceding review for *Mystère* and understand that everything said there applies here, except that this show takes place in, on, above, and around a 1.5-million gallon pool ("Eau" — pronounced *O* — is French for water), housed in an $80-million theater that nearly puts the *Mystère* one to shame. To say much more than that would be to ruin many a visual surprise. Don't expect a linear narrative, but do expect to get whiplash as you suddenly realize something else marvelous has quietly begun taking place on another part of the stage; don't be surprised if the sheer beauty of this extraordinary production makes you weep a little.

3600 Las Vegas Blvd. S. (in the Bellagio). ☎ *888-488-7111 or 702-693-7722. Reservations accepted up to 28 days in advance for general public, 90 days for guests of Mirage Resorts. (This is a very hot ticket so make those reservations as early as you can.) Admission: $90 and $100 (tax included). Show times: Fri – Tues 7:30 p.m. and 10:30 p.m. Dark Wed and Thurs. Showroom policies: Nonsmoking with pre-assigned seating. No tank tops, shorts, or sneakers. Attendees are asked to be seated half an hour before showtime.*

Danny Gans: The Man of Many Voices
Center Strip

Impressionist extraordinaire Danny Gans consistently rates as the "best in Las Vegas," according to local polls. Gans, a former Broadway theater star, does uncanny and hilarious impressions of great entertainers. The emphasis is on musical impressions (everyone from Sinatra to Springsteen), with some movie scenes (Hepburn and Fonda from *On Golden Pond,* Tom Hanks in *Forrest Gump*) and weird, fun duets (Michael Bolton and Dr. Ruth) thrown in. He performs a mind-boggling rendition of "The Twelve Days of Christmas" in 12 different voices. In the course of the show, Gans dazzles his audience with almost 80 different personas. Gans's vocal flexibility is impressive, although his impersonations can be hit or miss. Having said all that, I'm not entirely comfortable telling you he's worth his somewhat-high ticket cost — but he keeps selling out every night so many folks must think otherwise.

3400 Las Vegas Blvd. S. (at The Mirage). ☎ *800-963-9634 or 702-791-7111. Reservations accepted up to 30 days in advance. Admission: $67.50. Show times: Tues – Thurs, Sat – Sun at 8 p.m. Dark Mon and Fri. Showroom policies: Nonsmoking with pre-assigned seating.*

EFX
South Strip

EFX is Hollywood terminology for "special effects" and this show is, not surprisingly, loaded with them. It's a big extravaganza that celebrates dreams and the imagination; when one-time teen heartthrob David Cassidy starred in it, there was a nominal storyline, but when new talent took over (Broadway staple Tommy Tune, at the time of this writing), the show was modified accordingly. Still, expect time travel, visits with magical and mysterious folk such as Merlin, Houdini, and H.G. Wells, and singing, dancing, magic, acrobatics, and a slew of pretty remarkable (for Vegas theater) special effects. You can get away with sitting in the cheap seats; the view is just as good far back as it is up close (and that way, you won't get enveloped in fake fog).

3799 Las Vegas Blvd. S. (in the MGM Grand Hotel/Casino). ☎ *800-929-1111. Reservations accepted any time in advance. Admission: $51.50 – $72. Show times: Tues – Sat 7:30 p.m. and 10:30 p.m. Showroom policies: Nonsmoking with pre-assigned seating.*

Folies Bergère
South Strip

This topless revue is a veritable Vegas institution and one of the few remaining dinner shows in town. While it's not the Ultimate Topless Revue (I reserve that honor for *Jubilee!*), history has to count for something.

The show features beautiful showgirls dancing and singing while bedecked in lavish costumes (the headdresses aren't the largest in town — only the size of a two-seater). Scenes feature music from a variety of eras and styles (Parisian, American oldies, and so on) and are punctuated by acrobatic and comedy acts.

3801 Las Vegas Blvd. S. (in the Tropicana Resort & Casino). ☎ *800-829-9034. Reservations accepted up to seven days in advance. Admission: $39.95 – $54.95, including dinner and drinks at certain shows. Taxes and gratuities extra. Show times: Fri – Wed at 7:30 p.m. and 10:30 p.m. Showroom policies: Nonsmoking, pre-assigned seating.*

Jubilee!
Center Strip

This is what you envision when you think of a Las Vegas topless extravaganza. The show includes lots of singing, dancing, fantastic costumes, elaborate sets, and variety acts. And, oh yeah, bare breasts. Lot's of 'em. It's a huge show, with more than 100 dancers and over-the-top sets and I don't even know how many bare breasts. Wild production numbers abound, including Samson and Delilah, and a musical re-creation of the *Titanic* sinking (which prompted at least one recent attendee to comment "The effects are better here than in the movie"). I'm not saying it's good theater, but I am saying it's mighty good entertainment. If you want to see a classic, out-there Vegas show, this is the one. Heck, even if you never thought you wanted to see such a production, trust me, you'll want to see this.

3645 Las Vegas Blvd. S. (in Bally's Las Vegas). ☎ *800-237-7469. Reservations accepted up to six weeks in advance. Admission: Starts at $49.50, including tax. Drinks and gratuities extra. Show times: Wed – Mon at 7:30 p.m. and 10:30 p.m. Showroom policies: Nonsmoking with pre-assigned seating.*

Lance Burton: Master Magician
South Strip

This is the best of the city's big magic shows, by a sizable margin. Burton creates his magic inside a lush, Victorian-style music hall. The laid-back Kentucky native favors close-up magic over grand illusions. He also does a few big-set pieces, but Burton's laconic style makes even these routines seem less silly and overproduced than his competitors' shtick. Those looking for traditional Vegas pomp may find the show a bit modest, but, considering the very reasonable ticket prices, this may be the best value in Vegas productions and I highly recommend it.

3770 Las Vegas Blvd. S. (in the Monte Carlo Resort & Casino). ☎ *800-311-8999. Reservations accepted up to 60 days in advance. Admission: $44.95 – 49.95, including tax. Drinks are extra. Show times: Tues – Sat at 7 p.m. and 10 p.m. Showroom policies: Nonsmoking with pre-assigned seating.*

Legends in Concert
Center Strip

Arguably the best of the impersonator shows in Las Vegas, this fast-paced show has been continuously pleasing crowds since 1983. There's no lip-synching here; it's all live performances by impersonators of Liberace, Shania Twain, Prince, Bette Midler, and Elvis (performers rotate, so don't count on seeing these every night). Most of the performers look a lot like the celebrities they're impersonating — and act like them too. It's an entertaining night out and a lot of cheesy fun.

You can find many celebrity-impersonator shows in Las Vegas. Many of them, however, are pretty awful rip-offs featuring look-alikes lip-synching to prerecorded music. If you have discerning taste, be sure that any impersonator show you are going to see features actual singing and live bands.

3535 Las Vegas Blvd. S. (in the Imperial Palace). ☎ *702-794-3261. Reservations accepted up to 14 days in advance. Admission: $34.50, including two drinks. Tax and gratuity extra. Show times: Mon – Sat at 7:30 p.m. and 10:30 p.m. Showroom policies: Nonsmoking with maitre d' seating.*

Lord of the Dance
South Strip

No one was more surprised than I was to discover that this Celtic dance revue, which seems to run endlessly during PBS pledge breaks, was actually a worthwhile theatrical offering. These people are genuinely amazing dancers and they are coupled with some striking musicians (including, as this is written, two marvelously talented women who do a sort of Dueling Violin act) who play toe-tapping Celtic melodies. The show has a sort-of storyline — like every other show that attempts this in Vegas, it has something to do with Good battling Evil — but audiences come for the dancing and you should, too. It's a bit too long by half, but you don't need to be a Celt-o-phile to have a fine time anyway.

3790 Las Vegas Blvd. S. (in New York-New York). ☎ *800-693-6763. Reservations can be made 45 days in advance. Admission: $52 – $60 (includes tax). Show times: Tues, Wed, and Sat 7:30 p.m. and 10:30 p.m.; Thurs – Fri 9 p.m. Dark Sun and Mon. Showroom policies: Nonsmoking with pre-assigned seating.*

Siegfried & Roy
Center Strip

Lions and tigers and . . . magic, oh my! These two world-famous illusionists have been a Vegas institution for more than 20 years, and their $30 million show is a nonstop pageant of magic, dancing, explosions, special effects, and exotic animals. The highly stylized production is a bit overproduced, with so much going on that it's often easy to miss the important things (like an actual magic trick) because your attention is elsewhere. Many call this spectacle a must-see affair — and it does sell out every night — but tickets are exceptionally overpriced and your money is probably better spent seeing **Cirque du Soleil.**

3400 Las Vegas Blvd. S. (in The Mirage). ☎ *800-963-9634 or 702-791-7111. Reservations accepted up to three days in advance (and this is one of the hottest tickets in town, so act fast). Admission: $95, including two drinks, tax, and gratuity. Show times: Fri – Tues at 7:30 p.m. and 11 p.m. Showroom policies: Nonsmoking with pre-assigned seating.*

Tournament of Kings
South Strip

Kings in various distant lands gather together to compete in a highly choreographed tournament — and all the while, you eat dinner with your hands. Sound like fun? Well, it kind of is — I even got some too-cool teenagers to acknowledge they had a good time, and you know how hard that can be. The show is full-blown medieval tournament fare with audience participation encouraged to the point of overkill. There's a whole lot of hooting and hollering going on. Think of it as dinner theater mixed with professional wrestling. If you're into the WWF, Renaissance fairs, or you're just a child at heart (underneath your armor), you might find it entertaining. But actual children are the ones who most enjoy this show; their parents usually look like they'd prefer to be at *Jubilee!*

3850 Las Vegas Blvd. S. (in Excalibur). ☎ *702-597-7600. Reservations accepted up to six days in advance. Admission: $34.95, including dinner, beverage, tax, and gratuities. Show times: "Knightly" (their word, not mine) at 6 p.m. and 8:30 p.m. Showroom policies: Nonsmoking with pre-assigned seating.*

Headliner Showrooms

It used to be that Vegas' nightlife was dominated by showroom headliners — heard of the Rat Pack? — but while they are no longer the major players in town, they still offer great entertainment (especially in the rock music genre).

Describing the venues is really a waste of time; you're not going for the décor. Policies, prices, and show times vary by performer and venue, so call the showroom for information. I do give a few examples of the performers who have played in each place in order to give you a sense of the type and caliber of performers that management tends to book. Here's a list of the best of the bunch:

> ✔ **Bally's Celebrity Room,** in Bally's Las Vegas (3645 Las Vegas Blvd. S.; ☎ **800-237-7469**), offers 1,400 seats, and is where everyone from superstars to still-popular has-beens play: Hall and Oates, Barbara Mandrell, Liza Minnelli, Andrew Dice Clay, and George Carlin, among others have played here.

✔ **Caesars Circus Maximus Showroom,** in Caesars Palace (3570 Las Vegas Blvd. S.; ☎ 800-445-4544), is a 1,200-seat venue that has featured big-name headliners since 1966, including David Copperfield, Jerry Seinfeld, Julio Iglesias, Natalie Cole, and Rosie O'Donnell.

✔ The main competition for the Joint is the **House of Blues,** in Mandalay Bay (3950 Las Vegas Blvd. S.; ☎ 877-632-7400 or 702-632-7600). They both target the same kind of rock acts — when Alanis Morrisette played the Joint, her tour's opening act, Garbage, played the House of Blues. Other recent acts to play here include the Go-Go's, X, Taylor Dane, and the Neville Brothers. If you sit downstairs, be careful that you don't get stuck behind a stage-obscuring pillar, and note that upstairs has proper theater seating and is perhaps the best place in town to watch a show from.

✔ **The Joint,** in The Hard Rock Hotel & Casino (4455 Paradise Rd.; ☎ 800-693-7625), opened in 1995 with 1,400 seats. This is the place to see current rock headliners, including Melissa Etheridge, Marilyn Manson, Hole, Hootie and the Blowfish, Lyle Lovett, and even Bob Dylan. Note that sightlines here can be pretty tricky, since it's often general admission, standing room only. Still, this is where you can see big rock bands, who usually play much larger venues, but in a smaller-capacity show.

✔ At the **Las Vegas Hilton** (3000 Paradise Rd.; ☎ 800-222-5361), headliners are once again dominating the showroom where Elvis used to perform. Acts like Bill Maher, Johnny Cash, The Monkees, and Al Jarreau join the ghost of Elvis to fill the 1,500 seats.

✔ The 15,225-seat **MGM Grand Garden,** in the MGM Grand Hotel/Casino (3799 Las Vegas Blvd. S.; ☎ 800-929-1111) offers sporting events and the biggest pop concerts: Bette Midler, The Rolling Stones, Janet Jackson, and Elton John. Tickets are available through Ticketmaster (☎ 702-474-4000 or through your home town number). The 650-seat **MGM Grand Hollywood Theatre** is located in the same hotel. Here you can see smaller shows in a more intimate setting. It has hosted Wayne Newton, Dennis Miller, Randy Travis, and Las Vegas tapings of *The Tonight Show with Jay Leno.*

✔ The 450-seat **Orleans Showroom,** in the Orleans (4500 W. Tropicana Ave.; ☎ 800-ORLEANS), hosts acts like Chuck Berry, The Pointer Sisters, and The Oak Ridge Boys.

✔ The 750-seat **Sahara Hotel Showroom,** in the Sahara Hotel & Casino (2535 Las Vegas Blvd. S.; ☎ 702-737-2878), schedules musical acts and comedians such as Rita Rudner and Elayne Boosler.

Chapter 21

Partying the Night Away at the Best Clubs and Bars

L as Vegas is a 24-hour town, and so it goes without saying that the nighttime *is* the right time. This chapter explores some of your nightlife alternatives. No matter what's your bag, baby (obligatory Austin Powers reference), Vegas has something for you — and I've tried to list it (or a portion of it) here. Pry yourself away from the slot machines or the roulette wheel, if only to give your wallet (and wrists) a rest. It won't even cost you anything, if you choose; it's fun just wandering around, checking out the neon spectacle and barhopping from hotel to hotel.

Insomniacs rejoice! This city is the answer to your prayers. If you find yourself with a sudden burst of party energy late at night, you're in luck in Las Vegas. You can legally buy liquor 24 hours a day, and a lot of joints take advantage of that fact by never closing. Because of the late-night mentality that prevails in this city, you find that most bars and nightclubs don't really start jumping until late.

 A word to the wise: Nevada has extremely tough laws regarding drinking and driving, public intoxication, and disorderly conduct. It's fine to go out and have a good time, but don't think that absolutely *anything* goes — there are boundaries (and they are enforced), despite the hedonistic, party-zone atmosphere.

Las Vegas Nightlife

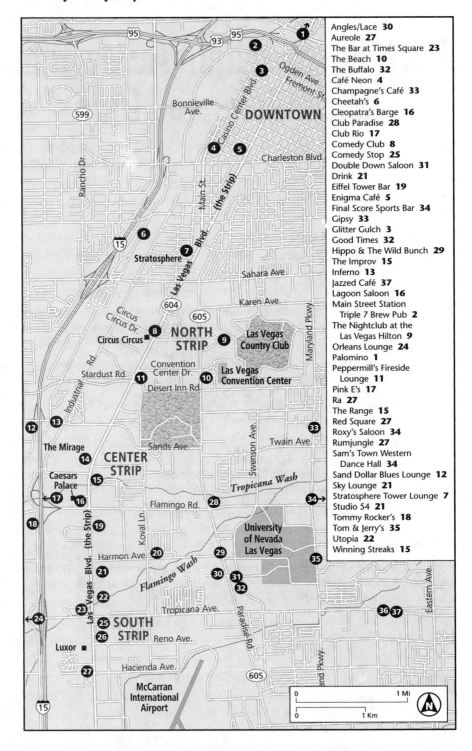

Angles/Lace **30**
Aureole **27**
The Bar at Times Square **23**
The Beach **10**
The Buffalo **32**
Café Neon **4**
Champagne's Café **33**
Cheetah's **6**
Cleopatra's Barge **16**
Club Paradise **28**
Club Rio **17**
Comedy Club **8**
Comedy Stop **25**
Double Down Saloon **31**
Drink **21**
Eiffel Tower Bar **19**
Enigma Café **5**
Final Score Sports Bar **34**
Gipsy **33**
Glitter Gulch **3**
Good Times **32**
Hippo & The Wild Bunch **29**
The Improv **15**
Inferno **13**
Jazzed Café **37**
Lagoon Saloon **16**
Main Street Station
    Triple 7 Brew Pub **2**
The Nightclub at the
    Las Vegas Hilton **9**
Orleans Lounge **24**
Palomino **1**
Peppermill's Fireside
    Lounge **11**
Pink E's **17**
Ra **27**
The Range **15**
Red Square **27**
Roxy's Saloon **34**
Rumjungle **27**
Sam's Town Western
    Dance Hall **34**
Sand Dollar Blues Lounge **12**
Sky Lounge **21**
Stratosphere Tower Lounge **7**
Studio 54 **21**
Tommy Rocker's **18**
Tom & Jerry's **35**
Utopia **22**
Winning Streaks **15**

Laughing Matters

A haven for stand-up comedians, Vegas has several hotel-based comedy clubs, and many prominent comics have paid their dues on the Vegas stage. Up-and-coming comics frequently perform in the Vegas clubs, so the performer you see may be that next sitcom star. Show times and prices vary, but I list the latest pricing information throughout this section.

Here's something cool to consider: Some big-name comedians are known to put in special, unannounced appearances at Las Vegas comedy clubs to test out new material. In fact, many of the jokes you hear from Jay Leno on *The Tonight Show* were told to Vegas audiences beforehand. The clubs don't tell you in advance, so you can't plan to see these "previews," but you may be in for a pleasant surprise.

- ✔ The **Comedy Club,** in the **Riviera Hotel & Casino** (2901 Las Vegas Blvd. S.; ☎ **800-634-6753** or 702-734-9301), features comics, hypnotists, and occasional theme shows (shock comics, X-rated, all gay, and so on) at 8 p.m. and 10 p.m. nightly, with a bonus 11:45 p.m. show on Friday and Saturday. Prices range from $15 – $20 and include one drink and tax. You can't call ahead and charge over the phone, so plan to buy your tickets at the box office. Oh, and it even includes maitre d' seating.

- ✔ The **Comedy Stop,** in the **Tropicana Resort & Casino** (3801 Las Vegas Blvd. S.; ☎ **800-468-9494** or 702-739-2411), has 8 p.m. and 10:30 p.m. shows nightly. The $17.50 cover includes two drinks, tax, and gratuities. You can charge tickets in advance, and there's maitre d' seating. This is the only comedy show in town that permits smoking.

- ✔ An offshoot of the famous New York City club, **The Improv,** in **Harrah's Las Vegas** (3475 Las Vegas Blvd. S.; ☎ **800-392-9002** or 702-369-5111), has a 400-seat showroom that often books the top comics on the comedy-club circuit. You can catch shows every day except Monday at 8 p.m. and 10 p.m. for $24.95 (tax and drinks extra). Call ahead to charge tickets. Seating is pre-assigned.

Looking for Tony Clifton

(Who? Tony Clifton was late comedian Andy Kaufman's alter ego, and arguably the most vile lounge act ever performed.) If you're looking for lounge acts, you don't have to look far: Just about every hotel has a lounge with some sort of live, nightly entertainment. There was a time when you could find a flood of top-drawer acts in hotel lounges, but these days expect stand-up comedy or impersonator shows. Some are good, some are comedic, and many are just plain campy. If you are looking for the latter, keep your eyes peeled for the dreaded — and delightful — **Cook E. Jarr,** a cult figure currently lauded as the worst, and yet, most special, lounge act in Vegas.

If you want some more solid musical entertainment, without the camp value, here are a few places to check out.

✔ For the dance/pop scene, one of the best is **The Nightclub at the Las Vegas Hilton** (3000 Paradise Rd.; ☎ 702-732-7111). This 350-seat venue has a large dance floor and recording artists entertain twice nightly. Cover charges and schedules vary, so call ahead for details. It's open nightly except Mondays from 8 p.m. – 2 a.m.

✔ Fans of salsa and reggae music should head to the **Lagoon Saloon,** located in **The Mirage** (3400 Las Vegas Blvd. S.; ☎ 702-791-7111). Here you can catch live lounge acts performing nightly in a tropical rain forest atrium. The club is open 24 hours, but band schedules vary; they usually play from noon until 2 a.m.

✔ Want to dance on a boat, but can't help but notice you are in the desert? No fear; **Caesars Palace** has provided **Cleopatra's Barge Nightclub** (3570 Las Vegas Blvd. S.; ☎ 702-731-7110). Yes, the dance floor (a small one) is on an actual, floating barge. No, you won't get seasick (although it can be an odd sensation if everyone is groovin' at once). It's pretty nifty. No cover; 2-drink minimum Fri – Sat. It's open nightly, 10:30 p.m. – 4 a.m.

✔ If you're looking for something different still, check out the zydeco bands at **Orleans** (4500 W. Tropicana Ave.; ☎ 702-365-7111). Zydeco is Southern Louisiana music combining French dance melodies, Caribbean music, and the blues. You can also hear other New Orleans sounds in the lounge next to the front doors. It's open nightly (except Monday), 9 p.m. – 3 a.m.

Shaking Your Groove Thang

You'll find plenty of places to dance the night away. In contrast to Las Vegas' normally casual atmosphere, the hot clubs have dress codes — some more strict than others. You'll also encounter a number of steep cover charges, and more than a little attitude. Call ahead to get the scoop on the details (although you may not find out about the attitude factor until it's too late!).

If you don't want to break the bank to have a good time at the local nightclubs, go earlier in the evening before cover charges go into effect. Yes, you may get there before the hoards of party-goers arrive, but you can also consider the lack of huge crowds on the dance floor to be a bonus. And doing so may help you get to bed at a more civil hour.

And, lastly, ladies look out! These places are major meat markets, so if you're not obviously with a date, you may be hit on endlessly. But, hey, you may be up for that sort of game! (If you want to avoid that, and you're just into dancing, you might check out **Gipsy,** a predominantly gay nightspot listed later in this chapter.)

✔ Party animals need look no further than **The Beach** (365 S. Convention Center Dr.; ☎ **702-731-1925**), located at the corner of **Paradise Road** across from the **Las Vegas Convention Center.** This tropical-themed, two-story mecca for fun-seekers has eight separate bars surrounding a giant dance floor. The crowd here is young, attractive, and mostly male; think of it as a giant frat party. Women in bikinis serve beer out of steel tubs when they aren't roaming the floor with other pricey drinks. The 24-hour club charges a hefty cover ($10), but the place packs them in.

✔ One of the hottest nightspots in Vegas is **Club Rio,** in the **Rio Hotel & Casino** (3700 W. Flamingo Rd.; ☎ **702-252-7777**). It's open Wed – Sat from 10 p.m. until around 4 a.m. It may have a little more class and is popular with the young and trendy, but I found a lot to dislike. There's a draconian dress code, a ridiculously over-priced cover charge of $20, the door people sport major 'tudes, and the wait time is interminable. And did I mention the music is kind of blah?

✔ Then there's the futuristic Egyptian-themed **Ra,** at the **Luxor** (3900 Las Vegas Blvd. S.; ☎ **702-262-4000**). Yes, Egypt *and* the future. Whatever. Swing bands, recorded techno, a major light show, and a heavy gilt interior are what you'll find here. They have made a definite attempt at creating a sexy, neo-mysterious vibe, and the place does pack in more locals than, say, **Studio 54** at **New York-New York.** Even better, the staff is actually sociable. The cover is $10 for men, $5 for women; it's higher for concerts and special events.

✔ The real hot ticket in town is for **rumjungle** in **Mandalay Bay** (3950 Las Vegas Blvd. S.; ☎ **702- 632-7408**). If you build it, they will come, and in this case, "it" means a fire-wall entrance that gives way to a wall of water; a bar holding hundreds of bottles of rum, each lit by a laser; dancing go-go girls; dueling congo drum-mers; grilled Brazilian food served on sword-like skewers; and live hot world music. The crowds here start at 10 p.m. and it stays packed until, well, I can't stay up that late anymore. The cover is $15 after 10:30 p.m.

✔ You've read the book and seen the movie, now come to the recre-ation of New York's legendary **Studio 54** in the **MGM Grand Hotel** (3799 Las Vegas Blvd. S.; ☎ **702-891-1111.**) Strangely, though Las Vegas is known as Sin City, this is a downright tame, strictly-for-tourists kind of place (but if you want to pretend, that's all right with me). Tennis shoes, baggy or ripped jeans, and hats (for men or women) are not allowed. Cover is $10 for men Sun – Thurs, $20 Fri – Sat; always free for women.

✔ A three-room home for the tragically hip, **Utopia** (3765 Las Vegas Blvd. S.; ☎ **702-740-4646**) is a veteran of the Vegas underground scene. Wed – Sat, the cool crowd heads here from 10 p.m. – 3 a.m. for an evening of techno-tribal-rave partying. There's no real dress code, but if you don't dress hip, you'll feel out of place. The cover varies, so call ahead.

✔ Now, since I've been a bit testy over some of these places, you may be wondering where I go to shake it up. The answer is **Drink** (200 E. Harmon Ave.; ☎ 702-796-5519). (No beating around the bush with the name, huh? I swear that's not what I'm doing there, but it's cool if that's what you do.) I love the groovy layout, with several different rooms, each featuring its own drinks and music. The Drink Vodka room has a mind-boggling array of vodka choices and alternative and retro music. Or you can check out the Drink Beer room, which seems to have almost every brew known to mankind. The rooms are always packed (bottlenecks in the hallways leading from one to the next are frequent), and they're set in a meandering layout surrounding a three-story, cave-like dance floor. You may even find a celebrity or two boogying the night away. The crowd and staff are friendly and the prices are actually affordable. It's open Thurs – Sat from 10 p.m. – 4 a.m. To find it, take Harmon Avenue east from the Strip (near the **MGM Grand**) to the next major street, Koval Lane. **Drink** is on the corner. There's free self-parking; valet parking costs $3.

Getting the Lowdown on the Hoedown

All the hotels and neon lights on the Strip may make you forget that you're still in the West, just a hop, skip, and a jump from cowboy country. If Garth Brooks is more to your musical taste than Madonna, you'll find more than your fair share of places to dance.

✔ You can act out your *Urban Cowboy* fantasies — assuming you've been harboring them for many years — at the one and only **Gilly's** (yep, the club from the movie), which has taken up residence in the **New Frontier Hotel** (3120 Las Vegas Blvd. S.; ☎ 702- 794-8200). Expect live and recorded country music, and yes, a mechanical bull. Ride 'em, cowboy. There is no cover, unless a headlining country act is performing (John Anderson was on a recent visit). It's open daily from 4 p.m. until whenever they decide to shut the doors, usually between 2 and 4 a.m.

Note that there is a chance that the New Frontier may be closing before the end of 2001.

✔ **Sam's Town Hotel & Casino** (5111 Boulder Hwy.; ☎ 702-456-7777) features two separate clubs for you to two-step the night away. **Roxy's Saloon** features live country bands and dancing (on a very small dance floor) daily from 12 p.m. – 6 a.m. **Sam's Town Western Dance Hall** has a huge dance floor and a DJ spinning the best country music from 9 p.m. – 3 a.m. Mon – Sat. Get here early to take the line-dancing lessons from 7:30 p.m. – 9 p.m. every night. Sam's Town is in the eastern part of Las Vegas and is best reached by taking Flamingo Road east from the Strip about 8 miles to Boulder Highway. Make a right, and you can't miss it on your left.

✔ If you follow the directions for Sam's but turn left on Boulder Highway and head north, you'll find **Dylan's** (4660 Boulder Hwy.; ☎ 702-451-4006), featuring the same kind of idea (country, dancing, lessons) but slightly more casual. It's open Thurs – Sat from 7 p.m. until around 3 a.m. Compare and contrast cowboys, why don't you?

Finding a Place to Hoist a Few

You may want your bars to come with personality, and so this may require leaving your hotel (in most cases) to search out bars that aren't generic watering holes. Your reward will be a glimpse of that rapidly vanishing true Vegas vibe.

✔ You can start at **Champagne's Café** (3557 S. Maryland Pkwy.; ☎ 702-737-1699). This is the sort of place those hip guys who made the movie *Swingers* just worship. It's so outmoded that it's hip again — they just don't know it (or, worse, think they never lost it) — and it serves ice cream shakes spiked with booze. You don't get this in a hotel bar.

✔ On the other hand, the **Double Down Saloon** (4640 Paradise Rd., at Naples; ☎ 702-791-5775), knows it's hip, but is too hip to let on (if you follow). There's no flashy décor (unless you count the "you puke, you clean" sign and the arty graffiti on the walls). Instead they let their jukebox — from the Germs and Zappa to Dick Dale and Rev. Horton Heat — do the talking. The clientele (including the late Timothy Leary and director Tim Burton) are listening.

✔ Back to dated views of hip — here's **Peppermill's Fireside Lounge,** inside the **Peppermill Coffee Shop** (2985 Las Vegas Blvd. S.; ☎ 702-735-7635), where romance is provided by a water and fire pit, a piece of kitsch you probably thought had gone the way of the dodo bird. Those basketball-sized drinks will put you into a stupor, after which the plush, cozy booths support you in womblike comfort until you feel (if you ever do) like moving on.

My snippy comment about generic hotel bars notwithstanding, there are a few worth seeking out — heck, even the locals do!

✔ A couple of these are actually housed in restaurants, and all are in the **Mandalay Bay** (3950 Las Vegas Blvd.). **Aureole** has a four-story glass wine tower, and bottles are fetched by comely young ladies wearing "Peter Pan" style harnesses that whisk them up and down as they fetch the bottle of a patron's choosing. The bar in the front, facing the wine tower, has become a nighttime hangout, with people ordering obscure wine just to send the damsels as high up as they can.

✔ You can keep your drink nicely chilled all night long on the ice bar at **Red Square,** created by water freshly poured and frozen daily. Or join the locals late at night feeling the blues at the small, bottle-cap bedecked bar in the corner of the **House of Blues** restaurant.

There's also the **Viva Las Vegas Lounge** at the **Hard Rock Hotel** (4455 Las Vegas Blvd. S.), which looks like a nothing little bar, but which is usually jumping late with locals — and at any time, with traveling rock musicians, in town for a gig.

✔ After about 9 p.m., the **Monte Carlo Pub & Brewery,** in the **Monte Carlo Resort** (3770 Las Vegas Blvd. S.; ☎ 702-730-7777) gets loud and hopping thanks to rock videos blaring forth from 40 monitors, and live entertainment of varying kinds, not to mention that microbrewery and a cigar bar. For similar action, check out **Main Street Station Triple 7 Brew Pub** (100 Main St.; ☎ 702-387-1896), inside downtown's **Main Street Station.** In addition to the micro-brewery, which has a good selection of ales, there's a sushi bar, an oyster bar, a grill, and two grand pianos, where someone tinkles the ivories nightly. It looks kind of yuppie-like (San Francisco post-modern warehouse) but it's also a bit of a break from claustro-phobic hemmed-in drinking joints.

Cool Clubs for the Special-Interest Set

Not everyone wants to spend the night bumping and grinding to the latest in hip-hop, and if you fall into that category, don't worry. Some Vegas clubs cater to specific groups, including college students, busi-nessmen, blues aficionados, and those looking for a less frenetic atmos-phere than the average club offers.

✔ If you want to join up with the Cliff Notes crowd, head for **Tom & Jerry's** (at 4550 S. Maryland and Harmon; ☎ 702-736-8550), whose location across the street from UNLV makes it understand-ably popular with college kids. The "drink cheap, be loose, have fun" party ethic also helps. There are several rooms with no atti-tude or pretensions, but plenty of the things that make a party: live dance music by cover bands, 20 pool tables, nightly $1 drinks specials, and weekly beer busts. There's a moderate cover that changes week to week.

✔ The TGIF crowd usually heads for **Tommy Rocker's** (4275 Industrial Blvd.; ☎ 702-261-6688). The owner (whose name is — surprise! — Tommy Rocker) plays at this beach-meets-frat-party themed club every Friday and Saturday night, mixing bar band standards with '80s and '90s hits. Strip musicians do join in once their own shifts are done, but otherwise, it's a one-man show, with Strip musicians dropping by after their own shifts are done. (Occasionally, local bands are permitted to play as well.) The crowd is former frat boys, happily continuing their education — or what they best remember of it — by drinking, dancing, and eating.

✔ Those sick of strict dress codes, lousy attitudes, and the collegiate crowd should think pink! Pink pool tables, lava lamps, furnishings — it's not hard to see how **Pink E's** (3695 W. Flamingo.; ☎ 702-252-4666), got, or at least keeps, its name. A DJ plays here on week-ends and you can chow down on retro diner food. Despite the gim-mick, or maybe because of it (pink is the new black, you know), this is actually a more grown-up destination in a town full of diversions for frat boys.

✔ If you're hankering for the blues, you can find zero ambiance but plenty of atmosphere at the stripped down **Sand Dollar Blues Lounge** (3355 Spring Mountain at Polaris; ☎ **702-871-6651**). It's funky and friendly, with a mix of locals and tourists, and is completely free of any theme (aside from blues bands), trend, or neon (unless you count beer signs). Doesn't that mean they should bulldoze it and put up a blues-themed amusement park? Live blues (and sometimes zydeco) bands play nightly.

A View to Kill For

Few cities have a skyline as unique and beautiful as Vegas', especially when night falls. Paris may be called the City of Lights, but nowadays, it has nothing on Vegas. For a perfect end to a day in Sin City, nothing beats a nightcap at a lounge that provides a panoramic view of the city.

✔ Ready to test your vertigo? The most memorable view in town is the nighttime vista from the cocktail lounge on the 107th floor of the **Stratosphere Tower** (2000 Las Vegas Blvd. S.; ☎ **702-380-7777**). It costs $6 to get up there and, while drinks are pricey, it's very cool to sip a martini while gazing down at the sea of neon displayed at your feet. The lounge, like the restaurant directly below, revolves slowly, so give yourself an hour to make a 360-degree trip around the city. It's open daily, 11 a.m. – 1 a.m.

✔ If you don't mind a drop in price and height, take the elevator in the **Polo Towers** to **The Sky Lounge** (3745 Las Vegas Blvd. S.; ☎ **702-261-1000**.) Sure, it's not the Stratosphere's view, or even the one from Paris' Eiffel Tower, but it's still pretty high up and pretty spectacular, especially at night, and all it will cost you is a drink. Gaze and linger. It's open 24 hours, 7 days a week.

✔ If you want to look down on the rest of the world, like a true Parisian, try the **Eiffel Tower Bar,** in **Paris Las Vegas** (3655 Las Vegas Blvd. S.; ☎ **702-948-6937**), in the restaurant on the 11th floor of Paris' half-size replica of the City of Lights' most famous landmark. It's cool and sophisticated. Bar hours are Sun – Thurs 5:30 p.m. – 12 a.m., Fri – Sat 5 p.m. – 1 a.m. No cover or minimum.

Root, Root, Root for the Home Team

The Sports Book at the major casinos are some of the best places to watch the latest sports action, but you can find some other great places to catch a game. (If you think lap dancing is a sport, check out "Scouting the Strip Joints" later in this chapter.)

✔ A great spot to catch a game or two is **Final Score Sports Bar,** located adjacent to **Sam's Town Hotel & Casino** (5111 Boulder Hwy., East Las Vegas; ☎ **702-456-7777**). It's a unique environment featuring interactive sports, video games, a basketball court, pinball, pool, an outside volleyball court, and dozens of televisions on which you can catch just about any major game from across the U.S. It's open daily from 10 a.m. – 4 a.m.

✔ Another cool sports spot is **Winning Streaks,** in **Harrah's Las Vegas** (3475 Las Vegas Blvd. S.; ☎ **702-369-5000**). Although more restaurant than bar, it's open to the casino and has a parade of televisions, yummy hamburgers, and some tasty specialty drinks. It's open 24 hours, 7 days a week.

Satisfying a Caffeine Craving

Yes, Vegas has a **Starbucks** — who doesn't? — but it also has a number of unique coffeehouses and it would behoove you to collect your cappuccinos in one of them.

✔ Situated in a funky space above the **Attic,** a vintage clothing store, **Café Neon** (1018 S. Main St.; ☎ **702-388-4088**), sports a truly local flavor. Live comedy is sometimes staged inside the café. It's located near **Charleston Ave.,** 5 blocks west of the Strip, and is open daily from 10 a.m. – 6 p.m.

✔ A calm, almost un-Vegas atmosphere marks the **Enigma Café** (918½ S. Fourth St.; ☎ **702-386-0999**), which offers a pretty, patio setting and is candlelit at night. This artist hangout has a huge menu of coffees and smoothies, plus an art gallery, live acoustic and folk music, and poetry readings. It's open Mon from 7 a.m. – 3 p.m., Tue – Fri from 7 a.m. – 12 a.m., and Sat and Sun from 9 a.m. – 12 a.m.

✔ The intimate **Jazzed Café** (2055 E. Tropicana; ☎ **702-798-5995**), is a European-style bistro — small but cozy, candlelit, and featuring nonstop jazz music. Their coffee is genuine Italian (try the Illy), and they have some excellent wines for such a small space. Be sure to browse their lovely — and inexpensive — menu of Italian cuisine. The café is located about 3 miles east of the Strip at Eastern Avenue and is open Tue – Sun from 6 p.m. – 3 a.m.

Checking Out the Gay and Lesbian Scene

Boys will be boys and girls will be girls, especially at the following places. *Note:* It doesn't matter which you prefer, as most of the gay/lesbian bars in town are straight-friendly. For non-gays who like to dance, but don't want to get hassled by the opposite sex all night, these are good spots to hang out in.

✔ Thanks to recent remodeling, longtime favorite, **Gipsy** (4605 Paradise Rd.; ☎ **702-731-1919**), once again reigns supreme. Nevertheless, it still has everything that made it popular for so long, including dancing, go-go boys, and shows. The interior sports plenty of glass and marble, and the dance floor has an odd Indiana Jones look. Most nights you pay a cover charge of $5 or $6. You'll find it just south of Harmon Road and it usually opens around 10 p.m. and closes whenever they feel like it — usually after the sun comes up.

✔ Right next door to Gipsy is **Angles/Lace** (4633 Paradise Rd.;
☎ **702-791-0100**), an upscale 24-hour video bar divided into two
parts: the predominantly male Angles and the predominantly
female Lace. The club sports a dance floor with a really loud
sound system and a game room that features video poker and
billiards. There's no cover or drink minimum.

✔ The leather-and-Levis crowd can go right across the street to **The
Buffalo** (4640 Paradise Rd.; ☎ **702-733-8355**), which often has beer
busts ($5 for all you can drink) on Fridays from 9 p.m. – 12 a.m.,
and is open 24 hours. There's no cover, drinks are cheap, and you
can try your hand at billiards, darts, and the ever-present video
poker.

✔ If you're looking for something a little more cozy, try **Good Times**
(1775 E. Tropicana Ave.; ☎ **702-736-9494**), a quiet neighborhood
bar with a small dance floor. The 24-hour spot has no cover
charge. It's located in the same complex as the **Liberace Museum,**
after which you may need a stiff drink.

For more information on what's going on in gay Las Vegas during your
visit, pick up a copy of the *Las Vegas Bugle* (☎ **702-369-6260**), a free
gay-oriented newspaper that's available at any of the places described
in the preceding list. For online information on the gay nightlife scene,
surf over to www.gayvegas.com.

Scouting the Strip Joints

Welcome to Decadence Central. Sex is a major industry in Las Vegas — it
isn't nicknamed Sin City for nothing — and on an evening's stroll down
the Strip, you're likely to have dozens of flyers advertising a strip of a
different sort shoved at you. If you've had even the slightest interest in
viewing naked, or semi-naked, women dancing and prancing onstage,
you've hit the jackpot. There are numerous topless, or totally nude, strip
bars from which to choose. Some are actually clean, respectable establishments — if, of course, your idea of respectability includes half-naked
women. The most prominent ones are generally the safest and nicest of
the bunch. You can find seedier places in this town — but you're on
your own.

Keep in mind that in Las Vegas proper, topless bars can serve alcohol,
but all-nude clubs cannot. Only the **Palomino,** an all-nude joint in
North Las Vegas, is allowed to serve stiff drinks (the exception due to a
grandfather clause in the Clark County ban). The rules and regulations
vary from club to club, so be sure to ask at the door if you want to stay
out of trouble. In general, note that touching the dancers in a strip club
is usually forbidden. Some clubs, however, allow a restrained bit of
physical interaction between clients and dancers.

✔ Featured in that masterpiece of bad cinema, *Showgirls,* **Cheetah's**
(2112 Western Ave.; ☎ **702-384-0074**) is a clean, jovial place
where many in the young, party sect hang out. Sure, it has a bit of
a frat-house atmosphere, but you're likely to see some couples

here having a bit of fun. Feel free to order up a table or couch dance. There's a $10 cover charge, and the club is open 24 hours. (Go to Western Avenue just east of I-15, and the club is between Sahara and Charleston Avenues.)

✔ Possibly the best of the strip joints, **Club Paradise** (4416 Paradise Rd., just north of Flamingo; ☎ **702-734-7990**) is a glitzy spot that attracts an upscale white-collar crowd, with bright lighting, a plush interior, champagne, and cigars. Oh, and topless dancers. Can't forget that. The dancers, called "actual centerfolds," are more likely to be cosmetically enhanced than in the other establishments. Hours are weekdays from 4 p.m. – 6 a.m. and weekends 6 p.m. – 6 a.m. There's a $10 cover charge, plus a two-drink minimum (drinks start at $4.50).

✔ A perfect place for the merely curious, **Glitter Gulch** (20 Fremont St.; ☎ **702-385-4774**) is somewhat of a downtown landmark located smack dab in the heart of the *Fremont Street Experience.* This place offers much of the same, but also includes a gift shop (you read that right) and limo service to and from your hotel. The club is open Sun – Thurs from 12 p.m. – 4 a.m. and Fri and Sat from 12 p.m. – 6 a.m. You don't have to pay a cover charge, but there is a two-drink minimum (drinks start at $6.75).

✔ The large, two-story **Palomino** (1848 Las Vegas Blvd. N.; ☎ **702-642-2984**) boasts a bunch of stages, semi-private rooms, and total nudity. It's somewhat seedy, but if you're looking for a private, totally nude lap dance, you can get it here. It's a straight shot up Las Vegas Blvd. (the Strip) past downtown, but it'll take 15 to 25 minutes, depending on traffic. It's open daily from 1:30 p.m. – 4 a.m. You pay a cover charge of $10, plus a two-drink minimum (drinks start at $6).

Part VII
The Part of Tens

The 5th Wave By Rich Tennant

"...and do you promise to love, honor, and always place maximum bets on the dollar slots?"

In this part . . .

Ah, tradition. The Part of Tens is to . . .*For Dummies* books what gambling is to Las Vegas — an integral part of the experience. This area of the book is where I feed you some useful and fun information, just to give you some interesting topics of conversation, if nothing else.

In the chapters in this part, you find out some of Las Vegas' great claims to fame and also learn some interesting facts about institutions that went the way of the dinosaurs.

Chapter 22

Ten Las Vegas Claims to Fame

Considering the city's reputation for doing things bigger — if not necessarily better — than anywhere else, it should come as no surprise that Vegas has secured a few spots in the *Guinness Book of World Records*. If this city loves anything, it's a challenge; right now, some new project is probably in the works that will eventually end up on Vegas' roster of larger-than-life achievements.

Lighting Up the Sky

It used to be that the Great Wall of China was the only man-made structure that could be seen with the naked eye from outer space. Naturally, it was only a matter of time before Vegas aspired to reach such stellar heights (although one wonders how long it will be before they attempt to "do" the Great Wall as a theme hotel), and it succeeded. From the top of the pyramid of the **Luxor** shines the world's brightest beam of light — using it, you could read a newspaper 10 miles in space. What a beam of light has to do with a pyramid I don't know, but you can see it from the space shuttle, so that's that.

Wide-open Spaces

As if having the world's biggest light beam were not enough, the **Luxor** is also home to the planet's largest indoor atrium! Housed inside the hotel's 36-story pyramid, the atrium measures 29 million cubic feet. You could fit nine jumbo jets inside the pyramid — if you wanted to, that is.

Larger than Life

Following the bigger-is-better theory (a much cherished ideal in this town), it's only natural that Las Vegas is home to the largest hotel in the world — at least in terms of number of rooms. The holder of this distinction is the appropriately named **MGM Grand.** It has 5,034 rooms, in case you're counting. And to put this number in perspective, think of this: It would take a person 13 years and 8 months to sleep one night in each of the hotel's rooms. If you stacked all the beds in those rooms up, the resulting tower would be ten times higher than the Empire State Building — the real one, not the one across the street.

No Room — Ha!

Okay, that may not be true — there have been numerous occasions when the odds of hitting it big on the craps tables were better than getting a room in Las Vegas, but that isn't due to lack of space. The city has more hotel rooms than any other — more than 120,000 at last count. And by the end of 2002, you'll be able to tack on 8,000 more places to park yourself while resting up for the next round of blackjack.

Money Is No Object

You can't accuse Vegas of cheaping out on the luxury hotel experience — okay, you can in some cases, but that's a totally different chapter — since it's home to the most expensive hotel ever built. **The Venetian** cost $1.5 billion, and that's only for its first phase of construction. Plans are in the works to add a second structure to the hotel (so far, no scheduled date for completion has been set), which will bring its grand total to a mere $2.5 billion. That's a lot of quarters!

Reach for the Sky

Move over, Seattle Space Needle. Las Vegas is home to the tallest building west of the Mississippi. The **Stratosphere** checks in at 1,149 feet, which also makes it the tallest observation tower in the U.S. It's also home to the world's highest roller coaster. Hope you don't have vertigo.

Going to the Chapel

Paris may have a better reputation for romance, but no city in the world hosts as many weddings as Las Vegas. Over 100,000 couples enter the bonds of holy matrimony here — and they call it Sin City! — each year. And it doesn't get more romantic in Vegas than on Valentine's Day, when more people marry here than anywhere else on the planet.

Reeling in the Dough

Las Vegas makes really big bucks! More than 85 percent of all visitors to the city spend at least some time courting Lady Luck. The amount of money spent annually on gambling in Vegas totals more than the gross national product of several small countries combined. In 1999, visitors blew $5.7 billion in the casinos. That's *billion*.

Just Visiting

Those Super Bowl commercials may have you believing that everyone is heading for Walt Disney World (and I'll concede they get more kids), but Vegas, the city that has been called an "adult's Disneyland," gets more visitors annually than all U.S. theme parks combined! Almost 34 million souls made a pilgrimage here in 1999. And you wonder why there's no elbow room at the craps tables?

A Golden Moment

Forget about Fort Knox, head for Las Vegas if you want to see the world's largest gold nugget on public display. The "Hand of Faith" nugget was discovered in Australia in 1980, and currently resides at the **Golden Nugget** (where else?) in downtown Vegas. It weighs in at 61 lbs., 11 oz.

Chapter 23

Ten (Or So) Las Vegas Institutions That Are No More

● ●

In This Chapter

▶ Disappearing hotels

▶ A legend lives on

● ●

*1*t would be hard to imagine New York City ever razing the Waldorf, or Paris tearing down the Ritz, but Las Vegas has brought down many of its historic landmarks without so much as a by your leave. Heck, by the 1990s, the city was promoting the destruction as a tourist attraction — at least if they had to go they went out in style. Here's a list of just a few of the oldies but goodies that got lost during the Strip's endless makeover.

El Rancho Vegas

Built in 1941, the **El Rancho** was the first hotel resort ever built on the Strip — not Bugsy Siegel's **Flamingo** as many people mistakenly assume. Its success launched a building boom on the Strip, a movement that is still going strong today. Alas, the hotel was destroyed by a fire in 1960 and was never rebuilt; all that's left of it is a big vacant lot at the corner of Sahara and Las Vegas Boulevard South.

The Other El Rancho Hotel

Not to be confused with the **El Rancho Vegas,** this place actually started out in the 1940s as the **Thunderbird** hotel before being re-named the El Rancho in 1982 after a series of ownership changes. Standing right across from **Circus Circus,** it closed in 1992 and remained empty and decaying until 2000, when it was purchased by Turnberry Place, the new $600 million condo development right behind it (just opposite the **Las Vegas Hilton**). The company says it will probably partner with a casino developer and build something there, but for now they just want to demolish the graffiti-covered buildings.

Dunes

A Strip fixture since the 1950s, the **Dunes'** claim to fame is that it was first to host that most Vegas of art forms, the topless showgirl review (in 1957). Purchased by former **Mirage** owner Steve Wynn in 1992, the Dunes at least got a proper Vegas sendoff. In 1993, more than 200,000 spectators watched as the Dunes imploded and it's famous neon sign exploded amidst a fireworks display that set Wynn back more than a million dollars. Wynn then spent more than a billion dollars putting up the **Bellagio** in its place.

Sands

This legendary spot made its debut on the Strip in 1952, but is most famous for hosting the "Summit Meeting" of the Rat Pack (Frank Sinatra, Dean Martin, Peter Lawford, and Sammy Davis, Jr.) in 1960. No show ticket since has been as hard to come by. Renowned for its entertainment, the **Sands** helped boost Las Vegas' reputation as a happening town. The hotel was reduced to a 30-foot-high pile of rubble in 1996 to make way for **The Venetian,** which memorialized the Sands by naming its convention center for it.

Hacienda

Another old-timer that went out with a bang, the **Hacienda** opened in 1956 and quickly became a Strip favorite. Known for its friendly service and old-style character, it simply couldn't compete with the mega-resorts that sprang up along the Strip in the 1990s. Hundreds of thousands came out to say goodbye to the hotel when it was blown up on New Year's Eve 1997 to make way for **Mandalay Bay.**

The Old Aladdin

Following the tradition of the **Hacienda** and the **Sands,** the **Aladdin** went up (or down, if you want to be picky) in smoke in 1998. Built in 1963, the Aladdin had major history behind it — Elvis married Priscilla here in 1967. Caught up in financial problems, it was finally decided to ditch the old resort and to replace it with a new and improved — and more expensive — version. The new **Aladdin** opened on the site of the old one in August 2000.

Vegas World

More notorious than famous, **Vegas World** sprang from the imagination of the casino maverick Bob Stupak, a PR master determined to take guests for every dollar that he could — he was eventually fined by the casino commission for false advertising. Calling the hotel a money pit would have been kind. As a marketing ploy, Stupak started building a large tower next to the hotel as a tourist attraction, but went bankrupt and was forced to sell out to Grand Casinos. Cutting its losses, the new owner stuck with the tower — today's **Stratosphere** hotel — and demolished Vegas World.

Desert Inn

When Mirage Resorts was acquired by **MGM Grand** in the Spring of 2000, Steve Wynn went looking for a new hotel to revamp and he settled on the **Desert Inn.** The venerable Strip contender had been losing money for a while, but unlike many of its megaresort competitors, it had class. With more than 50 years on the Strip, the historic hotel was home to Howard Hughes for most of the '60s. It gained major fame as the main setting for the '70s television show, *Vega$*. Although plans haven't been finalized, a new 59-story Desert Inn will take the legendary hotel's place. At press time, a major blowout — excuse the pun — is being planned for the hotel's demise.

Elvis

Okay. He isn't a hotel; but with all due respect to the King, he is a Las Vegas institution that did blow up there toward the end. And, like the Strip hotels that continue to re-create major landmarks and themes, Vegas is awash in Elvis impersonators who copy the legend — and with the same degrees of success. From his marriage to Priscilla in 1967 to his sold-out stints at the **Las Vegas Hilton,** Elvis did as much to promote the city as any hotel. Elvis may have left the building, but his presence is very much alive in Sin City.

Appendix

Quick Concierge

● ●

*T*his handy section is where I've condensed all the practical and per-
tinent information — from airline phone numbers to mailbox locations — you need to make sure you have a successful and stress-free
Las Vegas vacation. And for those of you who believe in being really
prepared, I also give you some additional resources to check out.

Las Vegas A to Z: Facts at Your Fingertips

AAA

The nearest regional office for the nationwide auto club is located in Carson City
(☎ 702-883-2470).

American Express

If you lose your American Express Travelers
Cheques, dial ☎ 800-221-7282 anytime, 24
hours a day. There's an American Express
Travel Services office in Caesars Palace
(☎ 702-731-7705) and at the MGM Grand
(☎ 702-739-8474).

ATMs

ATMs are everywhere, because casinos
want you to have easy access to your money.

Baby-sitting

Both Around the Clock Childcare (☎ 800-
798-6768 or 702-365-1040) and Children's
Babysitting Service (☎ 702-255-5955) have
experienced and licensed childcare available
24 hours a day. Their workers are screened
by the health department, sheriff, and FBI,
and provide extensive references upon
request.

Camera Repair

You can find photo and camera service in the
main gift shop of most major hotels. Check with
your hotel's concierge or guest services desk.

Conventions

Las Vegas is one of America's top convention
destinations. Much of the action takes place
at the Las Vegas Convention Center, (3150
Paradise Rd., Las Vegas, NV 89109; ☎ 702-
892-7575), which is the largest single-level
convention center in the world. Its 1.3 million
square feet includes 89 meeting rooms. And
this immense facility is augmented by the
Cashman Field Center, (850 Las Vegas Blvd.
N., Las Vegas, NV 89101; ☎ 702-386-7100).
Under the same auspices, Cashman provides
another 98,100 square feet of convention
space.

Doctors and Dentists

Most major hotels have physician-referral
services, but you can also call the free service
at Desert Springs Hospital (☎ 800-842-5439
or 702-733-6875) Mon – Fri 8 a.m. – 5 p.m.
For a dental referral, call the Clark County
Dentist Society (☎ 702-255-7873) weekdays
9 a.m. – 12 p.m. and 1 p.m. – 5 p.m.

Dry Cleaners

Most major hotels offer laundry and dry-cleaning services, but you may want to try Steiner Cleaners (1131 E. Tropicana at Maryland Parkway near Vons; ☎ 702-736-7474). Why? They were Liberace's personal cleaners — what else do you need to know? They're open Mon – Fri 7 a.m. – 6:30 p.m., and Sat 8 a.m. – 6 p.m.; closed Sun.

Emergencies

Dial ☎ **911** to contact the police or para-medics. You can get emergency service at any time, day or night, at Sunrise Hospital and Medical Center (3186 Maryland Parkway, between Desert Inn Road and Sahara Avenue; ☎ 702-731-8080). For less-critical emergencies, there's a 24-hour urgent care facility on the eighth floor of the Imperial Palace (3535 Las Vegas Blvd. S., just north of Flamingo; ☎ 702-731-3311). It's independently run, retains a full staff of doctors, and has all the latest medical equipment. No appointment is necessary.

Gambling Laws

You must be 21 years old to enter a casino area.

Highway Conditions

For recorded local information, call ☎ 702-486-3116.

Hotlines

In a crisis, you can contact the Rape Crisis Center (☎ 702-366-1640), the Suicide Prevention Hotline (☎ 702-731-2990), or Poison Emergencies (☎ 800-446-6179).

Information

All the major hotels have tour and show desks, but you can get additional information from the Las Vegas Convention and Visitors Bureau (3150 Paradise Rd.; ☎ 702-892-0711) or the Las Vegas Chamber of Commerce (3720 Howard Hughes Pkwy.; ☎ 702-735-1616).

The LVCVB is open Mon – Fri 8 a.m. – 6 p.m., Sat – Sun 8 a.m. – 5 p.m.; the LVCC is open Mon – Fri 8 a.m. – 5 p.m.

Liquor Laws

You must be 21 to buy alcohol — period. You can buy liquor at bars and stores 24 hours a day, including Sunday. You can even drink from open containers on city streets — a practice banned in most other cities.

Mail

The most convenient post office is immediately behind the Stardust Hotel (3100 Industrial Rd., between Sahara Avenue and Spring Mountain Road; ☎ 800-297-5543). It's open Mon – Fri 8:30 a.m. – 5 p.m. You can also mail letters and packages at your hotel, and there's a full-service U.S. Post Office in the Forum Shops in Caesars Palace.

Maps

All major hotels have basic city maps available to hotel guests. You can buy more-detailed maps at any hotel gift shop.

Newspapers/Magazines

Las Vegas has two major newspapers that you can buy in the city: *The Las Vegas Review-Journal* and *The Las Vegas Sun.* Both are available at almost every hotel gift shop. In addition, a variety of free local magazine publications have information on local happenings. The most prominent are *What's On Las Vegas* and *Showbiz Weekly*, available in hotels and restaurants throughout the city. For a totally unbiased, and more hip alternative opinion, try the free weekly papers *Las Vegas Weekly* and *City Life,* both of which are available at various record and used clothing stores and the like around town.

Pharmacies

Sav-On, (1360 E. Flamingo Rd. at Maryland Parkway; ☎ 702-731-5373), is part of a large national pharmacy chain and is open

24 hours. You can find a Walgreen's at 3765 Las Vegas Blvd, S. (at Spring Mountain). If you want to patronize an independent that is not part of a chain, try White Cross Drugs (1700 Las Vegas Blvd. S. just north of the Stratosphere Tower; ☎ 702-382-1733). The latter makes deliveries to your hotel, if you so desire.

Police

For emergencies, dial ☎ 911; for non-emergencies, dial ☎ 702-795-3111.

Restrooms

All the major hotels have public restroom facilities. They are, for the most part, clean and safe. Remember not to leave your children unattended, however.

Safety

As long as you stick to well-lit tourist areas, crime is usually not a major concern. However, pickpockets who target people coming out of casinos (or people in the casinos who are entranced by gambling) can be a problem. Men should keep wallets well-concealed, and women should keep pocketbooks in sight and secure at all times. Be warned — thieves tend to be particularly bold during outdoor shows like the Volcano at The Mirage or the Pirate Battle at Treasure Island. Many hotel rooms have safes for cash or valuables. If yours does not, the front desk can offer you a safety deposit box.

Note that the area northeast of Harmon and Koval has had increased gang activity of late. Either avoid the area or at least approach with caution.

Smoking

This is one of the few places in the United States where you aren't exiled to a space the size of a closet, or thrown outside, if you want to light up. Non-smokers beware: Smoking is not only permitted inside the casinos, it runs rampant.

Taxes

Clark County hotel room tax is 9 percent, and sales tax is 7 percent.

Taxis

Basic fare is $2.20 for the first mile, $1.50 for each additional mile, with time penalties for sitting still. Major operators include ABC (☎ 702-736-8444), Ace (☎ 702-736-8383), Checker (☎ 702-873-2000), Desert (☎ 702-386-9102), Henderson (☎ 702-384-2322), Star (☎ 702-873-2000), Western (☎ 702-736-8000), Whittlesea (☎ 702-384-6111), and Yellow (☎ 702-873-2000).

Time Zone

Las Vegas is in the Pacific time zone, three hours earlier than the East Coast (New York, Florida), two hours earlier than the Midwest (Iowa, Texas), and one hour earlier than the Mountain states (Colorado, Wyoming).

Transit Information

Call Citizen's Area Transit (CAT) at ☎ 702-CAT-RIDE.

Weather and Time

Call ☎ 702-248-4800 for an update.

Weddings

If you want to get hitched in the state of Nevada, you don't need a blood test nor to withstand a waiting period. Get your license at Clark County Marriage License Bureau, (200 S. 3rd St. at Bridger Ave., downtown; ☎ 702-455-3156), for $35.00. They are open 8 a.m. – 12 a.m. Mon – Thurs, and 24 hours a day on weekends and holidays. For more information, see Chapter 17.

Toll-Free Numbers and Web Sites

Airlines

Air Canada
☎ 800-776-3000
Internet: www.aircanada.ca

Alaska Airlines
☎ 800-426-0333
Internet: www.alaskaair.com

America West Airlines
☎ 800-235-9292
Internet: www.americawest.com

American Airlines
☎ 800-433-7300
Internet: www.americanair.com

American Trans Air
☎ 800-435-9282
Internet: www.ata.com

Canadian Airlines International
☎ 800-426-7000
Internet: www.cdnair.ca

Continental Airlines
☎ 800-525-0280
Internet: www.continental.com

Delta Air Lines
☎ 800-221-1212
Internet: www.delta-air.com

Hawaiian Airlines
☎ 800-367-5320
Internet: www.hawaiianair.com

Midway Airlines
☎ 800-446-4392
Internet: www.midwayair.com

Midwest Express
☎ 800-452-2022
Internet: www.midwestexpress.com

National Airlines
☎ 888-757-5387
Internet: www.nationalairlines.com

Northwest Airlines
☎ 800-225-2525
Internet: www.nwa.com

Southwest Airlines
☎ 800-435-9792
Internet: www.iflyswa.com

Trans World Airlines (TWA)
☎ 800-221-2000
Internet: www.twa.com

United Airlines
☎ 800-241-6522
Internet: www.ual.com

US Airways
☎ 800-428-4322
Internet: www.usairways.com

Car-Rental Agencies

Alamo
☎ 800-327-9633
Internet: www.goalamo.com

Avis
☎ 800-331-1212 in Continental U.S.
☎ 800-TRY-AVIS in Canada
Internet: www.avis.com

Budget
☎ 800-527-0700
Internet: www.budgetrentacar.com

Dollar
☎ 800-800-4000
Internet: www.dollarcar.com

Enterprise
☎ 800-325-8007
Internet: www.pickenterprise.com

Hertz
☎ 800-654-3131
Internet: www.hertz.com

National
☎ 800-CAR-RENT
Internet: www.nationalcar.com

Payless
☎ 800-PAYLESS
Internet: www.paylesscar.com

Rent-A-Wreck
☎ 800-535-1391
Internet: rent-a-wreck.com

Thrifty
☎ 800-367-2277
Internet: www.thrifty.com

Major Hotel & Motel Chains

Best Western International
☎ 800-528-1234
Internet: www.bestwestern.com

Clarion Hotels
☎ 800-CLARION
Internet: www.hotelchoice.com

Comfort Inns
☎ 800-228-5150
Internet: www.hotelchoice.com

Courtyard by Marriott
☎ 800-321-2211
Internet: www.courtyard.com

Days Inn
☎ 800-325-2525
Internet: www.daysinn.com

Doubletree Hotels
☎ 800-222-TREE
Internet: www.doubletreehotels.com

Econo Lodges
☎ 800-55-ECONO
Internet: www.hotelchoice.com

Fairfield Inn by Marriott
☎ 800-228-2800
Internet: www.fairfieldinn.com

Hampton Inn
☎ 800-HAMPTON
Internet: www.hampton-inn.com

Hilton Hotels
☎ 800-HILTONS
Internet: www.hilton.com

Holiday Inn
☎ 800-HOLIDAY
Internet: www.basshotels.com

Howard Johnson
☎ 800-654-2000
Internet: www.hojo.com

Hyatt Hotels & Resorts
☎ 800-228-9000
Internet: www.hyatt.com

ITT Sheraton
☎ 800-325-3535
Internet: www.sheraton.com

La Quinta Motor Inns
☎ 800-531-5900
Internet: www.laquinta.com

Marriott Hotels
☎ 800-228-9290
Internet: www.marriott.com

Motel 6
☎ 800-4-MOTEL6 (800-466-8536)
Internet: www.motel6.com

Quality Inns
☎ 800-228-5151
Internet: www.hotelchoice.com

Radisson Hotels International
☎ 800-333-3333
Internet: www.radisson.com

Ramada Inns
☎ 800-2-RAMADA
Internet: www.ramada.com

Red Carpet Inns
☎ 800-251-1962
Internet: www.reservahost.com

Red Lion Hotels & Inns
☎ 800-547-8010
Internet: www.redlion.com

Red Roof Inns
☎ 800-843-7663
Internet: www.redroof.com

Residence Inn by Marriott
☎ 800-331-3131
Internet: www.residenceinn.com

Rodeway Inns
☎ 800-228-2000
Internet: www.hotelchoice.com

Super 8 Motels
☎ 800-800-8000
Internet: www.super8motels.com

Travelodge
☎ 800-255-3050
Internet: www.travelodge.com

Vagabond Inns
☎ 800-522-1555
Internet: www.vagabondinns.com

Where to Get More Information

If you want more detailed information on attractions, accommodations or just about anything else in Las Vegas, you won't find it difficult to come by. In the upcoming sections I list some excellent sources for tourist information, maps, and brochures.

Las Vegas Convention and Visitors Authority

The Convention and Visitors Authority can answer any questions you have and can also send you a comprehensive packet of bro-chures, a map, a show guide, an events calendar, and an attractions list. They can also help you find a hotel that suits your needs and assist you in making a reservation.

3150 Paradise Rd., Las Vegas, NV 89109. ☎ 800-332-5333 or 702-892-7575. Internet: www.lasvegas24hours.com.

Las Vegas Chamber of Commerce

Another great source of local information, the Las Vegas Chamber of Commerce offers the *Visitor's Guide,* which contains extensive informa-tion about accommodations, attractions, excursions, children's activi-ties, and more. It will answer all your Las Vegas questions, including those about weddings and divorces.

3720 Howard Hughes Parkway, #100, Las Vegas, NV 89109. ☎ 702-735-1616.

The Las Vegas Review Journal

The largest paper in town, its *Neon* section has numerous listings for entertainment, dining, and nightlife. Web-savvy readers should head to its Internet site, where they will find a variety of pull-down menus with detailed descriptions of places of interest, such as the best romantic restaurant, best blackjack tables, best wedding chapel, and best roller coaster. A *Best of the Worst* section features such notables as the slow-est stoplight in town and the worst place to take visitors.

P.O. Box 70, Las Vegas, NV 89125. ☎ 702-383-0211. Internet: www.lvrj. com/lvrj_home/bestoflv/2000/index.html

Las Vegas Weekly

The Web site (www.lasvegasweekly.com) for this alternative weekly, which can be picked up in local shops and restaurants around town, offers reviews of bars, cafés, nightclubs, restaurants, bookstores, amusement parks, and shop listings. The dining listings are especially good if you're looking for an alternative to the touristy restaurants at the hotels.

A2ZlasVegas.com

This Web site lives up to its name. It's chock full of information on everything from hotels and guided tours to shows and getting married in Las Vegas. It even keeps tabs on the status of progressive slot machine jackpots in Nevada (to better help you budget in those winnings right away, of course). The hotel and dining reviews feature objective comments and ratings by fellow visitors.

Guidebooks

Get more information on Las Vegas from these IDG books: *Frommer's Las Vegas, Frommer's Portable Las Vegas, Frommer's Irreverent Guide to Las Vegas, The Unofficial Guide to Las Vegas,* and *Mini Vegas.*

Fare Game: Choosing an Airline

Travel Agency:_____ Phone:_____

Agent's Name: _____ Quoted Fare:_____

Departure Schedule & Flight Information

Airline: _____ Airport:_____

Flight #:_____ Date:_____ Time: _____ a.m./p.m.

Arrives in:_____ Time: _____ a.m./p.m.

Connecting Flight (if any)

Amount of time between flights: _____ hours/mins

Airline: _____ Airport: _____

Flight #:_____ Date: _____ Time: _____ a.m./p.m.

Arrives in:_____ Time: _____ a.m./p.m.

Return Trip Schedule & Flight Information

Airline: _____ Airport:_____

Flight #:_____ Date:_____ Time: _____ a.m./p.m.

Arrives in:_____ Time: _____ a.m./p.m.

Connecting Flight (if any)

Amount of time between flights:_____ hours/mins

Airline: _____ Airport:_____

Flight #:_____ Date:_____ Time: _____ a.m./p.m.

Arrives in:_____ Time: _____ a.m./p.m.

Notes

Fare Game: Choosing an Airline

Travel Agency: _____ Phone: _____

Agent's Name: _____ Quoted Fare: _____

Departure Schedule & Flight Information

Airline: _____ Airport: _____

Flight #: _____ Date: _____ Time: _____ a.m./p.m.

Arrives in: _____ Time: _____ a.m./p.m.

Connecting Flight (if any)

Amount of time between flights: _____ hours/mins

Airline: _____ Airport: _____

Flight #: _____ Date: _____ Time: _____ a.m./p.m.

Arrives in: _____ Time: _____ a.m./p.m.

Return Trip Schedule & Flight Information

Airline: _____ Airport: _____

Flight #: _____ Date: _____ Time: _____ a.m./p.m.

Arrives in: _____ Time: _____ a.m./p.m.

Connecting Flight (if any)

Amount of time between flights: _____ hours/mins

Airline: _____ Airport: _____

Flight #: _____ Date: _____ Time: _____ a.m./p.m.

Arrives in: _____ Time: _____ a.m./p.m.

Notes

Making Dollars and Sense of It

Expense	Amount
Airfare	
Car Rental	
Lodging	
Parking	
Breakfast	
Lunch	
Dinner	
Babysitting	
Attractions	
Transportation	
Souvenirs	
Tips	
Grand Total	

Notes

Making Dollars and Sense of It

Expense	Amount
Airfare	
Car Rental	
Lodging	
Parking	
Breakfast	
Lunch	
Dinner	
Babysitting	
Attractions	
Transportation	
Souvenirs	
Tips	
Grand Total	

Notes

Sweet Dreams: Choosing Your Hotel

Enter the hotels where you'd prefer to stay based on location and price. Then use the worksheet below to plan your itinerary.

Hotel	*Location*	*Price per night*

Sweet Dreams: Choosing Your Hotel

Enter the hotels where you'd prefer to stay based on location and price. Then use the worksheet below to plan your itinerary.

Hotel	Location	Price per night

Places to Go, People to See, Things to Do

Enter the attractions you would most like to see. Then use the worksheet below to plan your itinerary.

Attractions	Amount of time you expect to spend there	Best day and time to go

Places to Go, People to See, Things to Do

Enter the attractions you would most like to see. Then use the worksheet below to plan your itinerary.

Attractions	Amount of time you expect to spend there	Best day and time to go

Menus & Venues

Enter the restaurants where you'd most like to dine. Then use the worksheet below to plan your itinerary.

Name	Address/Phone	Cuisine/Price

Menus & Venues

Enter the restaurants where you'd most like to dine. Then use the worksheet below to plan your itinerary.

Name	*Address/Phone*	*Cuisine/Price*

Going "My" Way

Itinerary #1

☐ _____
☐ _____
☐ _____
☐ _____

Itinerary #2

☐ _____
☐ _____
☐ _____
☐ _____

Itinerary #3

☐ _____
☐ _____
☐ _____
☐ _____

Itinerary #4

☐ _____
☐ _____
☐ _____
☐ _____

Itinerary #5

☐ _____
☐ _____
☐ _____
☐ _____

Itinerary #6

☐ _____
☐ _____
☐ _____
☐ _____

Itinerary #7

☐ _____
☐ _____
☐ _____
☐ _____

Itinerary #8

☐ _____
☐ _____
☐ _____
☐ _____

Itinerary #9

☐ _____
☐ _____
☐ _____
☐ _____

Itinerary #10

☐ _____
☐ _____
☐ _____
☐ _____

Going "My" Way

Itinerary #1

☐ _____
☐ _____
☐ _____
☐ _____

Itinerary #2

☐ _____
☐ _____
☐ _____
☐ _____

Itinerary #3

☐ _____
☐ _____
☐ _____
☐ _____

Itinerary #4

☐ _____
☐ _____
☐ _____
☐ _____

Itinerary #5

☐ _____
☐ _____
☐ _____
☐ _____

Itinerary #6

- ❑ _____
- ❑ _____
- ❑ _____
- ❑ _____

Itinerary #7

- ❑ _____
- ❑ _____
- ❑ _____
- ❑ _____

Itinerary #8

- ❑ _____
- ❑ _____
- ❑ _____
- ❑ _____

Itinerary #9

- ❑ _____
- ❑ _____
- ❑ _____
- ❑ _____

Itinerary #10

- ❑ _____
- ❑ _____
- ❑ _____
- ❑ _____

Notes

Notes

Index

Accommodations Index

Restaurants Index

Discover Dummies Online!

The Dummies Web Site is your fun and friendly online resource for the latest information about *For Dummies*® books and your favorite topics. The Web site is the place to communicate with us, exchange ideas with other *For Dummies* readers, chat with authors, and have fun!

Ten Fun and Useful Things You Can Do at www.dummies.com

1. Win free *For Dummies* books and more!
2. Register your book and be entered in a prize drawing.
3. Meet your favorite authors through the IDG Books Worldwide Author Chat Series.
4. Exchange helpful information with other *For Dummies* readers.
5. Discover other great *For Dummies* books you must have!
6. Purchase Dummieswear® exclusively from our Web site.
7. Buy *For Dummies* books online.
8. Talk to us. Make comments, ask questions, get answers!
9. Download free software.
10. Find additional useful resources from authors.

Link directly to these ten fun and useful things at
http://www.dummies.com/10useful

For other technology titles from IDG Books Worldwide, go to
www.idgbooks.com

Not on the Web yet? It's easy to get started with *Dummies 101*®: *The Internet For Windows*® *98* or *The Internet For Dummies*® at local retailers everywhere.

Find other *For Dummies* books on these topics:

Business • Career • Databases • Food & Beverage • Games • Gardening • Graphics • Hardware
Health & Fitness • Internet and the World Wide Web • Networking • Office Suites
Operating Systems • Personal Finance • Pets • Programming • Recreation • Sports
Spreadsheets • Teacher Resources • Test Prep • Word Processing

IDG BOOKS WORLDWIDE BOOK REGISTRATION

Register This Book and Win!

We want to hear from you!

Visit **http://my2cents.dummies.com** to register this book and tell us how you liked it!

✔ Get entered in our monthly prize giveaway.

✔ Give us feedback about this book — tell us what you like best, what you like least, or maybe what you'd like to ask the author and us to change!

✔ Let us know any other *For Dummies®* topics that interest you.

Your feedback helps us determine what books to publish, tells us what coverage to add as we revise our books, and lets us know whether we're meeting your needs as a *For Dummies* reader. You're our most valuable resource, and what you have to say is important to us!

Not on the Web yet? It's easy to get started with *Dummies 101®: The Internet For Windows® 98* or *The Internet For Dummies®* at local retailers everywhere.

Or let us know what you think by sending us a letter at the following address:

For Dummies Book Registration
Dummies Press
10475 Crosspoint Blvd.
Indianapolis, IN 46256

...FOR DUMMIES™

BESTSELLING
BOOK SERIES